Idealism, Pragmatism, and Feminism

Idealism, Pragmatism, and Feminism

The Philosophy of Ella Lyman Cabot

John J. Kaag

LEXINGTON BOOKS
Lanham • Boulder • New York • Toronto • Plymouth, UK

Published by Lexington Books
A wholly owned subsidiary of The Rowman & Littlefield Publishing Group, Inc.
4501 Forbes Boulevard, Suite 200, Lanham, Maryland 20706
www.rowman.com

10 Thornbury Road, Plymouth PL6 7PP, United Kingdom

Copyright © 2011 by Lexington Books
First paperback edition 2013

All rights reserved. No part of this book may be reproduced in any form or by any electronic or mechanical means, including information storage and retrieval systems, without written permission from the publisher, except by a reviewer who may quote passages in a review.

British Library Cataloguing in Publication Information Available

Library of Congress Cataloging-in-Publication Data
The hardback edition of this book was previously cataloged by the Library of Congress as follows:

Kaag, John J., 1979–
Idealism, pragmatism, and feminism : the philosophy of Ella Lyman Cabot / John J. Kaag.
p.cm.
Includes index.
1. Cabot, Ella Lyman. I. Title.
B945.B894K33 2011
191—dc23
2011031883

ISBN 978-0-7391-6780-9 (cloth : alk. paper)
ISBN 978-0-7391-8598-8 (paperback)
ISBN 978-0-7391-6781-6 (electronic)

♾™ The paper used in this publication meets the minimum requirements of American National Standard for Information Sciences—Permanence of Paper for Printed Library Materials, ANSI/NISO Z39.48-1992.

Printed in the United States of America

Contents

Preface		vii
1	The Life of American Philosophy: The Education of Ella Lyman Cabot	1
2	Women and Forgotten Movements in American Philosophy: Ella Lyman Cabot and Mary Parker Follett on Growth and Creativity	33
3	Ella Lyman Cabot's Chance: The Nature of Contingency in the American Philosophical Tradition	63
4	*Everyday Ethics*: Morality and the Imagination	87
5	"How Does It Feel to Be a Problem?": Women in American Thought	111
6	Cabot on Peace Education: Moral Psychology, Ethics, and International Affairs (1906–1930)	137
7	"Thought Is Never at Rest": Ella Lyman Cabot and the Struggle of Idealism	163
Appendix: Selected Writings of Ella Lyman Cabot		177
Index		219
About the Author		223

Preface

Ella Lyman Cabot's story was not the one I expected to tell. Five years ago I intended to write a book about how the fathers of American philosophy—Ralph Waldo Emerson, William James, Josiah Royce, and Charles Sanders Peirce—addressed the concept of the imagination. As I sifted through the archives at Harvard University, however, paging through a notebook that Royce had used in teaching a metaphysics seminar in 1899, I came across a name that would dramatically alter the course of my research: "Mrs. Cabot." Royce, who was arguably the most recognized American philosopher at the turn of the century, repeatedly referred to this woman as the brightest star of the course, outshining classmates such as William Ernest Hocking, who would later join the ranks of the university's famous thinkers.

Who was this Mrs. Cabot? Of course I recognized her married name, a name that adorned many a street sign in Boston and that had defined the cultural and mercantile arenas of the Northeast since the 1700s. I had heard the rhyme: "Welcome to Boston, the home of the bean and the cod, where the Lowells speak only to the Cabots, and the Cabots only to God." I knew of James Elliott Cabot, the student of the German idealist Friedrich Schelling, and the friend and editor of Emerson. He was the one who brought Continental philosophy to America. I had a vague familiarity with his seven sons as well. Freethinking and free speaking, the Cabots had invaded nearly every corner of the Boston community. I knew one of them, Richard Cabot, was a disciple of the American pragmatists, the founder of social medicine in the United States, Harvard ethicist, and best-selling author in the early twentieth century; that is to say, I knew of Ella's husband. I also had some vague sense about Ella's family name, but only an inkling. Lyman: French, wealthy, aristocratic, Harvard bred, closely related to the Lowells. I guessed there was some truth to the rhyme.

My curiosity concerning Mrs. Cabot led me to the Institute for Advanced Study at Radcliffe, the onetime college that Ella Lyman Cabot had helped found. It was also where she had taken thirteen philosophy courses—and *only* philosophy courses—as a "special student." An author from the 1913 issue of the *Harvard Graduate Magazine* explains that this was the designation for students at Radcliffe who "regarded . . . degrees and other academic distinctions as of little importance."[1] In truth it was not considered proper for young women of Boston Brahmin families to place importance on such "unnecessary" formalities as degrees, and Radcliffe only began to confer degrees in 1895. Ella Lyman Cabot, like her Pulitzer Prize–winning cousin, Amy Lowell, played an integral part in the college's early life, but never received a formal Radcliffe degree. After Cabot's death, her godchild, Ada McCormick, would claim that this special student was "pure thought and soul," the archetype of a philosopher. The course themes buried in boxes at Radcliffe, developed by Ella between 1889, when she entered the College Annex, and 1903, when she finished taking formal classes, evidenced this fact. Astute, probing, and, at times, painfully personal, her unpublished essays rivaled many of her teachers' published tomes.

This rivalry, unfortunately, can be established only in hindsight. During her time, men dominated the discipline of academic philosophy. In light of this, the early contributions of this natural-born philosopher were almost wholly forgotten. Her seven published works on ethics and education, written between 1906 and 1934, have been overlooked by intellectual historians and philosophers alike, demoted to the status of "social commentary." In retrospect, however, Cabot's early themes, often focusing on the topics of creativity and personal growth, anticipated the work of her male counterparts by many years, a fact that is obvious in a careful comparison of her works and those of Josiah Royce and John Dewey. Likewise, her teaching and mentoring of many women who would rise in the ranks of progressive reformers has been lost as the discipline of philosophy turned away from teaching and mentoring. Her advocacy on the behalf of women on the Board of Radcliffe College and as a member of the Massachusetts Board of Education has been all but forgotten. Her own work in peace education between 1900 and 1930 has been eclipsed by other individuals—as if history has space for every warrior, but only a limited amount of room for peace reformers. What is also lost in losing the life and work of Ella Lyman Cabot is the sense that philosophy can, and must, make a difference in the world of non-philosophers. This remains a radical thought in a time when academic philosophy has jeopardized its own relevance by retreating to the small corners of large universities. This book about the philosophy of a forgotten philosopher is at once the story of a philosopher's engagement with the world and a story that might serve as a guide to those thinkers who still believe that philosophy is best done in the *agora*, in the field of everyday life.

This was a special student with a very special family. Ella Lyman Cabot was the grandniece of James Russell Lowell, the Romantic poet who introduced Dante to America in the mid-nineteenth century and who helped found the Saturday Club. This club—including Oliver Wendell Holmes, Henry Wordsworth Longfellow, Henry David Thoreau, and Ralph Waldo Emerson—drew together the best of classical American thought and created the breeding ground for what today is described as "classical American philosophy." Ella Lyman Cabot inherited her granduncle's Romantic streak, his intimate connection to the Transcendentalists, and his passionate admiration for Dante and Elizabeth Barrett Browning. When Longfellow vacated the Smith Professorship at Harvard in 1855, Lowell had taken the post and spent the next six years teaching Dante to a very small group of students. By the 1890s Dante's popularity had swelled, but his spiritual acolytes had declined in number. Arguably, there were only two: Ella Lyman and Richard Cabot. Ella Lyman Cabot would receive tutelage from the greatest philosophical minds of her day, but she would also reflect a deep heritage of Romanticism and idealism. She would channel all of these influences in an effort to clear a space for her own intellectual life and work. This effort would reflect the budding pragmatism and feminism of her day.

As I leafed through a philosophical essay written by Cabot titled "The Relation of Chance to Purpose and Invention," I smiled: here was a woman, at the turn of the nineteenth century, who was thinking through issues of creativity and individualism in ways that would remain unexplored until Dewey's *Quest for Certainty*, written two decades later. Here was a woman whose writings on chance and possibility were not bogged down by heavy metaphysical language, like Peirce and later Royce, but instead moved nimbly, negotiating the current affairs of her time. Here was a *woman* who wrote that, "Chance is always *my* chance!"—a personal, meaningful opportunity for growth. What kind of woman was this? What allowed her to make this claim at this time? Was it overblown idealism, polite defiance, feminist commitments, or extraordinary potential? As it turns out, it was a combination of the four. This book is the story of a woman philosopher that attempts to provide a new perspective on the development of the American philosophical tradition by addressing the ways this philosophical thinker was both nourished and stifled by the historical and cultural conditions of her time. In so doing it returns to, and re-turns, the question: Who is this Mrs. Cabot and why was she forgotten?

I sought the answer to this question in her 1884 journal titled "Hidden Passages," breaking the philosopher's first commandment: Thou shall not consider a thinker's personal life. On the first page of "Hidden Passages," I was warned against trespassing: "To read another's secret is a crime! Pause and reflect and do not do so!"[2] I, like her suitor, Richard, in 1896, disregarded this *caveat lector*, only to discover the poetic opacity that led

Ada McCormick, who began an unfinished biography of Ella in 1933, to call her a "hidden woman" and to claim that Emily Dickinson and Elizabeth Browning were her natural sisters.[3] I had to agree with McCormick.

As a nineteen-year-old, in the midst of reading Emerson's "Self-Reliance" for the first time, Ella Lyman pens the poem, "Reserve," which states, "We live alone, thoughts that are deepest drawn / And purest in our inner consciousness / Abide undreamed by the common throng / But to ourselves from God they wake to bless."[4] Yes, there really was something to that rhyme. Ella Lyman and Richard Cabot, as a couple, would together speak to God directly. Ella's sense of reserve and personal sense of religiosity was fortified during the months when she wrote this poem, but it was also tested. This was the first year that Ella spent extended time with the Cabot family, an American intellectual gang, led by a father who was in the midst of writing Emerson's biography. Every Sunday, on the way back from the Unitarian King's Chapel, Ella joined the Cabot boys for their discussions on ethics, religion, philosophy, and politics. It was on one of these first visits that she was introduced to Theodore and Richard Cabot. She would love both of these brothers, but marry only one. While the young Ella actively participated in these afternoon talks, she maintained her own unassuming bearing. In "Solitudes," she reflects on this fact: "Our lives are full of solitudes / And wild untrodden ways, / Of haunts where ardent fancy broods / And smiling memory plays. / And budding hopes dream in the shade, / Deep-hidden like wood-bound glade."[5] My intent in writing this book is to explore the intersection of philosophy, religion, and gender, three forces that continue to quietly determine our lives. Ella Lyman Cabot was not quiet on any of these subjects, a fact that makes her a perfect subject for this exploration.

The young Ella Lyman was not merely a brooding teenager, but an individual caught between the vision of the Victorian lady and the activity of the modern American feminist. She sought solitude not exclusively as a means of escape, but as a way of seeing clearly and making space for genuine creative activity. Her solitude did not mean that she was a solitary individual; she was continually transacting with the social and political issues of her time. From serving on the Massachusetts Board of Education with Alice Brandeis, to visiting Jane Addams's Hull House in Chicago, to inspiring Mary Foote and Mary Parker Follett in their respective works in literature and labor management, Ella Lyman Cabot's later projects were singular in their personal approach and the insight they inspired. Steeped in the pragmatic atmosphere of the day, Cabot insisted that insight have real consequences in the lives of individuals and communities. That is also to say that she insisted that the age of sentiment must give way or, more accurately, give rise to the age of action. And women, Ella hoped, were going to be front and center in this coming age. While her father had believed that women ought to have the same opportunities as men, Ella understood that most forms of patriarchy did not hold this position. Women would have to fight for the opportunity to exercise their strengths. This book draws Ella Lyman Cabot out of her "Hidden Passages," highlighting the way that her writing complements and occasionally contradicts the work of philosophers and women activists of her age, many of whom considered her a close friend and confidant.

After visiting John Dewey's school in Chicago in 1899, Ella commented that Dewey's philosophy was mechanical; it lacked tragedy and ecstasy. Her own life and writing were never lacking in this regard. Tragedy repeatedly gave way to ecstasy in the forty years of her marriage to Richard. Ella's professional successes were mixed and invariably complex. Despite the fact that decisions were a great struggle for her, Ella managed to write books on ethics that earned considerable acclaim during her life, repeatedly finding herself, unlike someone like C. S. Peirce, in the annual *Who's Who in America*. Her reputation, however, faded as philosophy took its unfortunate turn away from the affairs of everyday life. Cabot's works dare to make pragmatism practical and carefully apply the tenets of American thought to the events that defined the social and political landscape of her day. While contemporary philosophers might accuse Cabot of a lack of technical sophistication, it is clear that the philosophers of her time took her seriously and respected her work. George Herbert Palmer, Josiah Royce, John Dewey, Alfred North Whitehead, William Torrey Harris, and others read and reviewed her writings, reflecting the opinion that her sophistication could be subtle and, moreover, did not have to stand against practical purposes. This fact ought to give students of contemporary philosophy a moment of pause for at least three distinct reasons. Despite being overwhelmed by her husband's hyperactivity, Ella Lyman Cabot found unique outlets for her imagination and abilities. This being said, many of these outlets have remained private until this point. McCormick suggested in the 1930s that Cabot's books occasionally suffered from her attention to detail in the teaching of ethics and philosophy. McCormick, however, writes: "Her letters are very different. There she was larger and freer. She was herself, and wrote often as Whistler painted. You remember his words: 'As the light fades and the shadows deepen, all the petty and the exacting details vanish. Everything trivial disappears. And I can see things as they are, in great strong masses.'[6] I believe that McCormick is generally right when it comes to this point, and it has led me to employ large swaths of Cabot's unpublished work. I believe McCormick is right when she states, "I think if EC letters were edited and published that we would have a contribution to literature, the literature of spiritual direction." The contribution that these letters have to offer is also, I would argue, an important one for American philosophy.

This is an intellectual biography in the most literal sense. Rarely has a couple so thoroughly attempted to embody and live through the spirit of philosophy and religion. Even rarer is the opportunity to witness the consequences of such an attempt. As witnesses, we have three angles of vision. First, we can read the extensive writings of the Cabots, and particularly Ella Lyman Cabot, that reflect their feelings as they lived out their idealism, writings that reflect their immediate feelings concerning their lives together, their famous peers, and their culture. Second, we have a pool of remarks made by their contemporaries in philosophy that shed light on the way that the couple was situated in the wider intellectual and social circle of nineteenth-century America. Finally, and perhaps most valuably, we have a retrospective perspective, one gleaned from the extensive interviews that McCormick conducted in the 1930s with Ella, Richard, and a surprising number of their famous friends for a biography that was never written. McCormick, taking meticulous notes, asks these individuals to relive the most crucial decisions of their lives. Examining the difference between the living and the reliving of these moments is a study in the human person, an intriguing tale of hopes and false memories, and a testament to the life of the mind.

This book is meant to serve three interrelated purposes. First, it provides the necessary context in which to understand Ella Lyman Cabot's published works on ethics, civics, and religion in the period after 1906. My hope is that the resurgence of American philosophy—a resurgence that has been motivated by a small and dedicated group of scholars and that has entered the mainstream in recent years—can carry the work of Ella Lyman Cabot in its wake. This thinker deserves to be a part of the American philosophical canon, and I hope to create the context for her inclusion. Providing this context helps understand that her later work—books and pamphlets often characterized as "merely" Progressive reform literature—has its roots in philosophic and poetic reflections that before now have remained unpublished. These reflections turn on the topics of growth, creativity, and the imagination. I believe that Ella Lyman Cabot's writings reflect a unique dedication to idealism, pragmatism, and feminism—schools of thought that are often held in opposition. A close investigation of her work shows how she understood Roycean idealism as fortifying and securing the progressive impulses of pragmatism and feminism, providing the ideals and purposes that guide the "can do" attitude of these two more forward-looking temperaments. This investigation is possible because, unlike many of the women working in philosophy in the late 1800s, Cabot's papers have been saved and catalogued.

Second, Cabot's notebooks, written as a student at Radcliffe College and as a graduate student at Harvard, can teach us significant lessons about her teachers, many of whom are prominent figures in the American philosophical tradition. Her comments concerning John Dewey and Josiah Royce give us insight into the content and method of these thinkers' pedagogy. Additionally, her notes provide a snapshot of Royce's nascent thoughts that would later grow into works such as *The World and the Individual* (1901) and *The Philosophy of Loyalty* (1908). It is interesting to note how often Cabot identifies a kernel of meaning in her teachers' thought and anticipates the future course of their inquiry. I hope to bring Cabot into conversation with her famous teachers; in many cases, this will be a conversation that Cabot was never able to actually have herself because women were still so marginalized in the discipline of philosophy.

Third, and most important, this book is meant to expose another buried root of the American philosophical tradition. While her notebooks provide insight into the philosophy of her male contemporaries, Cabot's writing stands as an independent contribution to the American canon. Indeed, her writings self-consciously resonate with the voices of Ralph Waldo Emerson, Henry David Thoreau, William James, and Josiah Royce, but this resonance is given in a different key, one that is genuinely original and distinctly feminist in its perspective. Her thinking, presented prior to the 1906 publication of *Everyday Ethics*, exposes this fact. Struggling as a young woman philosopher in an unwelcoming intellectual atmosphere, Cabot's treatment of marriage, personal growth, unity, risk, loyalty, political unity, and international relations is expressed in, and as, a unique composition. Recovering this work grants us a better understanding of women's experience at the turn of the century, explains how it might have reflected the concepts of creativity and community, and suggests how this experience gave rise to unique forms of American philosophy.

This book consists of chapters that represent several distinct approaches to Cabot's work. Each chapter is meant to assist a reader in addressing and responding to Cabot's work. Additionally, the reflections and exegetical remarks in these chapters aim to open Cabot's writings to the field of contemporary philosophy. Versions of chapters 2, 3, and 4 have been published in the *Transactions of the Charles S. Peirce Society*. I would like to thank the editors of the *Transactions*, as well as the many other individuals who reviewed this book. Scott Pratt, Dorothy Rogers, Robert Innis, Carol Hay, Douglas Anderson, Charlene Seigfried, Marilyn Fischer, and Frank Oppenheim made many suggestions that proved invaluable in the book's development. I would also like to thank the American Academy of Arts and Sciences and the Harvard Humanities Center for sponsoring this research.

The first of these chapters orients a reader to the philosophical, cultural, and religious milieu in which Cabot's thinking developed. This thinker's early education was formative in her later work and reflects many of the positions expressed by feminists and pragmatists in the 1880s. This chapter will also address the relationship between Ella Lyman and Richard Cabot, the founder of medical ethics at Mass General and the Department of Social Ethics at Harvard in the early years of the twentieth century. This couple would marry but only after Lyman expressed very progressive feminist leanings in a paper they collectively termed "The Paper on Marriage." By way of this opening chapter, a reader can come to understand how philosophical issues of creativity, growth, unity, and imagination held a special place for Ella Lyman Cabot, for they spoke directly to her hopes and aspirations as a woman philosopher at the turn of the century.

The second of these chapters addresses Cabot's treatment of the concepts of unity and growth. Cabot's understanding of these concepts, reflected in notebooks written in 1892, matures in Josiah Royce's seminars at the turn of the century and is extended and modified in her *Everyday Ethics* of 1906. My intent is to listen for the resonances of Royce and others in Cabot's work but also to identify ways in which Cabot may have anticipated the moves of her male counterparts who become the "fathers" of American philosophy. Her writing evinces a pointed and continual care for the modes of human flourishing in which individual growth and interpersonal unity harmonize. This is a pragmatic but also particularly feminist concern; Cabot's personal experiences lead her to recognize the unfortunate tendency for communal unity to be achieved at the expense of the self-creation of a community's members. Her writing seeks to counteract this tendency. This chapter concludes by highlighting the ways Cabot's work sets the stage for the work of Mary Parker Follett.

The third chapter explores the relation between Cabot's work and C. S. Peirce's development of tychism, the doctrine of absolute chance. In 1906, Peirce suggests that chance ought to be regarded as some type of agency and must be understood in relation to the idea of purpose. This suggestion indicates Peirce's desire to avoid the determinism that characterized the twilight of the scientific revolution. Cabot's work in 1902 on the topic of chance, purpose, and invention serves as a useful complement and interesting harbinger to Peirce's observations concerning chance. This chapter demonstrates the way in which Cabot clears a middle ground between Royce, often regarded as a determinist, and Peirce, a follower of tychism. She exposes the complementary relation between purpose and chance events, while developing a position that is perhaps most akin to the position expressed in Ralph Waldo Emerson's "Fate" and "Power." Centrally, I argue in this chapter that Cabot's treatment of the question of chance is always at the service of a more particular and pressing question, namely the question of human conduct. Royce seems occasionally to forget this point, and Peirce usually misses it altogether. For Cabot, the question of chance is *always* the question of the ability to negotiate personal possibilities and seize unexpected opportunities. Having studied Emerson since her late teenage years, Cabot was well prepared to draw these three thinkers together on the topic of contingency. Indeed, these thinkers were already drawn together by the students of Cabot's time; for example, Emerson and Peirce both gave lectures in the Harvard University Lecture series established in 1870. This fact is often forgotten and can be recalled by Cabot's comments on issues that resonate closely with both thinkers.

Cabot describes this unique ability to seize unexpected possibilities as the process of the creative imagination. The fourth chapter examines her understanding of the imagination in relation to two figures of the American philosophical tradition, Ralph Waldo Emerson and John Dewey. Cabot, Dewey, and Emerson all broaden the definition of the imagination beyond its traditional rendering as an aesthetic faculty. Each of these thinkers, working in their own unique valence, argues that a particular conception of the imagination is a necessary force in a moral life. Cabot's thinking on the imagination is evident in her early poetry and is easily traced through papers such as "The Search for the Eternal" (1902) and "Different Forms of Unity" (1902). She explains the close relation between imagination and sympathy, while acknowledging that being imaginative is a necessary, but not sufficient, condition for being moral. Her work in *Everyday Ethics* coincides with large swaths of Dewey's writing and predates his observations on the imagination in *Art as Experience* and *The Quest for Certainty* by more than a decade. We are left to wonder why and how Cabot's work has been so systematically ignored.

The fifth chapter takes up precisely this issue by allowing Cabot's life and work to shed light on the intellectual cultural atmosphere of her time. Cabot's work provides a portrait of womanhood that helps explain the treatment and situation of women in society and philosophy at the end of the nineteenth century. This portrait is not, however, for many reasons, a cohesive whole. Sadly and frustratingly, its lack of cohesion often served as the grounds for its dismissal. In the convergence and divergence of her writings, we catch sight of a surprising picture of creativity and community—incomplete, striving, stifled, triumphant, ambivalent. Cabot forces us to face and re-interrogate the way in which social and philosophical commitments have the power to enable, but also severely limit, creativity and personal growth. Despite the limitations individuals face, Cabot maintains that they have a duty to express themselves, drawing on Kant's rendering of imperfect duties to support her argument. Additionally, Cabot suggests that a woman's self-expression must weigh carefully the duties to oneself and the duties to care for others. In effect, she provides a very early critique of what contemporary philosophers call the "ethics of care."

The sixth chapter examines Cabot's mature thought, focusing on the work in social and political theory reflected in *Everyday Ethics* and *A Course on Citizenship* (1913). In the latter work, Cabot works closely with Fannie Fern Andrews, who became one of the foremost peace advocates of the twentieth century. Both of these writings select an interesting array of "peace heroes" to guide a child's moral education. Cabot, following her mentor Royce, believes that ethical principles, and idealism more broadly, must be embodied in the lives of individuals and their social networks. Additionally, she suggests that imitation of exemplars may serve as the basis of early moral education. What is most striking in Cabot's account is the diversity of her exemplars, many of which span the cultural spectrum and defy gender stereotypes.

The book concludes by making the case that Cabot maintained the type of "idealistic pragmatism" that Mary Mahowald described in her early writings on the American philosophical tradition.[7] Many of today's philosophers would like to maintain that pragmatism can be divorced from idealism and, indeed, that idealism and pragmatism are necessarily antagonistic. This position is an anachronistic one that reflects an unfortunately common shortcoming of contemporary philosophy, namely a stubborn unwillingness to do the historical legwork that is required to understand thinkers on their own terms. While such an understanding is only ever partial, a good-faith attempt should be made. I hold that Ella Lyman Cabot was, in the end, an idealist who pursued practical projects of social justice and gender equality with varying success. Without succumbing to monism or determinism, a certain strain of idealism provides the purpose, direction, or cause that contemporary accounts of pragmatism often lack. Many of the causes to which Ella Lyman Cabot was dedicated remained lost causes, ones that could never be fully realized by a single individual. I will address the character and value of a lost cause and explain the role that pragmatism and idealism play in their pursuit. This final chapter also consists of reflections concerning the fate of women in philosophy and in academia more broadly construed. There is a deep sense of regret and ambivalence in Cabot's writings that deserves to be explored. It deserves attention for it sheds light on the *current* position of women in philosophy. Indeed, readers should listen for resonances of Cabot's frustrations in contemporary philosophy, in the experiences of women philosophers, who continue to face obstacles of gender discrimination and censure. There are still many hidden passages of American philosophy and philosophy in contemporary America.

The book concludes with an appendix consisting of selections of Cabot's writings. This appendix has been organized into two sections. The first section consists of poetry, selected journal entries, and correspondence; the second contains more formal philosophical material. Cabot's poetry, written principally between 1884 and 1899, serves as an opening that allows a reader to get a sense of the writer's intellectual temperament and early thought. The section that contains Cabot's philosophical reflections has been chronologically organized. In all cases, the works have been published with the permission of the Schlesinger Library at the Radcliffe Institute for Advanced Study.

A brief note about presentation is warranted. Because Ella Lyman took the Cabot name in 1894 when she married Richard Cabot, it is sometimes difficult to distinguish which Cabot is being referred to in the course of the book. In most cases, I have attempted to refer to her as "Ella Lyman" or "Lyman" in descriptions of her life prior to her marriage and "Ella Lyman Cabot" or "Cabot" in periods following her marriage.

NOTES

1. "The Radcliffe Special Student," *Harvard Graduate Magazine* (Cambridge, MA: Harvard Graduate Magazine Association, 1918), 379.
2. Many of the citations from Ella Lyman Cabot are from the unpublished papers housed at Schlesinger Library at the Radcliffe Institute for Advanced Study, Harvard University. Collected Papers of Ella Lyman Cabot. A 139/Folder 320. After this point, all citations will be made in call/folder style. Hence, A 139/320.
3. Richard Clarke Cabot Papers, Harvard University Archives. HUG 4255.80. Box 1. "ELC Part of Early Sketch."
4. A 139/320v.
5. A 139/320v.
6. Richard Clarke Cabot Papers, Harvard University Archives. HUG 4255.80. Box 1. "Research Material for Ada McCormick."
7. Mary Mahowald, *An Idealistic Pragmatism: The Development of the Pragmatic Element in the Philosophy of Josiah Royce* (The Hague: Martinus Nijhoff, 1972).

Chapter One

The Life of American Philosophy: The Education of Ella Lyman Cabot

DANTE AND BEATRICE—CABOT AND LOWELL

> *Welcome to Boston,*
> *The home of the bean and the cod,*
> *Where the Lowells speak only to the Cabots,*
> *And the Cabots only to God.*

It was a very odd way to consummate a marriage. Forty years later, Richard Cabot would look back on the bizarre passion, but also the tragic appropriateness, of that afternoon in the summer of 1894. Richard had waited a long time for that moment. She had kept him waiting. She had successfully eluded him for six years. It undoubtedly would have been longer had he not given in to *her* requests. High in the hills of Northern Italy, the couple stretched out on the grass. This was the place where two august American households—the Cabots and the Lowells—were to be united. The time had arrived. In the end, she was just aroused as he was—perhaps even more so. After all, every true philosopher loves a good book. And she was the truest, if the most unknown, of American philosophers. It was not physical intercourse, but philosophical discourse, that marked the culminating moment of their honeymoon. As Richard Cabot opened the book, the couple began to read aloud, *and began to live*, the story that would come to define their marriage—the story of the *Divine Comedy*.

The *Divine Comedy* is unapologetically idealistic. It is, after all, a story of the soul's journey toward God. It is, however, also a pragmatic story about the trials and tribulations of everyday ethics. Dante offers his reader a practical handbook that describes with nightmarish accuracy the potential pitfalls of moral life. The newly married couple was simultaneously drawn to its idealism and pragmatism and saw them as complementary rather than as antagonist. While underscoring the pragmatic and idealistic character of the *Divine Comedy* is not particularly difficult, it is more challenging to identify its feminist underpinnings. Indeed, Dante does a very good job of covering them up, obscuring them from view. It is possible that Richard Cabot did not even notice the fact that the driving force in the *Divine Comedy* is not a man, but a woman who appears only occasionally on the journey. This woman remains hidden and is rarely described in any detail. It is almost certain that Cabot's new wife took note of this fact. *She* is the main character of *this* book.

The *Divine Comedy* is not funny. In fact, it is somewhat nightmarish when Virgil leads Dante through the underworld: through limbo, reserved for those unfortunate souls who never made good on their lives; through purgatory, reserved for those who were still figuring out the meaning of goodness; and through the deeper reaches of hell, reserved for those who were downright bad. No, Richard Cabot would not end up in any of these places. Fiercely ambitious, like the rest of the Cabot family, Richard usually made good on the many opportunities that accompanied his life of privilege. He was also as pious as his liberal Unitarianism would allow. So purgatory and hell did not, at least at first glance, seem to be likely destinations. Richard did not empathize with any of the unlucky characters that Dante encounters but rather with his guide, and more significantly, the narrator himself. Indeed, Richard may have fancied himself a type of modern-day Virgil, embodying the ideals of philosophy, rhetoric, rationalism, culture, and piety. In the year of their marriage, Richard reflected on his promise and personal aspirations: "I feel that not to do something really great will be for me to have failed entirely. I have never heard or read of anyone with such advantages."[1] He was not alone in this assessment. Most of his contemporaries regarded him as a type of epic poet, ready to hold forth on any number of subjects, sometimes regardless of his expertise. William James would comment that Richard Cabot was "one of the most original minds and characters of Boston and *very good* . . . although he hates my philosophy. He has [put] a new moral tone into the whole medical professional life of Boston."[2]

The comparison between Cabot and Dante is deeper and more telling. Born into great fortunes, both men received educations that only great wealth can afford. These fortunes were tied to great merchant families that distinguished themselves by their political influence, their free thinking, and their free speaking. Like Dante's *Eloquence in the Vernacular*, Cabot's academic writing was geared to the common person, reflecting the pragmatic belief of his day that the life of thought could change the affairs of the world. Most significantly, both Cabot and Dante never really knew the woman they claimed to love. But here, the comparison breaks down. While Dante encountered his beloved only twice on the medieval streets of Florence, Richard Cabot, after many years of negotiating, had convinced his unknown love to marry him. While Dante's Beatrice remained forever unapproachable, enshrined in a book, Cabot's sat across from him on the grass, reading the *Divine Comedy*.

Beatrice Portinari is immortalized in Dante's epic poem, arriving late on the scene as the author's guide to the ten regions of Heaven. As the narrator directs his attention to the souls of the heroic men who inhabit Paradise, it is Beatrice that remains the enduring, but often forgotten, presence. Dante, however, cannot wholly forget. In Beatrice, we find the symbol of beatific love: sentimental, spiritual, pure, *chaste*. It is the sentimental Beatrice rather than the sensible Virgil who leads Dante to the freedom of salvation. Despite her importance as a symbol, the object of the poet's enduring affection remains just that—an object. Beatrice is more of an idealized figment of Dante's imagination than a person of flesh and blood. The woman who represents the divine freedom of humankind remains trapped, bound by the artistic imagination of a man. While Richard identified with the heroes of the *Comedy*, he was happy to identify his new wife with the symbol of the chaste and spiritual Beatrice, later referring to their marriage as the "Beatrice Relation."[3]

Ella Lyman Cabot was an American Beatrice. Her goddaughter would describe "Aunt Ella" as "pure spirit and thought," devoid of all things carnal and base. The philosopher Alfred North Whitehead echoed this sentiment by recounting Ella's first and only trip to a "sex-confessional," a practice of the Victorian era that satisfied both the Puritanical impulses of Bostonians, and also the voyeuristic drive that only religious repression begets. After listening quietly to the dirty secrets of her neighbors, it was Ella's turn to share. Whitehead remembers that she stood up and, in a voice just loud enough for everyone to hear, whispered, "My name is Ella Cabot. I am an earnest seeker of the Truth."[4] Then she sat down. That was it. There was nothing more to say. She was an American Beatrice: spiritual, pure, *chaste*.

There was, however, another side to Beatrice, a side that stood opposed to her virginal idealization. When Dante encountered the *real* Beatrice, she was walking freely in the marketplace that still bears her family name. She was flanked by two older women who shielded her from Dante's gaze. These women were not attracted to the symbol of Beatrice, but to her *person*. And this was a singularly wealthy, educated, and independent person. The Portinaris owned Florence—at least the half that the Alighieris did not claim. Beatrice's family had arrived in Florence in the eleventh century, well before the arrival of the more famous Medici clan, and had revolutionized its centers of education, industry, and commerce. This woman was to inherit her family's fortune. Yes, young Ella Lyman, heiress to the Lyman millions, was an American Beatrice. Like the heroine of the *Divine Comedy*, she would be caught between personhood and idealism, between personal freedom and the constraints of symbolism.

While the symbol of Beatrice was always at Dante's call, her person, the free woman who strolled with her friends, was never at his service. Ironically, it was this woman's independence and inapproachability that forced Dante to ensnare her in the idea of beatific love. That was, after all, the only way he could control her. Until that afternoon in Tuscany, Ella Lyman had always been flanked by her faithful friends and loving sisters. Indeed, she often called them her "maiden ladies." When her close friend Edith Paine had decided to marry, Ella had groaned, "Oh dear! She is the first of our old maid clique to go! The rest of the ladies must stick fast to their colors."[5] As Richard found out, these feminist colors did not fade easily. In the spring of 1892, Ella had impatiently responded to Richard's proposal and persistent advances:

> I have told you, I think, as clearly as I can, why I cannot marry now. It is love of my own life which at times makes anything else seem like tearing up my roots; and independence of temperament which makes marriage not a need as it would be with many people . . . my social atmosphere is so rich and free, I have in an unusual degree the maximum of doing what I want and the minimum of what bores me, and I know and love it through and through. I am close to people whom I know and draw my life from and yet my solitude is my own.[6]

In moments of personal crisis, the young Lyman's comments reflected the American philosophical and literary sentiments of her time, echoing Henry James's *The Portrait of a Lady* (1884) in Isabel Archer's assertion that, "I don't want to begin life by marrying. There are other things a woman can do."[7] Like Archer, Lyman took extreme and progressive measures to protect what she fondly called "my own life." She seemed to understand that her independence ran against the current of mainstream society, commenting to Richard that "perhaps it is difficult for a man to understand how independent a girl must insist on being."[8] She at last agreed to marry Richard only after an extended period of negotiations and only after he committed to "The Paper on Marriage," a prenuptial agreement that she wrote with the intent of undercutting the gender stereotypes of her time.

Looking back on her adolescence, Lyman would vaguely remember that there was much to love about her "own life." Born in 1866, her childhood had been split between 39 Beacon Street, overlooking Boston Common, the Lyman Estate, overlooking its 400 acres, and Southern France, overlooking the remnants of a romantic continent besieged by American industry and ambition. The Lymans, an American establishment, were a part of this beleaguered continent, and happily so. Ada McCormick, Lyman's goddaughter and a writer for *Harpers Magazine*, said that one could not understand Lyman's family without understanding the mood of French country life, and that one could not see "Ella's Mamma" without thinking of Parisian aristocracy. According to McCormick, Elizabeth Bancroft Lowell "belonged to the age of innocence, when French influence was strong on American families of wealth."[9] Ella Lyman's mother continued to dress her three boys in velvet and skirts, ignoring the fact that the mothers of Back Bay had long earlier accepted wool and trousers. Her four daughters also suffered the fashions of a bygone era, but it was a small price to pay. Ella and the other Lyman girls enjoyed quiet, European "freedoms": tutelage in the classics, instruction in the fine arts, and the support of parents who embodied the spirit of egalitarian enlightenment. Eventually, however, Ella, like the Old World with which she identified, would be freely occupied by American forces: the force of Richard Cabot.

And he was a force to be reckoned with. His six brothers came to understand this rather quickly. The Cabot boys were well-known for roughhousing in the large foyer of their parents' mansion. As Hugh Cabot would recall, the banister to the great stairwell was broken so often that his father gave up on its repair. More often than not, Richard Cabot was the culprit. These pitched battles had the dual purpose of releasing brotherly pressures and of training the Cabot men for a future campaign—the invasion of the cultural and intellectual centers of Boston. Richard would lead the charge, effectively reshaping the fields of medicine, pastoral care, and social ethics in America.

If he were sitting in the living room, James Elliott Cabot could have heard the rumble from the foyer. Perhaps he took some delight in the fact that his sons' interest in philosophy matched their interest in horseplay. In the 1850s, James Cabot, with the help of his brother Edward, had built the Athenaeum, Boston's largest private library and theatre, but thereafter had left architecture to return to the study of philosophy and religion. In his youth, he had studied with the German thinker Friedrich Schelling, and he was largely responsible for the importation of German Idealism to the United States. His friend, Ralph Waldo Emerson, was also involved in the American appropriation of continental thought, but Emerson typically deferred to the elder Cabot on the more technical matters of philosophy.[10]

James Cabot had served as Emerson's secretary when "dear Waldo" could no longer hold a pen and, in 1884, Cabot had undertaken the American scholar's biography. His own philosophical writings, short pieces published in Margaret Fuller's *Dial*, reflected his indebtedness to Schelling and Kant but also his abiding interest in the natural sciences of his day. This twofold commitment would define American Transcendentalism and the subsequent development of American pragmatism in the 1870s. Simply put, Schelling's idealism is the attempt to explain the relation between matter and mind, or in other words, between the real and the ideal. For Schelling, and his American progenitors, this relationship was not antagonistic but rather complementary. At the end of the nineteenth century, C. S. Peirce, the father of American pragmatism, would sum up this position rather nicely when he said that, "Matter is only partially deadened mind." This kernel of Transcendental wisdom is more easily digested in Peirce's pragmatic reformulation: *Thoughts matter!* Thinking should be judged on the ways that it *matters*—takes practical shape and physical embodiment—in the affairs of real people.

Peirce's pragmatic maxim was the unspoken rule in the Cabot household. The boys were continually encouraged to integrate their studies and beliefs into their very busy lives. Richard would recall how Ted, his athletic older brother, would lumber into the dining room, plop down in his wet football kit, and promptly ask his father a question concerning German aesthetics or English common law. During the 1880s, philosophy was not the dry, academic subject that is studied in today's classrooms. Classical American philosophy had not yet died. Instead it was alive and well and living at the Cabots'. It was the constant companion of the family and its visitors. It grew up in the same household, the same intellectual dwelling, that Ella Lyman and Richard Cabot would call their own. Thomas Davidson, the philosophy tutor of William James, Josiah Royce, and John Dewey, was especially fond of little Richard Cabot. With a Scottish joviality, Davidson, a frequent visitor of the Cabots, would throw the eight-year-old Richard on his shoulders and carry him triumphantly into the dining room where supper was waiting.[11] By the turn of the century, Richard would be the triumphant one, writing treatises on ethics and politics that stood on the shoulders of these intellectual giants. The house was frequented by giants, but also by less imposing figures, such as a young Ella Lyman. Every Sunday this quiet, yet oddly independent, thirteen-year-old would walk back with her family from King's Chapel to have supper at the Cabots' and witness the spectacle of another American establishment.

The education of Ella Lyman was defined by the budding pragmatism of the 1880s and 1890s, but also by the idealism and utopianism that sprung from the Transcendental movement led by Fuller and Emerson. These are not two independent lines of thinking, but strands that were intertwined in the making of American philosophy and, more particularly, in what would become the philosophy of Ella Lyman Cabot. Margaret Fuller's *Woman in the Nineteenth Century* was published in the *Dial* in the 1840s, and by the middle of the century had become standard fare for women intellectuals of the time. This book outlined new possibilities for identity that would free women from the gender stereotypes and submissive heterosexual relationships that had long defined Victorian womanhood. Ella Lyman, who read this work in her late teens and early twenties, undoubtedly recognized the similarities between the lives of Fuller's heroines and her own life.

Fuller's book reframes the myth of the feminine by concentrating on independent and highly educated women such as Miranda, a character who is developed as an autobiographical rendering of Fuller's own unique upbringing. Fuller describes this figure, explaining that "Her father was a man who cherished no sentimental reverence for Woman, but a firm belief in the equality of the sexes. . . . From the time she could speak and go alone, he addressed her not as a plaything, but as a living mind." This equality allowed Miranda to flourish in a number of fields that had typically been dominated by the opposite sex.

Arthur Theodore Lyman, like Fuller's father, thought it was very important for his daughters to receive a comparable education to his sons. In her *Temptations to Right Doing*, a book that she completed in 1929, Ella Lyman Cabot reflects on this fact, noting that her father encouraged her study of philosophy for the sole reason that his daughter seemed to have a special knack for the discipline.[12] The comparison, however, between the education of the young Ella and that of her brothers rests on shaky ground, however, because she had to eventually fight for the right to study philosophy, the quintessentially male discipline of the nineteenth century. Fuller comments that Miranda was the exception to the rule of sexism, and it seems that Lyman's painful journey to philosophy forced her to realize the difficulty of being this type of exception.

In addition to Miranda, another character from Fuller's work seems to resonate closely with the story of Ella Lyman Cabot. In part III of *Woman in the Nineteenth Century*, Fuller addresses the advantages and disadvantages of celibacy in women. She points us to a Native American story in which a woman is not united with another human being, but is betrothed to the Sun, dedicated to serving both God and truth. In this case, the sun worshiper builds her wigwam away from the rest of the community and pursues a life of personal and independent meaning. This is one case where celibacy was not only tolerated, but honored. The take-away message of this story was one that was taken to heart by Lyman: in order to protect their unique intellectual projects and spiritual pursuits, it was often necessary for women to retreat from the cultural expectations and familial obligations of their age. This would be the beginning of the "Paper on Marriage" that defined her partnership with Richard Cabot.

AMBIVALENCE: PHILOSOPHY AND WOMANHOOD

In 1894, Josiah Royce wrote to the newly married Cabots stating: "you . . . were born to philosophy. I was but driven to it by perplexity and defect of insight."[13] This comment speaks to Ella Lyman Cabot's proficiency in the formal philosophical studies that she took up in the early 1890s at Radcliffe College, but it fails to address the difficulty that the young woman had faced as she began to think through what it meant to be a woman philosopher. Ella Lyman's parents were products of European enlightenment, a fact that would account for their daughter's training in literature and the classics. Dante and Goethe were standard fare for Lyman, to which she added Emerson's essays in the 1880s, under the tutelage of the elder Cabot and his sons, primarily Ted and Richard. It is worth noting that these works formed the basis of every single "classical American" philosopher in the 1880s; Peirce, Royce, James, and Dewey were all brought up on a mix of German Romanticism and American Transcendentalism. The difference, however, between these men and Lyman was significant. There was, at least in Lyman's mind, a difference between reading philosophy as a hobby and doing philosophy as an original thinker. One seemed rather harmless and fit nicely with the late Victorian rendering of womanhood, the other stood to jeopardize this genteel tradition. Susan Cabot, Richard's younger sister, had begun to take classes with Royce at Radcliffe in the last years of the 1880s. Royce was a newcomer to Harvard at that point and was unusually welcoming to newcomers to philosophy, including the group of young women who took his courses at the Annex across Harvard Square. At the Cabots' encouragement, Lyman began to consider attending these classes as well.

In the summer 1889, at the age of twenty-three, Lyman might have been considered an adult—at least to the extent that she was of an age to marry and start a family, which was the "natural" terminus of adolescence for a woman in her day. At this point, however, Lyman was singularly uninterested in marriage, concentrating instead on the exegesis of T. H. Green's *Prolegomena to Ethics,* which her father had given her in the winter of 1889, and on the possibility of attending Royce's course in the fall of that year. This possibility, however, was a risky one. On August 14, Lyman writes to Richard Cabot:

> Sometime I want to know rather exactly about Royce's course. You think it is a tremendous gain, don't you? I feel sure of it, but what I have to do is to decide whether I can arrange it without hurting Mamma. If I decide against it, I shall very probably not even ask her about it because I can tell how she feels without.[14]

This comment reflects the tension between the methods of philosophy—a decidedly masculine pursuit—and the genteel idealization of womanhood that still held sway in the nineteenth century. Ella Lyman Cabot was thoroughly immersed in this genteel idealization—her education led her to adore Dante and Goethe throughout her life. This would prove consistently problematic in her studies of philosophy, and would produce a complex of cultural tensions that would emerge in her later philosophical writings.

For Cabot, and for women more broadly, European enlightenment meant freedom, but freedom within the constraints of rigid tradition. Attending classes in logic, argumentation, and metaphysics fell well outside the cultural limitations to which Ella's mother, Elizabeth Bancroft Lowell, was accustomed. The young Lyman and her female contemporaries worked through this tension as they gained varying degrees of access to the centers of classical American philosophy. It is worth noting that the idealization of women's identities and the oppression that it implied was internalized and self-imposed by women such as Lyman. The "hidden" character of women philosophers of the nineteenth century was a function of the cultural and intellectual prohibition that produced a narrow self-understanding, what Iris Marion Young would describe as "inhibited intentionality" nearly a century later. Lyman was self-consciously "closed off" from the intellectual centers of the time. This inhibition, this unwillingness to be known, is reflected in a journal dated 1889 and entitled "Hidden Passages." On the flysheet of the notebook, Lyman wrote, "To read another's secret is a crime. Reflect and do not do so!" Readers who ignore this *caveat lector* are faced with a scattering of philosophical reflections on womanhood, human nature, ethics, and metaphysics—the signs of a voracious mind getting its first taste of philosophy. Lyman, unlike her male contemporaries, was forced to keep these reflections in hiding, secrets that she held from her mother and the world at large.

The Forming of a Philosophical Temperament

Lyman's proclivity for philosophy was a *partially* kept secret. Prior to entering formal classes in the fall of 1890—beginning with a course on ethics given by George Herbert Palmer—she had engaged in philosophical dialogue with both Richard and Ted Cabot. The correspondence between Lyman and her early interlocutors exposes the obstacles that woman philosophers faced due to the disparities in educational access that cut along gender lines. In the course of their conversations on ethics and metaphysics, Richard Cabot often failed to recognize this discrepancy, criticizing the young Lyman for her lack of philosophical expertise and intellectual confidence. Lyman reminds him of her educational background, stating, "I believe you hardly realize how on various subjects on which we talk, I have never thought definitely and I have literally no opinion at first. . . . It makes me indignant now to think how little at school we were made to use our own minds."[15] Lyman, however, was a quick learner. Indeed, even as she downplayed her abilities to think independently, she began to develop original arguments concerning the value and method of philosophy. For example, she criticizes Richard Cabot's tendency, shared by so many in a male-dominated intellectual field, to judge a book before understanding it. In grappling with Royce's *Religious Aspect of Philosophy* (1888), Lyman writes to Cabot:

> My first thought on a new subject or book is never criticism. That comes later; it is what I call insight. I seek instinctively to make myself one with it; to *share its feeling* through realization, and then gradually to judge it. In questions about which I have thought really carefully this is, of course, not so, but in a book like Royce's I let myself be carried far along by the baffled searching skeptic before I even tried to find the answer that I felt innate assurance of.[16]

Intellectual charity and sympathy was part and parcel of womanhood in the late Victorian period, and Ella Lyman's comments may be interpreted along these lines. This being said, the ability to realize the intent and purpose of another individual through the establishment of sympathetic relations appears as a common concern for many American thinkers of the time, reflected in such works as Jane Addams's *Democracy and Social Ethics* (1902) and William James's "On a Certain Blindness in Human Beings" (1899). Richard Cabot was slow to cultivate this sort of insight, and Lyman repeatedly lashed out at him during their long courtship: "The main lack that I sometimes feel with your letters is that they are too analytic constantly. One needs freedom from inspection in order to grow; one feels like the watched pot which cannot boil when people are looking at it."[17] This was not merely a personal complaint about the way that Cabot tended to scrutinize Lyman's intellectual positions. It was also the preliminary articulations of Lyman's stance on the point and purpose of philosophy. In Lyman's day, and in our own, it is often forgotten that the point of philosophy, at its best, is to pursue mutual understanding and the expansion of ideas. According to Lyman, philosophy often devolved into a type of disciplinary infighting that yielded much heat and little light. The light of philosophy could be realized, according to Lyman, only by way of charitable readings and dialogue that attends the unexpected turn in another's argument. In her journal, she writes to this effect:

> I never have any fixed plans for treating people. . . . Anticipation helps tremendously, but it is never definite anticipation or arrangement such as: "When they say so and so I will say this." It is trying to enter into their feeling and point of view and its relation to me; and at the time of action I am absolutely conscious of their every motion and eagerly awake to possible new light which may of course alter my whole conduct. We must act and judge and criticize and assert but we must make full allowance for the elements of change and growth and welcome the unforeseen and bring it within the limits of our plan.[18]

This intellectual flexibility was already underpinned by her belief—one shared by Emerson and William James—that human growth depended on an experiential openness to novelty and unexpected occurrences. This point would receive full development in her formal philosophical work.

In 1891, Richard Cabot asked Lyman to give him an honest assessment of his character, to make note of his faults, and to suggest a way forward in his personal growth and development. She obliged, leveling a criticism that could have easily applied to many of the philosophers working in Cambridge at the time:

> You were, I think, not patient enough to wait for the other person's point of view. Your arguments tend to be too hard and fast, too analytic and one-sided. They are lacking in delicate insight and spirituality and artistic feeling, without which we cannot possibly reach the whole truth. You incline not to appreciate your opponent's point of view and to assert your own aggressively so that unless he knows and cares for you he is repulsed and thinks you dogmatic.[19]

This assessment of Cabot's philosophical demeanor and approach to intellectual disagreements rang true of the general philosophical atmosphere in Boston during the 1890s, a fact that was not lost on either of these students. In the spring of 1891, Lyman's teacher and lifelong friend, Josiah Royce, had engaged in vicious philosophical combat with Francis Ellington Abbott in what became known as the Abbott-Royce controversy. Accusing him of plagiarizing and of misunderstanding Hegel, Royce came very close to slandering Abbott in public and in print. Abbott, an individual who C. S. Peirce claimed was one of the most original minds of his day, would never recover from this argument, and never assumed a permanent position in philosophy at a college or university. Abbott, one of the most tragic figures in American philosophy, would commit suicide in 1903.[20] The Abbott-Royce controversy reverberated through the halls of Harvard and Radcliffe in the early 1890s, drawing figures such as James and Peirce into the mix. It seems likely that Lyman was well aware of this intellectual cockfight; what is more certain is that this thinker, throughout her lengthy career, would emphasize insight over criticism in her philosophical works.

What becomes apparent in an analysis of Ella Lyman Cabot's writings is that American philosophy emerged not fully formed in the writings of a number of distinguished individuals, but rather in a series of ongoing conversations and controversies that were at once personal and philosophical. For example, a year after the Abbott-Royce debacle, George Santayana came to stay with the Lymans at Waltham, Massachusetts. Santayana was a good friend of Ella Lyman's older brother, Herbert, and reflected upon the friendly rapport between himself and Herbert's younger sister as well. At this point, in 1892, Santayana turned a critical eye back on Royce's *Spirit of Modern Philosophy* (1892). Recounting her interaction with Santayana, Ella Lyman writes:

> I asked him about Description and Appreciation [a distinction that Royce makes in the *Spirit of Modern Philosophy*] and he said that he thought that Royce exaggerated its importance tremendously. He said that Royce was a solitary man, meaning that he was very little affected by other men's work, and that thereby he hurt his philosophy very much. The historical side, for example his account of Spinoza, was unfair [overaccenting his mysticism] and the constructive side, though his main doctrine of the Absolute was true, he gave it a religious glamour which made Santayana angry. . . . [M]en complained that Royce's teaching was vague and confused."[21]

Today it is easy to get the impression that classical American philosophy emerged fully formed in a very select number of essays and books—Peirce's "Fixation of Belief" and "How to Make our Ideas Clear," James's *Pragmatism*, and Dewey's *Democracy and Education*. In truth, it emerged slowly and sporadically in the course of complex conversations—both formal ones such as the conversations that Margaret Fuller held through the 1840s, and in less formal ones such as those between Lyman and Santayana and between James and Royce as they walked to Harvard every morning.

This American strain of philosophy stemmed from conversation in another important, albeit usually forgotten, respect. American thinkers were in constant contact with the religious, literary, scientific, and historical centerpieces of their time. In these years, philosophy had not marginalized itself to arcane reaches of the university, but stood aside other disciplines to make its case and to converse with these intellectual and spiritual players. Today, if we overlook the broad interdisciplinary character of American thought, its conceptual intricacies and historical backing, we run the very real risk of, in the words of William James, "thinning out" our intellectual memory in order to fit it into the philosophical narrowness of the present. Focusing on the life and work of Ella Lyman Cabot is one good way to avoid this risk. Cabot was deeply enmeshed in the everyday conversations that gave rise to classical American philosophy. She was engaged with both the persons and the subjects that helped form its history. In looking carefully at her life, we have the opportunity to understand the depth and richness—the culture—of American thought. In her personal reflections, we receive a reflection of the vibrant intellectual community, with all of its tensions and proclivities, that formed this intellectual tradition.

While the young Lyman was engaged in the conversation of philosophy, it is worth noting that she often remained detached and reserved, apparently willing to document philosophical disagreements of her day without passing immediate judgment on the parties involved. She often served as a participant–observer, or witness, to the intellectual workings of her day. Along these lines, this young student in philosophy was probably not quick to argue with Santayana over the shape or existence of the Absolute, or to butt heads with Richard over formal philosophical issues. This hesitancy to critically assess her interlocutors on formal philosophical grounds may be traced to the gendered norms of her time, but it would be a mistake to construe the young Ella Lyman as a pushover. She was not. She merely chose her battles carefully. At this point in her life, Lyman reserved her animus for more important and practical matters such as defending the rights of the disadvantaged, and more immediately, defending her own right to personal growth. What we find in this defense is a practically oriented feminism, underpinned by the philosophical arguments of pragmatism and idealism. Lyman's argument against marrying Richard Cabot, expressed in the "Paper on Marriage" reveals her formal philosophical training and her ability to translate theory into meaningful human practice.

THE "PAPER ON MARRIAGE"

> In 1889, prior to attending Royce's lectures, Lyman wrote in her journal that, "A girl's life is indefinitely harder than a man's in some ways. His sacrifices hard though they are, are only for some end he really believes better, while hers are often the bearing of the loss of helpful and joy-giving intercourse with nothing in her life to take its place."[22]

On the threshold of womanhood, Lyman assessed the dangers. In the same year that Charlotte Perkins Gilman would begin her publishing career, a young Lyman articulates a thesis very similar to the one found in Gilman's "The Yellow Wallpaper"(1892), a story of a woman's descent into hysteria, precipitated by the inactivity and domestic confinement that was prescribed as the "rest cure" for a nervous disposition. Serving as a harbinger to Gilman, Lyman laments the expected passivity of womanhood:

> She has constantly to resign and without the relief of activity; to readjust herself to loss, to fill up the gaps of loneliness. A man does this naturally by work, a girl has to resolutely face the loss and patiently bear it. Then again a man's work is finished at night while a girl's is perfectly indefinite and largely intangible.[23]

Here Cabot, echoing the newly forged Chicago school of philosophy, led by John Dewey, and the Cambridge pragmatists, led by William James, suggests that the "nature" of personal identity is not something immutable and naturally constrained, but something cultivated and trained in a social setting. This is not to say that these cultural roles are not often regarded as innate dispositions. They often were, and are, and to very poor effect. This being said, just as Jane Addams and John Dewey claimed that education and democratic practice could leave an indelible mark on human nature, Cabot implies that re-visioning the cultural roles of womanhood could rework the "natural" dispositions that had defined Victorian society. She concludes her journal entry along these lines:

> Men meet in business on an impersonal basis; girls have to keep a perpetual cruse of tenderness to oil the jarring tempers. And because she needs to be more alive to the feelings of others a girl is more quick to be hurt, more sensitive. Is it strange that girls are more subject to moods than men?"[24]

According to Lyman, the "moods" of women, so long regarded as a function of nature, were in fact a function of the societal expectations placed on a particular group of individuals. Cabot's observation here is not merely a passing philosophical musing, but rather motivated a commitment that remained central throughout her life. This centrality is patently obvious as she optimistically concludes her assessment of womanhood: "Yet *I* will be under the control of no such influence."[25] For many women of her era, this spirit of independence would have remained a "diary dream," but for Lyman, it motivated many of her most personal decisions and determined her professional goals. Heiress to one of the largest family fortunes in America, Lyman maintained a type of financial independence that allowed her to strive for personal independence.

Richard Cabot proposed to Ella Lyman in June of 1892 after reconnecting with her in Royce's seminars in the early 1890s. As it turned out, these seminars, many of which focused on the concepts of tragedy and romanticism, were a fitting venue for the formation of this couple. Ella's response to Richard's proposal was appropriately philosophical: "Choosing to marry is choosing to live a dual life, to bring two different lives into union and we don't do that unless the tie that unites them, the life in common, is holier and higher that the work of either apart."[26] This comment cuts in at least two directions. First, and most obviously, marriage is the union of two individual lives. But for an individual in Lyman's situation, marriage also initiated her into the "dual life" of womanhood. On the one side, were the traditional Victorian expectations of domesticity and motherhood, while on the other were the possibilities, just beginning to show themselves, afforded by the women's rights movement. While many activists, such as philosopher C. S. Peirce's ex-wife Melusina Fay, suggested that a happy union could be established in this dual life by elevating housework to the level of a respectable profession, Ella Lyman begged to differ.

In responding to Richard's continued courtship, Lyman wrote the "Paper on Marriage" a detailed discussion of the power dynamics that defined marriage at the turn of the century. Lyman drafts this paper in a notebook for Royce's 1892 seminar, demonstrating a willingness to understand Royce's thinking, and philosophy on the whole, as the outcome of individuals thinking through the most meaningful questions of living:

> This is what makes the question of marriage such a tremendous one. For here, we deliberately unite our ends to each other's ends, and unless each feels the other's ends are as real and sacred as his own, they will conflict.[27]

Here it is clear that Lyman's framing of an equitable marriage draws heavily on her recent studies of both Kant and Hegel. First, Lyman conceives of marriage as a type of "kingdom of ends," which Kant describes as a "union of different rational beings" in an organization that would honor each of these beings as able to set ends for themselves. In another of her formulations, marriage is a kingdom, or community, of two people in which each participant has a moral obligation to act only on principles that could be accepted by the other member of this community. This "other member" is one who has equal share in legislating the principles of the marriage. Lyman's remarks reflect not only Kant's ethical thought, but also the strain of Hegelian thinking that she is picking up from Royce who was immersed in the *Phenomenology* at this time. Lyman echoes Hegel and Royce in her belief that individuals need robust communities in order to flourish and grow. Personal growth depends in large part on the recognition of others and by others. Lyman suggests that the recognition involved in an ethical marriage is a tenuous process, one that can easily slip into the unfortunate dialectic of master and slave or the emotional cul-de-sac of unhappy consciousness. In order to avoid this, recognition in marriage requires willing and equal participation by both parties as they negotiate common and individual interests and goals. Lyman translates these points from the German philosophical canon into a progressive feminist position. Opening the "Paper on Marriage," she writes that in an equitable union,

> the man may be right in one way, to regard his vocation first, but he must remember, all the time, that he is dealing in a personal partnership with one who has a life of her own to lead as freely as he has. And the woman must remember that the man's relation to her is only part of his activity. The man has no more right to sacrifice her interests to his business than to sacrifice his business to her interests.[28]

This position, one that suggests that men and women should be regarded as ends in themselves who have lives to lead as freely as possible, can be read as an expansion and application of Kant's formulation of humanity, but I believe it is more accurate to trace Lyman's remarks to T. H. Green's *Prolegomena to Ethics*, a book that she and Richard Cabot discussed at length in the early 1890s. Green, along with Royce, was one of the last defenders of idealism in the Western world who attempted, with varying degrees of success, to refashion idealism in order to counter the assaults that modern science and Biblical criticism had made on this foundering tradition in the nineteenth century. In his *Prolegomena*, Green repeatedly argues that a human self is necessarily a social self, steeped in the complex recognition of others. The admix of Kant and Hegel which Lyman developed in her early writing may be borrowed from Green who, as Simhony recently observes, "grounds the Kantian community of rights (respect for persons) in the Hegelian-inspired community of mutual recognition."[29] More broadly, Green suggests that individual well-being is only realized in the negotiation of collective interests and pursuits. Describing this type of well-being, Green writes that "his own permanent well-being he thus necessarily presents to himself as a social well-being."[30] This would be a point that Lyman would adopt in her later writings on ethics and political theory. For Lyman, however, this point remained problematic insofar as the societal relations of nineteenth century America were stacked against the free expression of women such as herself. She makes this clear in her "Paper on Marriage" when she turns to rights of women in the workplace, stating:

> If he (the male partner) needs to be in Heidelberg to study law and she (the female partner) in Paris to study art, there is no reason why one career should yield to the other unless both recognize the work of one life as higher than that of the other. This was fairly simple in the past, for a woman was never treated as equally a very active being with the man. She was always made to subordinate her place to his business and follow where he led. It was enough for her to be his servant, his love and the mother of his children. My work comes first man says to his own satisfaction and feeling unselfish that he does not indulge his inclination. But so is the woman's work first, and there cannot be two firsts. Either the man's work must be the first and the man himself his wife's first or two equally free persons meet each with their own life to lead.[31]

Several important points deserve to be underscored in this passage. First, it should be noted that Lyman is not making a clean break from the gendered expectations of her day. The example that she gives of a woman being drawn to art and a man to the law recapitulates the gendered vocations of the late Victorian era. This being said, Lyman maintained that these vocations deserve equal respect; this is a move to counteract the prevailing sentiment that women worked at mere hobbies while men responded to important callings. She elaborates on this point, drawing her reader's attention to the subordinate status of women in previous generations. It is no longer satisfactory, according to Lyman, for women to be regarded solely as servants, lovers, or mothers. Her grouping of these roles is an implicit critique of both the patriarchy of her day and the sex roles that attended it. These roles, buttressed by an ethic of chivalry that continued to hold sway in the late nineteenth century, were said to benefit women by making their lives easier and by satisfying *their* desire to rely on a male partner. Lyman, along with other early American feminists, takes issue with this claim. Assessing the claims of Robert Louis Stevenson, she writes:

> Stevenson says marriage is almost always a gain for women. It may be true to facts, but it is rather a sad state of facts. The reason marriage is thought to be a gain is that women are thought incapable of living an eager active life apart from it.[32]

A growing number of women in Lyman's day were willing and able to live without the false partnership of most heterosexual unions. These individuals disrupted the cultural expectation that women were to remain at home and were to forego meaningful vocations if their pursuit ran counter to those of their husbands.

As one of the most educated young women of the Boston elite, Lyman was painfully aware of the double bind that such an education presented. On the one hand, married women who abandoned what Lyman called "impersonal work"—that is, professional work that did not explicitly focus on the tending of family, friends, and loved ones—lost valuable opportunities to make their mark in American culture and commerce. On the other hand, those women who remained unmarried in order to fulfill their professional dreams were derided in a society that continued to associate womanhood with the family. In light of this double bind, Lyman describes the psychological tension of an educated woman, explaining that,

> her instincts are harder to find; it is more of a question for a woman whether to marry or not, as she identifies herself more and more with impersonal work, a far harder question than with men who have only to ask whether it is on the whole conducive to their already formed plan of life.[33]

As Marilyn Frye explained nearly a century later, oppressed women have been subject to this double bind for a very long time: either women "participate in [their own] erasure" as moral subjects by complying with cultural expectations of docility and domesticity or they are "perceived as bitter, angry and dangerous" when they reject these expectations.[34] Men, whose occupational and personal trajectories do not conflict, experienced, and continue to experience, no such tension.

Given this situation, an ethically permissible marriage must, on Lyman's terms, be made under very specific circumstances. She writes that, "marriage is the chosen deliberate admission of another equally living self into the closest relation with you." She is, however, well aware that this is far from the reality of nineteenth century matrimony. She speaks directly to Richard, underlining a man's ability to set the conditions of this union: "In doing up this tie you can say to the woman, 'I want you to marry me provided that you will always subordinate your life to mine, your interest and plans to my work.' That is practically the present state of affairs, but it is an unfair one."[35] At this juncture, Lyman drives the point home for her suitor by insisting that, "a man who realizes a woman's life as real as his own, who honors her nature, her capacities as he does his own cannot say, 'I want you to marry me provided that you subordinate your life to mine.'"[36]

In Cabot's day, and in our own, women were and are encouraged to prioritize the interests of others over their own, to be selfless and caring. This prioritization makes it nearly impossible for individuals to grow and flourish. Cabot acknowledged this difficulty and listened carefully when she read Green's *Prolegomena* when he insists that a human subject must be "conscious at once of himself as an absolute end and of a life of becoming of constant transition from possibility to realization and from this again to a new possibility a forecast of a well being that shall consist in the complete fulfillment of himself."[37] Thanks to her wealth, social status, and intellect, the possibilities for Ella Lyman might have seemed endless, but her gender made realizing these possibilities highly problematic. It is likely that she read on with growing frustration as Green continues his analysis of self-culture: "Now the self of which a man thus forecasts the fulfillment is not an abstract or empty self. It is a self already affected in the most primitive forms of human life by manifold interests among which are interests in other persons."[38] This point had *always* been driven home for women—that their self-realization depended on the degree to which they adopted the interests of others as their own. What Lyman seemed to crave was a society, or marriage partnership, in which men came to regard women's interests as real and meaningful. Elaborating on this position in her "Paper on Marriage," Lyman writes:

> He must say: "Henceforward your life shall be as dear to me as my own, your ideals my ideals, and my ideas your ideas." At bottom, we aim at the same ideal, otherwise it would be absolutely wrong to marry. If my expression of my ideal, my work, cut off your expression, I shall have the right to say "My work is first." It is no more first than your work. Down below both is something which unites them, an ideal in which we both agree. By this alone can we tell whether my work ought to yield to your work or yours to mine.[39]

More than a decade before Royce begins to explain the importance of loyal devotion to a cause in his *Philosophy of Loyalty*, Lyman, one of his students, was working through the way that the tension between two individual interests, the tension that accompanies any dyadic relation, might be mediated by a third, overarching cause that granted the possibility of mutual cooperation. In 1908, Royce writes that, "where there is an object of loyalty, there is, then, a union of various selves into one life."[40] This is an apt description of what Lyman envisioned in her analysis of marriage. If the individual interests of one party are to be elevated over another, it is only ever on the grounds that the higher purpose and cause to which both parties strive might be better pursued in light of this disparity. If the pursuit of this higher ideal—an ideal that both individuals share equally—is not facilitated by any given individual action, that action can be deemed as inappropriate in the common life of the marriage.

For Lyman, the question of marriage does not turn on the attraction between two people, but rather on the sober assessment of the life goals of each individual and the common cause that might unite their respective pursuits. "Sober" is the operative word here, for it is no easy matter to determine individual and collective goods. Lyman explains:

> Marriage is a searching and deep act because it takes the tremendous step over the gulf that separates us from all mankind and makes another living will a double of our own. There may be no conflict of wills or plans; if there is we must first search for the union which underlies the division; but if your work seems to you to express the ideal better than union and like verse and they are incompatible, then one or the other must sacrifice tenderly and truly even what he thinks is best to the tie which unites his life to another. In this sense, I believe marriage ought to be first. If we deliberately chose to join another life with its reason and will inseparably into our life, then we must accept the necessity which may cause you to sacrifice even what he thinks right or what she thinks, or more truly our private opinion to a life together.[41]

What is most notable in this section is Lyman's insistence that the sacrifices entailed by loyal devotion must be shared equally by the parties of the marriage. At other points in her writing, she notes that the sacrifices entailed by heterosexual partnerships have been shouldered almost exclusively by women. Even at this relatively early age, Lyman jabs at Richard Cabot, quipping, "'When two men ride on a horse one rides behind.' This is the past history of marriage. But if the woman is man's equal, she cannot ride behind." For Lyman, if a woman could only ride behind her husband on the steed of marriage, it was better to walk on her own:

> And for a number of women, it will in the future when they have found their way to self-expression in creative work, be wrong to marry because as far as I see, marriage will always mean putting impersonal work in the second place, not perhaps as it happens so as to prevent their doing other things, but with the claim of their home and family first.[42]

This section places the responsibilities of household duties, often placed on women of Lyman's day without their consent, against freely chosen projects that remained unimagined in the nineteenth century narrative of womanhood.

Lyman's "Paper on Marriage" reflects the transitional character of women's roles at the turn of the century. It could have been written by any number of early feminists: Victoria Woodhull, Susan B. Anthony, Charlotte Perkins Gilman, or Jane Addams. What separates Ella Lyman from these figures is the fact that she did, after eighteen months of deliberation, decide to marry, and indeed remained in a very unique marriage for forty years. Instead of escaping or rejecting normative values regarding women's role in relationships, Lyman assumed the perhaps more difficult task of remaking these norms while also dedicating herself to a relationship with Cabot that was well ahead of their time.

The Specifics of the "Paper on Marriage"

So how was this relationship forged? Between 1892 and 1894, Lyman and Cabot corresponded constantly, and through their letters developed what might be called the logistical side of the "Paper on Marriage." Theirs was a unique prenuptial agreement. Informal contracts regarding the character of marriage were not unique to this couple; many wealthy women of the nineteenth century drafted documents that usually aimed to regulate finances and household responsibilities. The Lyman-Cabot agreement, however, was more complex and considerably more controversial. It formally separated the couple's finances and specified that Lyman would be in charge of her own investments and accounts. It carefully outlined a division of household responsibilities, and stated clearly that both parties would pursue individual occupations. Lyman explains her motivations for writing the paper in the following manner:

> I wrote the paper because I had been feeling doubtful whether you had any right to say that your work must always come first. It hurt me, not from selfishness or jealousy, but because it seemed to say: marriage then means the deliberate subordination of your work to your husband's.[43]

While resembling other prenuptial agreements of the time in certain respects, the Lyman-Cabot agreement departed radically from the norm in others. At the heart of this document was the idea of celibacy, the understanding that Ella would not bear children and that the couple, *out of principle*, would not have sexual intercourse. This self-restraint would be exercised in the name of self-liberation—Ella's liberation. Lyman's idealism sought to reverse the historical understanding of childlessness. The clinical term for childlessness, during Ella's time and in our own, is *nullapara*, derived from the Latin "zero," "void," "absence"—as in a woman who has never been pregnant.

This expression evolved, or devolved, into many different portrayals: the barren crone, the sterile spinster, the infertile woman.[44] Only recently has the *choice* of childlessness connoted the fecund possibilities that women might explore within the companionship of a relationship but beyond the strictures of motherhood. Lyman's case is a very early instance of this turn in thinking. She writes to this effect in a letter dated 1893:

> Marriage does not and ought not to exist merely for the sake of children, that it may be right to marry with the intention of not having children, that there is no reason for not taking our lives into our own hands in this respect as well as every other, that this changes the relative sacrifice that women make as compared with men.[45]

Her pointedly progressive rationale, like the reasoning of an increasing number of married women in the twentieth and twenty-first centuries, is directed at changing the "relative sacrifice that women make as compared to men." Lyman understood that this rationale ran counter to the ideals of her parents' generation; indeed, it remained out of kilter with the American cultural norm for nearly a century. It is in this respect that she observes that it would "kill Mama" to know that the couple had intentionally avoided childrearing in order to ensure *her* daughter's occupational and intellectual opportunities. The irony of this situation was not lost on Ella Lyman, who forewent bearing children in order to give birth to creative projects that had hitherto been the exclusive province of the opposite sex.

PRAGMATIC IDEALISM EMBODIED—READING THE LIFE OF ELLA LYMAN CABOT

Regarding celibacy and childrearing, it would at first glance seem that Richard Cabot took a small yet decisive detour in reaching the agreement with Ella Lyman: "I conceive that two people might find that they can be better *servants of God* by living and working together in a house of their own and belonging specially to each other, who yet found it expedient not to have any children."[46] The theological underpinnings of Cabot's opinion are not surprising; as a teenager, he intended to enter the Unitarian ministry and he remained committed to a particular vision of Christianity through his life. With the passing of the Comstock Laws in 1873, which forbade the distribution of contraceptives and other "licentious materials," the Victorian ideals of purity and chastity were written into the legal code of New England with an unprecedented rigidity. In the face of the dehumanizing force of industrialism and modernization, late Victorians across the Northeast embraced the ideals of asceticism and self-control as a way of reaffirming the primacy and importance of the human will.[47]

For Cabot, a vision of ascetic religious service, rather than the prospect of Lyman's free activity, determined his decision to remain celibate. As he slowly became the spokesperson for their decision, his piousness and proclivity for courtly love seems to have gradually overshadowed her early feminist conviction. In May of 1893, in a series of lectures given at Harvard on the topic of imitation and love, Royce echoes similar sentiments to an audience that most likely would have included one, if not both, of the Cabots. Indeed, he seems to be speaking directly to the couple. He states that,

> The lover as such is a very imitative being. He is not only disposed to a considerable extent to conform to the tastes and ideals of his beloved; but he is also an imitator even in the very act itself of falling in love. Nobody falls in love until he has first often heard that one can fall in love. Think how many lovers have been educated to their nobler passions by Dante's *Vita Nuevo* or by the other classic love poetry.[48]

Royce's comments reflect a sentiment of the time, one that Richard seems to have embraced wholeheartedly, that beatific love could be realized in abstinent repose. Here, we must pause and assess the role that religious considerations played in Ella Lyman's decision to remain celibate. As the marriage developed, she does temper her comments concerning the social and intellectual freedom implied in celibacy by remarks that speak to its ascetic and spiritual appeal and its virtue as the path of devout religious service. During the months when Ella Lyman and Richard Cabot crafted their prenuptials, it seems that they slowly arrived at an agreement that reflected Royce's general position.

To say that she adopts the rhetoric of religious devotion in defense of her unique marriage does not necessarily indicate that Ella Lyman Cabot became less of a feminist in her later life; indeed, it is only at the turn of the century that she actively worked on behalf of the political and intellectual lives of women. It does, however, suggest a particular tension. On the one hand, Lyman had to consistently struggle against the idealization of women that was imposed from her cultural surroundings. On the other hand, the only strain of American feminism that was readily available to her was closely allied with the religious and spiritual idealism of the time, especially the Unitarian-Universalist traditions that found their home in New England. This complicates the story of early American feminism. The practical pursuit of social and political equality for Ella Lyman Cabot, and perhaps for many other women, was enacted in the name of an idealism that took its cues from a particular reading of Christian fellowship and service. This point comes home to us if we return to Green's *Prolegomena* for a moment. This book, one of the most formative in Lyman's philosophical education, concludes with Green stating that a "good will" is realized in the "willingness to endure even unto complete self-renunciation, even to the point of forsaking all possibility of pleasure—the willingness to do this in the service of the highest public cause which the agent can conceive, whether that be the state or the cause of the kingdom of Christ."[49] Today, many feminists would cringe at the idea of Ella Lyman taking up Green's call for "self-renunciation, even to the point of forsaking all pleasure"—their legitimate concern being that this is merely the call to a stereotypically feminine version of self-sacrifice and self-effacement. Lyman's case, however, is unique insofar as her self-renunciation was enacted in the rejection of precisely those matrimonial relations that were geared toward the subjugation of women. In effect, Lyman revises the standard account of Christian piety in order to fashion a genuinely feminist life project. Lyman may have been the first American thinker to self-consciously embody this approach to feminism and Christian idealism, but she was not the first American philosopher to take this general conceptual turn. Royce makes a similar move that is worth exploring in brief.

In an 1881 essay that is often overlooked in the history of American philosophy, Royce highlights the intersection of George Eliot's work as a women's reformer and the religious idealism of the nineteenth century. Indeed, "George Eliot as a Religious Teacher," published after Royce's death in 1916, depicts many of the same ideas found in Ella Lyman Cabot's later writings on ethics and social and political issues. It is no wonder that Cabot states that Eliot's works "had a great impression on me."[50] In his essay on Eliot, Royce says that "the search for what is essential in the religious consciousness became for her a practical necessity," and that her aim was to depict this consciousness without the trappings of myth, superstition, or Christian dogma.[51] This was also certainly the case for Ella Lyman Cabot, who aimed to translate religious idealism into everyday life, and in so doing, affirm her own sense of independence and moral strength. Eliot's dismissal of Church doctrine and tradition coincided with her insistence that religious consciousness could be reflected in a variety of individuals regardless of gender or class. Eliot turned to religious idealism as a practical way of overcoming roles that oppressed the women of her day. Royce picks up on this, noting that her search for spiritual truths led Eliot's characters away from positions of subordination and away from the teachers they had once admired: "the awakened soul . . . must learn to live . . . in the power of self-sustained enthusiasm."[52] Continuing, Royce writes that in the pursuit of religious ideals apparent in so many of Eliot's works, we must learn to outgrow the direct influence of the teacher, just as Janet outgrows the need for her pastor, as Romola outgrows Savonarola, as Deronda learns to do without the prophetic voice of Mordecai, or as Gwendolen hopes to do without the personal magnetism of Deronda.[53]

Royce's suggestion rings with a feminist intonation, for the characters that he cites are women who find independence in a masculine world in the name of religious service.

To fully grasp the resonances between Royce's comments here and the life and thought of Ella Lyman Cabot, a bit more might need to be said in reference to Eliot's characters. Janet Dempster appears as the heroine of Eliot's "Janet's Repentance," a short piece included in the *Scenes of Clerical Life*, Eliot's first published book. Janet is an abused woman—she is beaten by Robert Dempster, who is arguably the most violent of all of Eliot's male characters. He is unarguably the most dramatic figure of male hegemony in her works. In an intoxicated rage, Robert repeatedly hits Janet, accusing *her* of being drunk. This scene is doubly ironic for Janet *does* give herself to alcohol as a way of numbing the pain of subordination experienced by women in the daily life of rural Europe. Janet's repentance is enacted in her total abstinence from alcohol and her turn toward Christianity, first inspired by her pastor. As the story comes to a close the power of this repentance is seen: Janet distances herself from the pastor and quietly triumphs over Robert Dempsey who dies from injuries when he is thrown from a carriage due to his drunkenness. In the final scene, a reader looks on as Janet prays next to Robert's deathbed, consecrating her newfound independence with a prayer. The reader is left to wonder if the prayer is meant for the dying husband or as a word of thanks to God for the freedom that is realized in his death. This confluence of religious submission and personal strength is seen in the other characters that Royce draws from Eliot's writings as well. Romola, first drawn to the zealotry of Savonarola, is at last repelled by his desire for political power; Eliot suggests that Romola frees herself from Savonarola's allure only by way of her steadfast devotion to religious ideals. Gwendolen, likewise, is the true heroine of *Daniel Deronda*. Her love for Deronda is eventually transformed into an ability to live independently and, in her words, "unselfishly." All of these women realize strength and freedom in the name of religious or spiritual dedication. This was also true in the case of Ella Lyman Cabot. Her reflections on marriage and God, her approaches to chastity and charity, and her dedicated work in ethical and religious scholarship all point to a unique idea in American feminism: that a woman could maintain her independence from her husband and from a dominant society through her embodiment of certain religious ideals.

This is a difficult idea for many contemporary theorists to swallow, and for Cabot and Eliot, the overlap between religious idealism and feminism appears to have been at once both problematic and beneficial. It was problematic in the sense that these women remained unwilling to claim certain freedoms on their own account (without the language of Christian religiosity), but beneficial to the degree that idealism masked or excused practices that would have otherwise received disapprobation in the still conservative centers of New England. This approach to American feminism emerges in one of Lyman's early reflections on marriage, written in 1889. She opens her comments with a type of religious dedication: "I think it is in some ways harder to live a married life in single minded service of God than as an unmarried woman."[54] In the same quotation, this religiosity, however, gives way to her very practical concerns about the ways in which women of her time have been made slaves to household duties:

> I have dread of either becoming frittered away in the innumerable petty claims of a woman's work or of growing slack and slipshod in it . . . Some women think all day about their parlour curtains, and others leave their windows unwashed for weeks. Mamma does neither, but she has given up her life to her family. I want money not to have luxuries, but to prevent giving brain work and time to petty questions of economy. I can't afford to haggle over the question of having salad or not for dinner. It is hard enough not to get narrowed in our interests.[55]

Lyman does not explain how her aversion to domestic obligations might coincide with her "single minded service to God," but her claim does seem to suggest that she envisions this service as being performed in the realization of new possibilities for womanhood rather than in the traditional roles of the late Victorian era. In the preceding decades, the duties of the household had doubled as the duties of "womanly" service in Protestant New England. In her marriage and in her later life, Ella Lyman Cabot would draw this elision into question by maintaining that loyal religious service, in the Roycean sense, must by definition be *freely* and thoughtfully given rather than forced by custom or norm.

Her conception of womanhood and its various possibilities would be underpinned by Royce's early understanding of loyalty (developed in his classes in the mid-1890s) but also by Emerson's rendering of God and religiosity, a rendering that remained starkly radical in comparison to the sermons given at Kings Chapel. In 1908, Cabot reflects on her indebtedness to Emerson's works, writing that, "Reading Emerson's Oversoul, Self-Reliance, and the Divinity School Address at about 16 first changed my conception of God; first prepared me to think of God as a whole of which we are true fragments than as a separate father."[56] For Emerson, involvement in the religious spirit required the embodiment of freely chosen purposes by way of self-reliant action. Cabot's appeal to religion must be understood in this context rather than as harkening back to a more conservative and traditional mode of spirituality. This becomes obvious as Cabot continually criticizes the patriarchy of the Church history and doctrine. Describing the formation of her religious beliefs, she writes that as a girl she was, "shocked and hurt by the old man picture of God in a good many of the religious pictures of Europe."[57] If Cabot was reticent to allow an "old man" to be her eternal God, she was even more reluctant to allow a man to be her worldly master. The "Paper on Marriage" should be regarded as the practical attempt to pursue transcendental ideals of freedom, creativity, and originality. It is in this sense that Cabot's feminism, in line with Royce's philosophy of loyalty, was a type of pragmatic idealism.

Both in her writings and in her daily activities, Cabot reflected a reverence for the relations of life—those freely constructed bonds that Royce described as the tethering of the individual to wider and more meaningful selves. This being said, Cabot departed significantly from Royce in her emphasis on the sanctity of possibility, chance, and a particular conception of autonomy. In a journal passage written while honeymooning in Italy, she states: "The central blessing of our lives that which holds our marriage in its peace is that we can help each other continually serve God better. *It is our sacred and awful trust to hold ourselves and one the other to growth and eager embracing of opportunity.*"[58] Ella Lyman Cabot's take on religiosity turned on the ability to pursue opportunities that fell outside the everyday habits and domestic limits of womanhood. At a relatively young age she understood that ideals such as social–political opportunity and gender equality could neither be realized in the quiet writings of one's journal nor in the mere talk of social reform. Instead, these ideals had to be pursued practically and doggedly in the course of daily life.

The Portrait of a Pragmatic "Lady"

Cabot's journals throughout the 1890s serve as an anthropological sign of this type of feminist activity. Next to her intellectual positions on marriage and gender norms, we find the markers of the practical ways that Cabot sought to counteract these norms. Immediately after their marriage on October 26, 1894, the Cabots traveled to northern Italy to begin their lives together. This is where the two would read the *Divine Comedy*; Richard Cabot undoubtedly understood his newly formed relationship in terms of this classical piece of literature. However, another more recent book could just as easily have served as the guide for Ella Cabot's trip to the continent. Henry James's *The Portrait of a Lady*, written a decade earlier, had quickly become a part of the cultural milieu of Boston at the end of the century. It is the story of a young woman's unusually free spirit, which is tragically tamped down, despite her greatest efforts, by a society that is still ill-prepared for a woman's liberation. It is the story of Isabel Archer's opportunity and personal growth, cultivated and protected by a great fortune, but eventually destroyed by a man who drains Isabel's finances and thereby robs her of her independence. Isabel meets this man, Osmond, in the hills of northern Italy; and it is here that a newly married Ella Cabot finds herself in 1894.

The similarities were obvious. While both Lyman and Cabot came from families of great wealth, it was patently obvious that Ella Lyman's fortune dwarfed her future husband's. Indeed, by the time of her death, her estate was one of the largest held by a woman in the United States, easily topping one and a half million dollars. If her aspirations for intellectual and personal freedom were to be more than an empty idea, Cabot realized that she had to avoid the fate of Isabel Archer—taking control of her life by taking control of her practical affairs. One would expect that a journal kept during a honeymoon might be a testament to romance and commitment. We find something quite different in Ella Lyman Cabot's diary from November 1894: "November 13, 1894 . . . Richard owes me—10 francs (4fr. for the carriage, 3 for photos, 3 borrowed) . . . November 14 . . . R. owes me 2.5 for photos, 1fr. borrowed."[59] This is a small artifact of a feminist at work. The account and ledger continues for many pages, always in the same manner. Richard Cabot repeatedly borrowed money, and Ella Cabot kept meticulous care of the money she lent him. Her life seems to anticipate Gilman's words from *Women and Economics* (1898): "Marriage is not perfect unless it is between class equals. There is no equality in class between those who do their share in the world's work in the largest, newest, highest ways and those who do theirs in the smallest, oldest, lowest ways."[60] According to McCormick, sex and money were the two things of which the Cabots never spoke. This twofold silence is telling. These were the two subjects that were to ensure gender equality in the relationship, and it seems clear from the writings of Cabot, Gilman, and other early feminists that American culture at the turn of the century was not yet ready to hear about this sort of parity.

CORRIDORS, PASSAGES, AND DEAD ENDS

In the fall of 1906, William James gave a series of lectures at the Lowell Institute that would become *Pragmatism*, a centerpiece of classical American philosophy. In his second lecture, he suggests that pragmatism was a thoughtful way of moving through a meaningful intellectual life, between the various projects that occupied the time and efforts of the American scholars of his day:

> [Pragmatism is] like a corridor in a hotel. Innumerable chambers open out of it. In one you may find a man writing an atheistic volume; in the next some one on his knees praying for faith and strength; in a third a chemist investigating a body's properties. In a fourth a system of idealistic metaphysics is being excogitated; in a fifth the impossibility of metaphysics is being shown. But they all own the corridor, and all must pass through it if they want a practicable way of getting into or out of their respective rooms.[61]

This corridor of philosophy opened out into rooms occupied by men at work—philosophizing, investigating, praying. These men "all own the corridor," that is to say that they owned the method by which ideas could be realized, distinguished, and judged by their practical consequences. Men owned this corridor of philosophy by which they could make their way into any thoughtful pursuit. Ella Lyman Cabot only occasionally traversed this highly trafficked passageway in the "hotel" of American intellectual life. In this hotel, she appeared and disappeared, giving the impression of an infrequent visitor *en route* to her permanent and comfortably domesticated home. In truth, Cabot was always there, making her way through hidden passages.

Through these passages Ella Lyman Cabot arrived at workrooms that have generally been forgotten in the history of classical American philosophy. Here she developed six published books on ethics and education between 1906 and her death in 1934 that expand and anticipate the philosophical works of many of her male contemporaries. The published contributions that Cabot made to the philosophical canon are tied closely, tied pragmatically, to what she would describe as a continued attempt to further the moral and intellectual development of young women. In the year that *Pragmatism* was published, Cabot reflected that her work had been "for the sake of helping the girls who are facing in lonely battle all their life problems . . . [and that] ever since I studied ethics twenty years ago this desire to help girls who are puzzled has been strong."[62] Cabot's published and unpublished materials turn on the broad philosophical topics of her day: the status of possibility in the universe and moral life, the questions of creativity and unity, the cultivation of virtue in a world without absolutes. These are issues that Peirce, Royce, James, and Dewey would take up, but never with the same practical commitments to the lives of women. The stakes in this sort of philosophy would always be higher for Cabot. When she looked back over the twenty years of her studies, her gaze came to rest on herself as the twenty-three-year-old who stated that "a girl's life is indefinitely harder than a man's in some ways." Her life remained harder in many ways as she faced poor health, depression, indecision, and the type of apathy that is produced when idealism is twisted by, and eventually succumbs to, reality.

Looking down a hidden corridor is often a matter of facing an unsettling darkness. This darkness can be unsettling in at least two respects. First, the obscurity of such passages, the fact that they appear unexplored, may lead one to assume that such little hallways must inevitably terminate in a series of dead ends. This particular feeling of being unsettled is frequently provoked in the task of recovering the work of Ella Lyman Cabot. In many cases, her philosophy is tucked away in journals and unpublished seminar papers. Often, Cabot will lead a reader down a promising intellectual path only to stop short, cutting herself and the reader off from the philosophical account that is all but promised in the course of her discussion. Facing the frustration of being both philosopher and woman in 1908, Cabot apologizes to her reader, stating, "There are times when any advance seems beyond my reach. I can just hold on to what I know and appear outward by the same constant effort."[63] The darkness of private hallways is unsettling in another respect. This darkness brings up a number of questions—Why are these passages not public? Why is there no lamp here to light the way? Will I like where I am going?—that repeatedly surface in the course of investigating Cabot's work. To answer these questions is to address the cultural and intellectual climate of Cabot's time. It is also to grapple with the fact that women continue to be marginalized in the discipline of philosophy. There is, according to Cabot, good reason to face this darkness. After admitting that many projects and ideas lie beyond her reach, Cabot provides a Thoreauvian affirmation that drives her reader forward:

> Still I believe that the things learned in silence and almost in the dark may be the most deeply rooted. Only keep your eyes open: it is not the night in its darkness that is harmful, for the day will again dawn; but only the bleedings of eyes that will not open to the light.[64]

Opening one's eyes to a new subject, like the life and work of Ella Lyman Cabot, can be extremely disorienting. Exploring the life and work of any member of the American philosophical canon is to take account of a variety of historical, personal, cultural, and intellectual factors that have been written out of our contemporary understanding of the movement. This rendering of the philosophy of Ella Lyman Cabot is an attempt to reacquaint us with these factors and recognize the rich intellectual heritage that was once identified with the American philosophical tradition. In large part, it is an effort to identify a number of forgotten individuals who tread lightly, but frequently, through the halls of this philosophical tradition.

NOTES

1. Richard Clarke Cabot Papers, Harvard University Archives. HUG 4255.80. Box 1. "Notebook 1."
2. Cited in Linda Simon, *Genuine Reality: A Life of William James* (Chicago: University of Chicago Press, 1999), 358.
3. Richard Clarke Cabot Papers, Harvard University Archives. HUG 4255.80. Box 18. "On the Beatrice Relation."
4. Alfred North Whitehead, *The Dialogues of Alfred North Whitehead* (David R. Godine Publisher, 2001), 31.
5. Collected Papers of Ella Lyman Cabot. A 139.
6. A 139/34. "ELC/RCC corr. 1893."
7. A 139/34. "ELC/RCC corr. 1893."
8. A 139/33. "ELC/RCC corr. 1892."
9. Richard Clarke Cabot Papers, Harvard University Archives. HUG 4255. Box 1. "ELC Ch. 1 and 2."
10. This is apparent in the correspondence between Emerson and James Elliott Cabot. See *Cabot Family Papers, 1786–1945* housed at Schlesinger Library at the Radcliffe Institute for Advanced Study, Harvard University. A 99/123. See also *Emerson, Ralph Waldo, 1803–1882. Letters to James Elliot Cabot* housed at Houghton Library. Harvard University. MS Am 1718.
11. Richard Clarke Cabot Papers, Harvard University Archives. HUG 4255.80. Box 8. "RCC's Youth."
12. Ella Lyman Cabot, *Temptations to Rightdoing* (New York: Houghton Mifflin, 1929), 160.
13. Cited in John Clendenning, *The Life and Thought of Josiah Royce* (Nashville: Vanderbilt University Press, 1999), 205. This note is written by Richard Cabot in response to the announcement of his wedding to Ella Lyman, in which Cabot writes, "You are a sort of philosophic father to both of us [Lyman and himself]—both of us took our first taste for speculation from your Religious Aspect." HUG 1755. Box 121. Folder 121.
14. A 139/32. "ELC/RCC corr. 1888–1889."
15. A 139/32. "ELC/RCC corr. 1888–1889."
16. A 139/32. "ELC/RCC corr. 1888–1889."
17. A 139/32. "ELC/RCC corr. 1888–1889."
18. A 139/278 V, 1908.
19. A 139/278 V, 1908.
20. It should be noted that Royce was, at this point in his career, still grappling for a foothold as the preeminent philosopher of history—a fact that might have contributed to his vitriol. Later in his life Royce would temper his own definition of philosophy, stating in a lecture course at Smith College: "[T]he very essence of philosophy is the spirit of earnest toleration—the reasonable respect for the man that differs from one's own views—the readiness to treat individuality reverently, even while one contends for one's own view of the truth." In "Philosophy and Life" (1909), in the Lectures to Smith College. The Papers of Josiah Royce, Harvard University Archives. 1755. Box 77. p. 39. This comment, however, came only after the suicide of Abbott in 1903. Abbott remained disturbed by his rejection by the Harvard community and was distraught by the recent death of his wife.
21. A 139/33. "ELC/RCC corr. 1892."
22. A 139/16. "Scattered pages of APM ts. notes for ELC biography."
23. A 139/16. "Scattered pages of APM ts. notes for ELC biography."
24. A 139/16. "Scattered pages of APM ts. notes for ELC biography.
25. A 139/16. "Scattered pages of APM ts. notes for ELC biography."
26. A 139/34. "ELC/RCC corr. 1893."
27. A 139/320v. "Philosophical reflections on God, Josiah Royce, etc. 1892."
28. A 139/320v. "Philosophical reflections on God, Josiah Royce, etc. 1892."
29. Avital Simhony and David Weinstein, *The New Liberalism: Reconciling Liberty and Community* (Cambridge: Cambridge University Press, 2001), 80.

30. Green elaborates on this point: "This well being he doubtless conceives as his own but that he should conceive it as exclusively his own in any sense in which it is not equally and coincidentally a well being of others would be incompatible with the fact that it is only as living in community as sharing the life of others as incorporated in the continuous being of a family or nation of a state or a church that he can sustain himself in that thought of his own permanence to which the thought of permanent well being is correlative." See Thomas Hill Green, *Prolegomena to Ethics* (Oxford: Clarendon Press, 1906), 273–74.

31. A 139/320v. "Philosophical reflections on God, Josiah Royce, etc. 1892."
32. A 139/320v. "Philosophical reflections on God, Josiah Royce, etc. 1892."
33. A 139/320v. "Philosophical reflections on God, Josiah Royce, etc. 1892."
34. Marilyn Frye, *The Politics of Reality* (Berkeley: The Crossing Press, 1983), 2–17.
35. A 139/320v. "Philosophical reflections on God, Josiah Royce, etc. 1892."
36. A 139/320v. "Philosophical reflections on God, Josiah Royce, etc. 1892."
37. Thomas Hill Green, *Prolegomena to Ethics* (Oxford: Clarendon Press, 1906), 229.
38. Green, *Prolegomena to Ethics*, 229.
39. Green, *Prolegomena to Ethics*, 229.
40. Josiah Royce, *The Philosophy of Loyalty* (New York: Macmillan, 1920), 54.
41. A 139/320v. "Philosophical reflections on God, Josiah Royce, etc. 1892."
42. A 139/320v. "Philosophical reflections on God, Josiah Royce, etc. 1892."
43. A 139/34. "ELC/RCC corr. 1893."
44. Laurie Lisle, *Without Child: Challenging the Stigma of Childlessness* (New York: Routledge, 1999), 5.
45. A 139/34. "ELC/RCC corr. 1893."
46. A 139/34. "ELC/RCC corr. 1893."
47. For a detailed account of Victorian sexual attitudes, see James Adams, "Victorian Sexualities," in *A Companion to Victorian Literature*, ed. Herbert Tucker (New York: Wiley-Blackwell, 1999), 128.
48. HUG 1755. Box 64. "Lectures to Teachers (1893)."
49. Green, *Prolegomena to Ethics*, 280.
50. A 139/14–20.
51. Josiah Royce, *The Fugitive Essays* (Cambridge: Harvard University Press, 1920), 283.
52. Royce, *The Fugitive Essays*, 283.
53. Royce, *The Fugitive Essays*, 283.
54. A 139/16. "Scattered pages of APM ts. notes for ELC biography."
55. A 139/16. "Scattered pages of APM ts. notes for ELC biography."
56. A 139/278 V. "April–July 1908; includes diary entries 1910, 1914."
57. A 139/278 V. "April–July 1908; includes diary entries 1910, 1914."
58. A 39/16. "Scattered pages of APM ts. notes for ELC biography."
59. A 139/274v.
60. Charlotte Perkins Stetson, *Women and Economics: A Study of Economic Relation Between Men and Women as a Factor in Social Evolution* (New York: Small, Maynard and Co., 1898), 220.
61. William James, *Pragmatism* (London: Longman, Green, and Co. 1907), 54.
62. A 139/278V. "April–July 1908; includes diary entries 1910, 1914."
63. A 139/278V. "April–July 1908; includes diary entries 1910, 1914."
64. A 139/278V. "April–July 1908; includes diary entries 1910, 1914."

Chapter Two

Women and Forgotten Movements in American Philosophy: Ella Lyman Cabot and Mary Parker Follett on Growth and Creativity[1]

> We need the past, every bit of it, for the sake of all our future. We cannot afford to forget although there must be many things that we store away till we are capable of assimilating them. We need all we can digest. For some experiences we must wait till our digestion grows stronger.
> —Ella Lyman Cabot, 1899 Notebook[2]

"MOVING" IN THE CORRIDORS OF AMERICAN PHILOSOPHY

Men, and men alone, frequented the "corridors" of classical American philosophy. This belief remained wholly unchallenged for much of the twentieth century and was only fully debunked in the last two decades. How it was established in the first place is a question that deserves greater attention, for it might explain why figures such as Ella Lyman Cabot were marginalized and then forgotten in the "silver age" of American philosophy. In 1952, Joseph Blau wrote *Men and Movements in American Philosophy*.[3] As the title indicates, Blau suggested that the work of men—from Ralph Waldo Emerson, to William James, to Josiah Royce, to John Dewey—provided the motivating force in the development of classical American thought. The author claims that his intent is to present "the more formal side of our formal philosophical history, to provide a general reader and the beginning student an introduction which will enable them to read further in and about American philosophy."[4] Throughout his account, Blau seems to forget the many movements that women philosophers made in this development of our philosophical history. Of course Blau is not wholly, or even largely, responsible for the marginalization of women in the American canon. His book, however, extends a pattern of scholarship, established in the first decade of the twentieth century, which served to eulogize and enshrine the work of men such as James and Royce while largely overlooking the contributions of women in the field. This neglect can be set in context if one remembers that women were not the principal *teachers* of philosophy in the golden age of American philosophy, and subsequently they had no students to carry on their legacies. It is easy to forget the role that the students of James and Royce played in maintaining the reputation of their teachers' "greatness." Figures such as Ralph Barton Perry, William Ernest Hocking, and Richard Cabot spent time and energy establishing a philosophical "cult of the dead" that kept their former teachers' writings in circulation and restated their importance. This effort was largely responsible for creating the canon that Blau worked through in his well-known survey.

Since the writing of *Men and Movements*, however, various attempts have been made to counteract the marginalization of women in American philosophy. Charlene Haddock Seigfried's work in the 1980s set the stage for a countermovement by scholars who have recently tried to expose the buried roots of the American tradition.[5] Judy Whipps and Marilyn Fischer have joined Seigfried in successfully creating a space for Jane Addams in the field of American philosophy and in the broader context of social and political thought.[6] Dorothy Rogers has assumed the important but relatively thankless task of remembering the forgotten thinkers who were the first women to teach philosophy in American universities in the mid-nineteenth century.[7] In so doing, she has re-membered the American canon, providing space for younger scholars to explore these women's writings in greater detail. This sort of investigation is also under way in the writing of Scott Pratt and Erin McKenna, among others. Pratt's *Native Pragmatism* makes the case that American philosophy should be understood as emerging from the experiences of a diverse group of individuals, including women and others who have been routinely excluded from the discipline of professional philosophy.[8] McKenna's *Task of Utopia* undertakes a similar project by concentrating on women, such as Charlotte Perkins Gilman, who have been written out of the history of philosophy but who deserve inclusion due to their embodiment of sophisticated and novel ideals.[9]

I take my cues from these scholars who have refigured the American philosophical tradition by including thinkers who have hitherto been excluded from this relatively narrow canon. This book stands as a small contribution in this larger project of recovery by addressing the writings of a woman who worked amidst the "movers and shakers" who are usually cited in the formation of this philosophical tradition. The works of Ella Lyman Cabot invite us to reinterpret the direction and content of American pragmatism as it emerged in the academic circles of New England at the turn of the twentieth century. Not only did her thinking influence the philosophical musings of her male counterparts—a fact that is consistently ignored—but it stands in its own right as a unique turn in American thought. This woman turned toward philosophical issues of creativity, invention, and social unity in ways that remained unexplored by the mainstream.

In this chapter, I will first discuss the Cabot papers, a selection of which have been presented, all of which are housed at the Schlesinger Library at Radcliffe College. I will concentrate on the material written between 1887 and 1902; these are Cabot's early papers. During this period Cabot writes extensively on the concepts of growth and wholeness. Much of her early work responds to lectures that Royce gave in the 1890s. During this period, Cabot continually asserts that creativity and spontaneity must be the defining characteristics of the natural and social spheres and appears to have served as a helpful interlocutor for Royce as his thinking matured during this decade.[10] This supposition is borne out by a comparison of Royce's *The World and the Individual* (1899–1901) and Cabot's contemporaneous writings and is also presented in Royce's own notebooks that he kept while Cabot was his student.[11] In the earliest years of the twentieth century, Cabot wrote "Wholeness in Relation to Growth." In this unpublished work, and in a variety of earlier notebooks, she extends and complements Royce's thinking on unity and growth. These early works by Cabot give us valuable insight into her teacher's intellectual development but also provide the necessary context to understand her *Everyday Ethics*, published in 1906 as a manual on pedagogical methods and the ethical upbringing of children. This work reflects Cabot's willingness to translate metaphysical and theoretical issues into the language of the "every day." In effect, she is willing to make the philosophy of pragmatism truly practical.

In 1924, Mary Parker Follett published *Creative Experience* and dedicated it to her friend and mentor: Ella Lyman Cabot. In the opening pages, she thanks Cabot for her "faith in the crescent power of the human spirit" that she attempts to give expression in *Creative Experience*. I will briefly address Cabot's legacy, as extended in Follett's work. This chronological leap—from 1902 to 1924—is intended to expose the way in which Cabot's early work, written in a time where women were just gaining access to the field of philosophy and the social sciences, resonates closely with her peer, who had the privilege of working more actively in the next generation of women scholars. Follett inherits her mentor's abiding interest in the relation between spontaneity, growth, and purpose but, more significantly, understands that this interest is vitally important to the revision and flourishing of the social sphere. By juxtaposing the early work of Cabot and the mature work of Follett, one comes to see just how forward looking the young Ella Lyman Cabot was. Both women went on to write books in ethics and political philosophy in the aftermath of World War I, and they were some of the first pragmatists to suggest that conceptions of social progress and growth must be rethought if we are to avoid international conflict and to encourage the flourishing of viable communities. This suggestion is the product of genuinely feminist thinking. Follett's treatment of creativity repeatedly points to the political and phenomenological experience of women in the attempt to explain the way in which creative progress—often construed as the project of solitary individuals—might be reframed as the project of coordinating communities. I will concentrate on her 1919 "Community as Process" and two sections of *Creative Experience* titled "Experience as Creating" and "Experience in Light of Recent Psychology: The Gestalt Concept, Integrative Behavior, and Circular Response." Here, Follett reveals herself as an important figure in the formation of first- and second-wave feminism and in the history of American thought, demonstrating a broad understanding of the work of Royce and James but, more important, a willingness to employ pragmatic sensibilities in novel ways in addressing feminist and social-political concerns.

This analysis reveals a woman who *could* have changed the character of classical American thought—but did not. Cabot's social position, her emotional disposition, and the scholarly climate of her day (and ours) have largely allowed her to be forgotten in our accounts of American intellectual history. While recovering her works stands as an important philosophical project, it is also a chance to access the cultural-academic patina of her time. As John Dewey says, philosophy is always a reflection of culture; this fact is placed in stark relief as one explores Cabot's work.

ROYCEAN INTERPRETATIONS: THE EARLY NOTEBOOKS OF ELLA LYMAN CABOT

Ella Lyman Cabot's undergraduate notebooks from the 1890s reflect a vibrant intellectual dialogue with Richard Cabot, a Harvard professor of sociology and medicine, whom she would later marry in 1894, but also a sustained engagement with the principal figures in the American philosophical tradition, most notably Josiah Royce. She "attended" Royce's seminar on metaphysics in 1888 by way of her correspondence with Richard Cabot and began to attend classes in person in 1890, beginning with Herbert Palmer's class in ethics. She took a variety of other courses with Royce over the next twelve years. Both of the Cabots participated in the "Philosophical Conference" of 1903 and 1904, which Royce organized at his Irving Street home. William James comments that these conferences were in fact motivated by the Cabots' desire to spend more time with Royce, mocking that "the Conference is a queer illustration of the Cabots' inability to live without Royce."[12] Ella Lyman Cabot's correspondence with Royce would last nearly four decades, and Royce repeatedly sought the Cabots' advice over this extended period.[13] When Royce begins to develop the "Lusitania Address," his last public lecture, it is Ella Lyman Cabot who is consulted for guidance.

In the later stages of her career, Cabot published several works on the education of children that continually reversed standard pedagogical assumptions: instead of discussing how teachers ought to instruct their students, she explores what *educators* might learn from their *students*. In the spirit of this work, I hope to explore the lessons that Cabot's notebooks, written as a student, teach us about the development of American philosophy but also the way in which her notebooks make an original contribution to the canon. This investigation is not intended to expose the way in which philosophy devours its young, nor the way that the young minds of Cambridge sought to overthrow their teachers. Indeed, what is perhaps most apparent in Cabot's work is a sustained affection for learning and, by extension, for her teachers and their thoughts. Cabot's criticism is always tempered by a remarkable intellectual charity. This charity survives even when she struggles with her professors, and, in fact, her struggles often turn on the issue of charity. In 1892, she wrote:

> Dewey perhaps understates what Royce dwells on too much—the storm-stress aspects of life. Dewey's attitude is tremendously healthy . . . and he is not without feeling and appreciation as the half-unintentional touches in his books show. But could he possibly have such a wide sympathy as Royce with mystics and romanticists? Could he be as fair to them as Royce is? And if not is his position the best one! A healthy scorn for all things abstract and spiritual is a bracing tonic, but passion and pathos and the tragedy and mystery of life are real and sometimes so life-giving as to be the only world we can see and they must be met with understanding criticism not mere condemnation.[14]

In this rich passage, we come to understand Cabot's generous approach to her teachers' positions but also her insistence that philosophy must be charitable to the experiences that seem so real and "life-giving" in our world. These are experiences of "passion, pathos, and tragedy" that the "mystic and romanticist" typify but, more important, that many people meaningfully embody in their daily pursuits. This passage gives us an idea of Cabot's philosophical temperament but also her abiding concerns, namely, her interest in giving philosophical form to pathos and tragedy. In Royce, Cabot finds a teacher who speaks directly to this interest.[15] In Cabot, we find a participant-observer in the field of classical American thought who recognized and described the tension that slowly developed through the 1890s between Royce's idealism, which still took the problem of evil seriously, and Dewey's instrumentalism, which tended to gloss the problem by focusing on providing creative and pragmatic solutions to the problems of the real world. Cabot is not happy with this disciplinary either-or and is able in the first sentence of this passage to critique *both* of these famous thinkers—Royce for dwelling on the problem too much, Dewey for neglecting it.

This being said, Cabot was often inclined to take Royce's position and to appreciate his courage in facing existential crisis. Through Cabot, we come to see Royce's struggle with the problem of evil and the character of the tragic through the 1890s. She writes in 1892:

> We owe Royce a very deep debt of gratitude for the courage and simplicity with which he has told of his own spiritual experiences. It is doubly convincing and inspiring because it is far more real when a man tells you in what a close way his philosophy coincides with his life. It helps me when I feel the faith, confidence and courage that his thought of the Absolute self gives to me. It moves me with grateful trust when he says: "I have often found it deeply comforting in the most bitter moments."[16]

Cabot, however, is never fawning in her gratitude.[17] While the thought of a unifying Absolute occasionally gave her confidence and courage, she seems to hold reservations in regard to a particular strain of monism that considered the Absolute as an all-encompassing entity or consciousness. This is to say that Cabot never fully accepted all of the points of Royce's idealism. Instead, she was more open to Royce's later suggestion that the Absolute ought to be understood as a well-ordered system or community of interpretation. Cabot, however, curbs her enthusiasm and remains reticent to embrace an ideal of an ordered community on the grounds that order, at least at first glance, seems to impede personal invention and the growth of particular individuals.

This reticence seems to stem more from her immediate experience as a woman in the social sphere of nineteenth-century New England than from any esoteric commitment. Struggling with the cohesion and expectations of her own community, Cabot writes in April 1892: "The danger in living in a family and state surrounded by customs that seem *unalterable and part of nature* is that that very influence which is such an essential factor in one's development retards our swift advance."[18] This is a remarkable comment. Not only is Cabot ahead of her time in drawing out the dangers of naturalizing cultural norms, a point that would be made in detail by Charlotte Perkins Gilman and Alain Locke at the turn of the century, but her comment sets her off from many of her male teachers, who remained relatively quiet on the subject of oppression and alienation. The one notable exception was Royce, who understood the pitfalls of institutional norms, standards that maintained their power at the expense of personal creativity and originality.

Throughout her life's work, Cabot continues to express concerns about the tension between ordered unity, belief in which allows Royce to weather the tragic storms of his life, and the idea of personal growth and development. As Frank Oppenheim notes, this is a tension that resides at the heart of Royce's thought through the late 1880s and early 1890s. His experience as an outsider—*inside* Harvard—resonates closely with Cabot's own experience as a talented woman in an unwelcoming intellectual sphere. John McDermott has repeatedly underlined this aspect of Royce's writings.[19] In reflections that respond to their existential and political situations, Cabot and Royce, in varying degrees, realize that a philosophy of community cannot be a philosophy that stifles newness, possibility, and creativity. In an early notebook (1892), Cabot suggests that personal growth and the growth of community are compatible ideals, stating:

> *The art of living is becoming other people.* We are unfit to deal with the tragic vital world until we can see through others lives that we may anticipate, grapple, and respond to their need—living lives with absolute understanding so that we can see all their point of view and beyond to what they really stand for. Oh God! Ever this lesson sink in deep![20]

The opening line of this passage can cut in one of two directions. First, the art of living is becoming other people in the sense that each of us discovers ourselves in the midst of a process of creation and self-transcendence. I grow. I mature. I become another person. Second, the art of living is becoming other people in the sense that our growth and maturation are always contingent on our ability to find ourselves in a wider community of interpretation. In effect, the art of living is always a collective and interactive affair that seeks to sympathetically integrate—not arrogantly assimilate—the purposes of others. The "other people" that we become in our creative enterprises seems intentionally ambiguous. It is true that I become other than I am at present but also that I do so only by way of my involvement and empathetic actions with others. It is worth noting that this passage of Cabot is written in the early 1890s, well before Royce had fully developed his thinking on loyalty and communities of interpretation. It stands to reason that Cabot's thinking on these issues may have contributed to this development. Royce thanks her in the acknowledgments of the *Philosophy of Loyalty* (1906) and the *Problem of Christianity* (1913). We now have the opportunity to understand his gratitude. This point will be developed in the coming sections.

In reading the early Cabot notebooks, it is often difficult to determine the source of the philosophical voice—whether this is the voice of the student, Cabot, or the teacher, Royce. In either case, it is possible to glean particular insights from these papers. On the one hand, we may be reading a genuine contribution to the canon that was alternately appropriated and forgotten. On the other hand, we may be getting a chance to see the message that Royce was expressing in his lectures, if not in his published works, in the early 1890s. At least one important point the latter case may obtain. Cabot describes Royce's lectures on ethics in detail, stating:

> Insight and order Royce said are the elements essential to morality. Moral conduct involves 1) the power of appreciation of interests outside of your own, the recognition of the interests of others as real and 2) the ordering of our world out of chaos into self-possession. These are the two factors that cause all problems and all advance. We grow by newly acquired insight into moral truth by so enlarging our private self through love such that it becomes more and more a social self, bound up with the life of others—and by ordering our insight so that it becomes our permanent possession . . . *Royce's ethical motto: "Act so as to make more ties and stronger ones . . . that is be LOYAL and loyalty includes sympathy and order."* [21]

This reflection was written on March 8, 1892, more than fifteen years before Royce's writing of the *Philosophy of Loyalty* (1908). There are two ways of understanding this comment. First, thanks to Cabot, we get a snapshot of Royce's early thinking on the issues of loyalty and the ideal of the community; this is a snapshot that provides additional evidence for the position, expressed by Oppenheim and Anderson, that Royce's metaphysics grows increasingly personal, centering on the relations between finite individuals and a personal God.[22] Additionally, her reflections allow us to dispel any lingering suspicions that Royce was an esoteric "head-in-the clouds" metaphysician. Royce appears to be constantly testing his ideas in the classroom, always interested in the traction that philosophy might have in the ethical affairs of daily life. Second, the vignette of Royce that Cabot renders is itself a type of Roycean interpretation, an original contribution to the development of American thought. In her engagement with Royce's work, we get a real sense of Cabot's willingness to engage in the interpersonal relations of a Roycean community.[23] The loyalty to which Cabot refers may have been discussed at great length in Royce's early seminar, or it could be the case that Cabot herself is adding the emphasis on the topic of loyalty and feeds it back to Royce as an extension and modification of his thinking. This is reasonable given that the *Philosophy of Loyalty* is dedicated to Ella Lyman Cabot. In any case, at the very least we hear a genuine interpretation of Royce, provided by a devoted student who integrates Royce's interest in the relation between the concept of unity, what

Cabot later calls "wholeness," and the concept of creative growth in her own projects and pursuits. Indeed, questions of creativity and integrity seem to define not only her academic writings but her most personal thoughts and actions.

A final point needs to be made on the topic of Cabot as providing an interpretation of the American philosophy of her time. Ella Lyman Cabot lived, studied, and wrote at a very unique time in American intellectual history. Her proximity to Royce and James allows her to witness, and reflect upon, the profound tension that had emerged between the idealism of the past century and the pragmatic instrumentalism that was to define the coming one. Indeed, the 1903 Philosophical Conference that the Cabots helped organize serves as a watershed moment in the thinking of James and Royce. James did not participate in the Conference consistently, suggesting that it was merely a small group of philosophical idealists who remained committed to a moribund philosophy that had little practical effect. He expressed this position at the one meeting that he did attend where he presented the work of John Dewey's Chicago School. Here, James is ecstatic to think that pragmatism had found a home in the Midwest and that a genuine school of American philosophy had emerged under Dewey's watch. When he presents the material at Royce's conference, it is obvious that James had set Royce's idealism and Dewey's instrumentalism in opposition: Royce was the old-fashioned metaphysician who remained detached from the affairs of the world, hung up on the religious questions of evil and salvation; Dewey was the up-and-coming thinker who successfully attempted to integrate theory and practice. Despite the close friendship between James and Royce, James seems to take more than a little bit of delight in using Dewey as a tool against his Irving Street neighbor. He muses to both F. C. S. Schiller and to Dewey that Royce was "extremely cut under" by Dewey's insistence that philosophy was to be judged by its ability to reconstruct human experience in the concrete. James thought he had given Royce's idealism a good thrashing and reflected that Royce was taking the beating as "benightedly as possible." Ella Lyman Cabot was present at this thrashing and watched her mentor reel in the wake of James's presentation of the Chicago School.[24]

Dewey's work was bold in its willingness to face concrete social issues. At least at first glance, its methodology seemed at odds with the careful deductive system building that often defined Royce's work. The mild antipathy that emerged between Royce and Dewey can be traced to a difference in philosophical disposition but also to the fact that Royce may have grown frustrated by having tried, unsuccessfully, to put forward a type of idealism that was amenable to social reform, to concrete political practices, and to the type of meliorism that would define James's later work and Dewey's social and political thought. As Cabot's comments from the 1890s seem to demonstrate, Royce maintained that idealism only "makes its philosophical living" in the activities of individuals and their communities. Indeed, Royce opens the 1903 Philosophical Conference with a wish to make idealism practical:

> I would express a wish to have more of applied philosophy than the seminary gives me, and more of a somewhat practical kind of discussion than it is proper to emphasize in ordinary philosophical theses. This more is what I hope to get in company with you.[25]

Cabot reiterates this point, stating that Royce's ethical motto, one that he repeats throughout his classes, is "Act so as to make more ties and stronger ones . . . that is be LOYAL and loyalty includes sympathy and order."[26] Most commentators agree that Royce makes a "pragmatic turn" in his later *Philosophy of Loyalty* in 1908, but it seems likely from Cabot's comments that Royce was in the process of amending and embracing strands of pragmatism in the 1890s. At the turn of the century Royce had ramped up his efforts to develop a complementary relationship between idealism and pragmatism, underscoring the point that human beliefs and practical purposes are, in Peirce's words, "the inseparable aspects of the same thing."[27] His efforts go relatively unnoticed by James and Dewey, but C. S. Peirce, in an unpublished reflection, writes: "I think Royce's conception in *The World and the Individual* (although I do not assent to the logic of that work) comes nearer to the genuine upshot of pragmaticism than any exposition that a pragmatist has given . . . that any *other* pragmatist has given."[28] Ella Lyman Cabot was pointedly aware of the tension—both personal and intellectual—between pragmatism and Royce's idealism. She was also aware of the way in which her mentor attempted to wed idealism to the pragmatic maxim. She takes on the difficult task of extending a type of idealism in the concrete activities of ethicists and educators.

CABOT'S VOICE: AN ORIGINAL COMPOSITION

Cabot's papers may at points provide us a type of Roycean interpretation, but, like any true interpretation, they do not speak in the voice of repetition but in that of careful originality. Ella Lyman Cabot was what I might call an interpretative thinker, one who reforms, rethinks, and returns the insights of the past in genuinely novel ways. This is also to say that she was a genius of a certain Kantian strain. Creative activity for Cabot was never an isolated affair but always situated as a moment of both inheritance and radical extension. Her writings have Roycean undertones but also reflect the poetic qualities of Thoreau and, at moments, the signs of urgent zest that define C.

S. Peirce's work in the 1890s. Listening to Cabot's voice, therefore, reveals an original contribution to, and an original composition of, American philosophy.

For Cabot, it is clear that the "art of living," like the pursuit of any art, carries with it a type of acute interest, ardent sincerity, and lingering skepticism. In 1893, she writes:

> Moral sleeplessness may, I think, be a danger for me. To be awake is good. To be sleepless is bad. It does not mark Richard because he is made so that alertness is food and refreshment. But not to have mental rest and quietness may be a strain for me. I can't physically bear very high or very continual mental pressure.[29]

Some commentators might claim that, like Thoreau's "Walking" and Royce's "The Problem of Job," Cabot's passage reflects the risk of social detachment that is occasionally experienced by all of us but that is confronted head-on in the task of philosophizing: "I am sure it is the danger I run, as shown in sharp headaches and in the craving of my whole nature for solitude and the wild woods at times."[30] This is not the sign of a weak disposition but rather a very strong and honest one. The danger of isolation and solitude implied in the task of American philosophizing is one that Cabot experiences acutely and provides the impetus for her later work on unity and growth. The moral sleeplessness that Cabot suffers may be caused by her involvement in American philosophizing, but it may not be the restlessness experienced by her male peers. After all, she observes that her husband, Richard, a philosopher in his own right, experiences no such difficulties. "Alertness," for him is "food and nourishment," but for "Mrs. Cabot" the interest in, and attunement to, her situation often leaves her hungering for more.

A week later, Cabot continues to face the condition of her moral insomnia, whether brought on by her American philosophizing or her gendered circumstances: "Poor instincts how you ache as you lay crushed and creased and scarred and bruised as they drag you out of view. Surely it is a strong love of truth which is willing to endure so much tugging and straining after the meaning of my buried life."[31] As she turns toward philosophical skepticism, her frustration and exhaustion repeatedly emerge, manifesting themselves in simultaneous reflections on the nature of truth and human finitude. In a passage that reveals the existential ground of philosophy, she writes: "Oh! Why can it [truth] not be given out and held forever to enrich the world? Why does God give us glimpses of eternity and let them vanish? Why will it ooze away until only its shadowy name is left? It *cannot* be wholly gone."[32] It may not be wholly gone, but the truth is not to be wholly realized by human beings and their particular communities. Here

Cabot is facing the skepticism and fallibilism that would become hallmarks of classical American thought. The Cambridge pragmatists held that truth is situational and arises, for the time being, in relation to particular human purposes. Our understanding of truth, therefore, is always provisional and ongoing. This stance may seem to fit fairly well with the cultural and epistemic relativism of our own day, but classical American thought did not foreclose the possibility of finding truth. Instead, it emphasized the tragic difficulties of its pursuit. Pragmatism is usually, and inaccurately, rendered as a cheery "get things done" philosophy, but behind this misinterpretation is a deep-rooted question concerning the prospects for human knowledge. James and Dewey may encourage us out into the projects of world, but there are *absolutely* no guarantees about the success of these undertakings. Indeed, in a buried manuscript, Peirce wrestles with the doubt, epistemological and existential, that Cabot touches upon in her writing:

> Do you, Reader, happen to know what "doubt" means? Do you know it, I mean, in that sense of "knowing" in which we say that few boys know what money means? If you do you have attained man's estate in philosophy, and won't grow much more, though you will gain strength and maybe art. Before I made its actual acquaintance, as applied to pragmaticism, I had printed over a score of logical and epistemological papers containing the majority of the original thoughts that I have as yet set forth, and had preached pragmaticism for over ten years. Very ignorant persons confound doubt with disbelief. Many others think simple unbelief constitutes doubt. What "doubt" really denotes is to be insupportably discontent to dispose for oneself of the proposition that is said to be "doubted," in any suggestible way whatever, whether it be to affirm it to oneself, or to deny it, or yet to leave the question of its truth unsettled. The abstract definition is easily apprehended; but an intimate, pillow-sharing acquaintance with the thing must come when living experience brings it.[33]

Cabot had this "pillow-sharing acquaintance" with doubt, the kind of acquaintance that keeps one up at night. Throughout her career, Cabot's writings reflected doubt, in the Peircean sense of the word, in regard to most propositions that she would discuss in her writing. Occasionally, this doubt would be interpreted as a "feminine" mannerism, as hesitancy, or as ambivalence. There is more than a shard of truth in all of these interpretations. Ella Lyman Cabot was wary to commit to a position or, as the case of Richard Cabot demonstrates, to another person. Following Peirce, she understood that the fixation of belief reflected in mindless commitment brings an end to philosophical inquiry. Cabot's doubt, however, is more complex than Peirce's in an important respect. The doubt that she expresses is not a purely academic one concerning the possibility for humans to acquire stable knowledge but also the self-doubt experienced by individuals who are unable to realize their projects and pursuits due to societal restrictions or prejudice. Despite this doubt, Cabot continues to work against these restrictions and to write in academic fields that would never welcome her.

American philosophy has flourished only when it preserves the willingness to doubt and the willingness to search for truths or solutions, *in spite of this doubt*. This is no easy task. The fallibilism that Peirce advances is one in which truth may always evade an inquirer or the community of inquiry in which she belongs. In Cabot's words, truth will "ooze away until only its shadowy name is left." If this is the case, one might rightfully ask: Why bother? Why go on searching for a truth that may never be found? These questions plagued most of the American philosophers of Cabot's day, but especially Peirce and Royce, who would serve as Cabot's mentor for most of her years in philosophy. The mutual influence between these two thinkers has been examined in recent years but mainly in terms of their later correspondence, after 1902. One of the abiding similarities between Peirce and Royce is their wide-eyed acknowledgment of human error and fallibility. Cabot seems especially drawn to Royce's ability to recognize, and respond to, the fragility of human inquiry and human life more broadly construed. In an unpublished manuscript that would eventually become his *Religious Aspects of Philosophy* (1884), Royce gives an unusually dark rendering of the prospects for human inquiry, expressing a sentiment that echoes Cabot's position. Royce leads into the question that Cabot expresses: "Why should we be truth-seekers?":

> To this problem we are led thus irresistibly. Here is a chaos of various minds, whose simpler ideas seem to vary very greatly, whose feelings grow so far asunder that each man becomes a mystery to his neighbor, whose conflicting opinions in consequence are all the results largely of accident, and certainly of narrowness of view. Yet it seems to be thought an excellent thing for each one of them to form fixed opinions about at least some matters, a sane undertaking of them to look for some sort of abiding truth, and a grand act to suffer loss or even death for the sake of the strongest and highest at least among one's beliefs. Why should this be the case? What is the use of truth-seeking, when so little truth will ever be found on this planet? What is the worth of remaining true to one's opinions, when everything tends to make them fleeting? These questions must, I think, come into the mind of every active person at some time during his life. I have not in the foregoing stated the skeptic's case nearly as strongly as I could state it. The more you consider human knowledge the more you will see that some of the dearest pretenses are found upon examination to be only pretenses. And when you see this you are, if of vigorous mental constitution, once for all aroused from what a great philosopher called the "dogmatic slumber" and sent out upon a new search. The questions you then propose to yourself can thus be stated: What kind of truth may I hope to discover? In what spirit ought I to search for truth? Am I to hope for much success? And to bear myself as one to whom truth will certainly

be revealed if he but work for it? Or shall I in a humbler spirit say that I am probably to remain in doubt so long as I live? Or finally shall I, neither confident of success, nor resigned to defeat, rise with all my strength and declare that whether finding or baffled, whether a wanderer forever or one who at last is to reach secure harbor of faith, I will through confidence and through doubt, through good and through evil report, search earnestly for truth though I never find anything that it is worth my while to call abiding?[34]

Here we come to hear the appreciation for the tragic that draws Cabot to her teacher. Here we come to appreciate the intellectual kinship between the two thinkers, one of whom was acknowledged, the other forgotten. Both are struggling with this social marginalization and catching sight of the painful limitations of human knowledge. It could be argued that Royce's early writing was an attempt to revive and revise standard conceptions of God in order to save himself from the nihilism that often attends extreme skepticism. Cabot often follows Royce's lead in the early 1890s in expressing a hope that the pursuit of truth and the art of living are not wholly futile endeavors, for she continues: "Somehow, somewhere, it [truth] must *live as music* sent up to God."[35]

Cabot's hopes for inquiry and the art of living are often modest, practical, and turn on the meaning-making involved in a particular type of creative activity. In these cases, her hopes are not hinged on theological belief or salvation. On April 24, 1893, Cabot describes the temporal and personal unity that is achieved in creative events, a unity that is distinctly open-ended:

Live in the past! Live in the present! Live in the future! How impartial and unsatisfactory all of these are. Rather live as one being, for rationality consists precisely in that: in not forgetting, in not ignoring the past, present or future, but bringing all into the unity of a single purpose which is leavened in the past, is created in the present, and is growing toward, looking toward its future.[36]

In 1889, Cabot's summer reading list includes several selections from Ralph Waldo Emerson, and perhaps we hear the echoing of "Experience," in which one finds herself on stairs that stretch two directions without end. To *find* herself on these stairs of time and circumstance, in Cabot's words, to live as this "one being," takes purpose and creative insight. When purpose is curtailed and insight is obscured—either by disposition or social circumstance—one is bound to languish. She explains that

to use the past—inherited physique, or brain, culture, joy, agony—so that it disentangles and liberates instead of enthralling, that is creative life. The same net which trips and tangles us may be used to drag the great waters and hoist the shining salmon. That is the relation between past and present that reconciles them.[37]

Meaning-making, however, does not trade merely on the unity that might be established between the past and the present. Cabot insists that this unity must provide space for, indeed enable, the growth of novelty. Here she integrates her own philosophical insight with Abraham Lincoln's comment on the "stormy present":

> [We must] gather in all the significant and relevant past to a focus so that the alchemy of the newly emerging fact shall crystallize it into a unique and unheard of deed. The dogmas of the stormy past are inadequate to the stormy present. If the occasion is new so we must think anew and act anew.[38]

In *The World and the Individual* (1901), Royce complements this passage nicely in describing temporal unity and novelty to the extent that he suggests that "[w]hat we find must indeed be *new*, and, nevertheless, be capable of being linked to the old. For, after all, even mere discrimination is an expression of the will, which seeks novelty."[39] Both Royce and Cabot hope to preserve genuine creativity while making it at home in a wider historical and social sphere—in a wider community.

With these comments in mind, it seems clear that examining the passages that reveal Cabot's moments of existential crisis have not lead us astray in our discussion of her philosophical treatment of unity and growth. Addressing Cabot's existential insecurities allows us to place her squarely in the tradition of American philosophy, a tradition that maintains that the live concerns of individuals and communities must be the starting point and touchstone of philosophic inquiry. Exploring the relation between growth and wholeness is not a strictly academic exercise for this student; it is, rather, her forthright attempt to understand the relation between creative growth— *her* creative growth—and the collective inheritance that both limited and enabled it.

CABOT ON GROWTH AND WHOLENESS

In a scribbled draft of a letter written in 1892, Cabot thanks Royce for his guidance and encouragement offered in a seminar earlier that year. At this point, Royce had begun to think through *The Spirit of Modern Philosophy* (1892). She writes to Royce that "It was a great surprise that you thought my work on growth to be worth publishing. I shall hope and work very hard to do it if I can."[40] The fact that Royce considered Cabot's work publishable is not surprising; what is surprising and slightly disturbing is that her work remains buried in unpublished folders at Radcliffe. It is unfortunate that there is such a dearth of material that reflects Cabot's work on growth in the late 1880s and early 1890s—only one notebook dated 1892.

At its best, intellectual history involves what C. S. Peirce might have called abduction, that is, a type of educated guesswork that aims at a working explanatory hypothesis by identifying possible relations between objects and ideas. It is with this in mind that I will claim that Royce's interest in Cabot's work turned on her negotiation of a question that perplexed him during the writing of *The World and the Individual*. It is a question with which American pragmatists continue to grapple, namely, the question of the relation between the concepts of growth and wholeness. Framed in another way, the question asks how it might be possible to hold on to the fact of unity and the fact of creative newness, two facts that many individuals are reluctant to abandon.

In 1899, Cabot prepared a talk that she titled "Wholeness in Relation to Growth." In her notes she writes:

> In digging the soil about the roots of my concept of Growth I have several times struck hard against a rock too heavy for me to move. When one does this repeatedly there are two alternative courses of action, one can move to another country and abandon the rocky soil or one can ask the help of all one's neighbors in hoisting the rock. As I am attached to the concept of Growth and don't want to move, I have adopted the latter course and shall tonight make a small effort to lift the rock with the hope of being aided by everyone present. The rock whose face I am first of all to dig out from the surrounding soil is called Wholeness.[41]

In typical pragmatic fashion, Cabot proceeds to reframe the philosophical tension between growth and wholeness as a tension produced by our adherence to particular conceptions of these terms. She begins by examining our frequent and uncritical usage of the term "whole" by underscoring several suggestive variations of meaning. First, it is commonplace to believe that to know the whole is to know that beyond which there is nothing else. Second, Cabot notes that "closely related to this usage is that of completion." She expands on this typical and misleading usage: "[t]o know the Whole is to know that which is total and undiminished, from which nothing has been subtracted. The whole is that which is perfect, finished, forever the same."[42] She notes at the outset that these definitions of wholeness stand opposed to the idea of creative growth, describes in detail the logical failure of the these two definitions, and finally suggests that these definitions are out of kilter with our experience of unity. At the expense of detail, I have tried to select an illuminating section of her argument that appeals to the experiences of her listeners. She skeptically writes:

> To know the whole is to know all there is? This is very comforting, nothing more could be asked. I remember an organist who at the end of each recital used to announce, "That is all." It was thoroughly reassuring. There was no

> danger of missing encores. But after all, was it true that we knew the whole of the concert? We had come at the very beginning, and stayed through the middle to its very end. Yes, but might it not have been that just because we had heard every single note we did not know the whole. Who of us has ever really heard the Whole of the Walküre? Is an aggregate, a sum total of an opera, the whole of an opera? Assuredly not.[43]

In parentheses, beneath this long quotation, Cabot writes, "The whole of that opera is the universe." In this selection, we hear Cabot dismiss the quantitative approach to understanding unity and catch a glimpse of her understanding of the universe—that is Wholeness—as a qualitative and creative integrity.[44] It is the whole of the opera, not its discrete notes, that constitutes a meaningful unity. It is worth noting here that music, once considered a fanciful pastime of women, is slowly drawn into the grave and weighty issues of philosophy and metaphysics.

As Cabot's description of the "art of living" indicates, she is well primed to employ the allusion of music that Royce uses effectively in the 1880s and 1890s. Cabot looks to the making of music as a way of explaining the development of organic unity but also the phenomenon of growth. Indeed, she suggests that the ideal of unity, like the unity of a musical harmony, is necessary in order to distinguish between the growth of this harmony and dissonance or "degenerate change." Here, in an 1899 notebook, she very likely echoes Royce's thinking for the Gifford Lectures:

> In the creation of the work of art we have perhaps clearer growth than anywhere else except in the execution of a well-conceived purpose. In each case we recognize growth as growth and not degenerate change because we made and know the ideal toward which we are working. We correct our failure by an appeal to an ideal. True, the ideal is a great deal more than we know and it also grows clearer when we express our aim but it is essentially ourselves and hence we can judge its progress or loss. . . . [E]thics as well as art appeals to a whole [ideal] without which growth may be degeneration or rather all is chaos.[45]

Whereas growth stood opposed to the uncritical definitions of wholeness described earlier, Cabot and Royce's descriptions of unity enable the prospect of growth and novelty. This, however, is not to say that there is not a tension between improvisational creativity and the course of an ideal harmony. Indeed, Cabot maintains that "[i]n the creation of the work of art as in the creation of any purpose there is struggle and a sense of finitude and contrast with the ideal."[46] She seems to understand that the struggle of individual growth is painfully real, "but when we dwell in the whole we turn from the struggle to the completion involved in that struggle if it is true in itself—to the finished work of art and to religion."[47]

Most of these comments resonate with Royce's comments in *The World and the Individual* and in earlier works in which he suggests that the dynamic and integrity of music might serve as a helpful analogue to the Absolute.[48] In her 1899 paper, "Wholeness in Relation to Growth," Cabot continues to jab at the mistaken conception of wholeness and growth as the mere conservation of an aggregate by remarking that

> [t]here are people who want to keep everything in an aggregate. It is for them a pity to lose even a fragment, they want the whole. They preserve their pressed flowers, their old shoes, every letter of business or pleasure, every scrap of twine. Nothing indeed is lost, except the wholeness that they sought. That is crowded out by an aggregate of rubbish.[49]

Cabot refuses to admit that wholeness is realized in conservation, in the mere stockpiling of an aggregate. Instead she states that "we are driven to a conception of wholeness which shall welcome instead of repel growth."[50] She presents this conception, writing, "A whole is a system of ordered parts and as order involves purpose. Any whole is the expression of a purpose and any purpose implies growth."[51] Here many scholars might listen for the echoing of Alfred North Whitehead or Royce, two of Cabot's teachers. For example, Cabot's comment on unity and purpose coincides with Royce's description of the cohesion of ideas: "By the word Idea . . . I shall mean in the end any state of consciousness, whether simple or complex, which, when present, is then and there viewed as . . . the expression or embodiment of a single conscious purpose."[52] But instead of relying on Royce to clarify Cabot, I am more inclined to amplify her own examples in elucidating her claims on unity and growth. She states that there are "several interwoven strands" in her notion of Wholeness. Here are but two strands. First, she states that "the whole in any ordered system is immanent i.e., the process is organic to the end."[53] Second, "the whole is transcendent, or creative in that it rejects the irrelevant and develops the new."[54] Implicit in this two-sided remark is the suggestion that wholeness is to be considered a type of organic creativity. Cabot once again appeals to lived experience in demonstrating the seemingly contradictory statement that wholeness is both immanent-organic and transcendent-creative. As a helpful example, she urges us to consider the way in which a "person of integrity" is "welded to wholeness by linking its changes into a unity, by opening out new reaches of effort, by preventing disintegration, by excluding irrelevancy."[55] Her character study of Ulysses S. Grant highlights this point—that the man of integrity, the man of wholeness, is by definition also a man of growth. She writes that

> We see him first as a drifter, dissipated and rapidly going to pieces. The swift disintegration of his career is about to wash away all traces of his name. Later, we see him again as the man with a single controlling purpose. He has begun

to be the man of integrity. Wholeness and purpose are one. . . . Instead of the dissipation of the nightclub or the passive morning at home in an armchair we see him doggedly setting off to his office day after day. He has formed the purpose of earning enough money to be able to marry. It is not attained, but he has, as we say, identified himself with it. It controls him and moulds him. A friend asks him to go hunting. He hesitates, but refuses. "On the whole, I think I had better not." To the whole he refers as his guide—it surrounds him as his most familiar presence.[56]

Cabot is careful in clarifying her description. It is not the case that Grant would achieve the whole in attaining his goal of marrying. She pointedly says that the end of the process "is not attained." Instead we are continually in the process of making ourselves whole in the genuine engagement with our purposes in the world. Cabot, like Royce, repeatedly insists that our purposes are never wholly our own but always situated in wider and more inclusive purposes. It is in this sense that Cabot writes that "any persistent purpose opens out to infinity."[57] The meaning of wholeness is this creative "opening out."

At the end of her talk, Cabot states that "the whole is the ongoing process of creation through an ordering and rejecting purpose." This conclusion must have given Cabot some trouble since beneath the final typed phrase is written, "Wholeness is the process of self-creation through purpose." It is this sentiment—one that refigures the relationship between growth and wholeness—that guides her social activism but also lays the groundwork for the social–political thought in *Everyday Ethics* (1906).

THE PURPOSE OF PRAGMATISM: *EVERYDAY ETHICS*

As mentioned earlier, Ella and Richard Cabot were among the participants of Royce's "Philosophy Conference," a fortnightly gathering of friends at Royce's home at 103 Irving Street in 1903. John Clendenning notes, quite accurately I think, that the "central purpose of the gatherings was to make practical applications of speculative problems."[58] It is a purpose that seems to have been carried forward in Cabot's *Everyday Ethics*, a work that sought to reframe the speculative issues of growth and unity in terms of the ethical issue of creative loyalty. This reframing seems to have come naturally to Cabot, who repeatedly uses real-world examples to shed light on more abstract themes.

Before addressing *Everyday Ethics*, let us take a moment to dwell on the description of Ulysses Grant that Cabot gives in 1899. This description was meant to unwind a highly intricate intellectual issue, namely the knotty relationship between unity and growth. It makes a meaningful attempt in this regard, but it also serves as a practical description of loyalty that bears an uncanny resemblance to the version that Royce develops in the *Philosophy of Loyalty* (1908). Remember that Cabot identifies loyalty as being central to Royce's thinking as early as 1892. In 1908, Royce defines loyalty as "the willingness and thoroughgoing devotion to a cause. . . . [The person of loyalty] expresses his devotion in some sustained and practical way, by acting in service of this cause."[59] To say that Cabot's Grant remains committed to his unifying purpose is also to say that he remains loyal to his ideal of making a living. Cabot may have realized, along with her male contemporaries, the value of negotiating the speculative issues of classroom philosophy by looking to the mundane affairs of contemporary society.

In *Everyday Ethics*, Cabot is explicit in her attempts to foster the personal temperaments and practical attributes that contribute to loyal behavior. Just as Royce intends *The Philosophy of Loyalty* to "win hearts for loyalty," she intends to outline an educational program that would cultivate loyal purposes in schoolchildren. The seeds of this work seem to have been sown very early in her career. In 1892, Cabot writes:

> The moral life is a carrying out of purposes. . . . [I]t is in this insight that knowing your purposes is the one thing for every mother to teach in a myriad of ways and educational influences and for every boy and girl to endeavor to learn.[60]

Cabot makes sense of this claim in *Everyday Ethics* by explaining the difference between a purpose and a fact by noting that a purpose, as opposed to a fact, has "a kind of hunger or desire." The fact rests in the present, "settled back comfortably in its chair." The purpose, in contrast, "leans forward eagerly . . . and stretches forward into the future." According to Cabot, "the fact is one with itself, the purpose is never at one with itself: it yearns toward what it is not itself."[61] This comment reverberates with her suggestion that the "art of living is becoming other people"; such an art turns on the acting out of a purpose that always looks beyond itself.

Cabot suggests that the practice of ethics rests, in large part, on the ability to judge the worthiness of purposes. An entire chapter of her work is dedicated to this topic, and I will address the philosophical value of interests and purposes in chapter five. For now, however, I will concentrate on the section of *Everyday Ethics* titled "A Good Purpose Is Carefully Chosen and Loyally Followed." Here, Cabot writes that, "the good purpose is perfectly fitted to the man, fully faced and loyally held. In order to carry it out he exercises courage, patience, imagination, resolution, industry, unselfish devotion, self-forgetfulness, [and] persistency."[62] Purposes are necessarily transcendent, directed beyond their current self-definition. This being said, true purposes are not absorbed in the group-think that some communities exhibit. "The good purpose then for each man is his own, and so is different in each case."⁶³ Cabot envisions a type of self-creation without the selfishness that shrouds the modern individual. She cites Royce in her attempt to show how loyal purposes strip away the mask of selfishness, stating that "Prof. Josiah Royce in a stirring chapter in the 'The Religious Aspects of Philosophy,' says that all selfishness is due to an illusion."⁶⁴ She then continues in an original interpretation of Royce:

> It is only through sympathy that we reach the truth, or as we accurately say, realize things as they are, see and feel them as real and not as shadows or masks. There are people whose lives are real to us as our own. These we call friends and brothers, for they are realized as human and so akin, but the outer circle of our acquaintance . . . are often far less real than the sparrows at our feet. We think of them as mere means to our ends, or vaguely and dimly as strangers.⁶⁵

Indeed, this interpretation written in the years prior to 1906 anticipates many of the themes that Royce will develop in *The Philosophy of Loyalty*, especially his emphasis on the sympathetic temperament that is required in genuinely loyal acts. Cabot is aware not only of her intellectual affinity with Royce, but also her indebtedness to William James's discussion of the self in his *Principles of Psychology*.⁶⁶

There is no doubt that Royce reads Cabot's manuscript of *Everyday Ethics* in 1904. In this year, he writes on behalf of Cabot to a Boston publisher concerning her work titled *The Secret of Power*.⁶⁷ Royce is extremely supportive of the project and only recommends that Cabot change the title to *Conduct and Power*. Cabot finally decided that the title *Everyday Ethics* best conveyed the pragmatic purpose of her book. This cursory treatment of *Everyday Ethics* demonstrates large swaths of common ground between this work and Royce's *The Philosophy of Loyalty*. This is ground that deserves careful exploration in the future and will receive greater treatment in coming chapters. What will become especially apparent is that Cabot's book anticipates many of the moves in ethical theory that idealists, such as Royce, and pragmatists, such as Dewey, make in their later works.

Cabot's writing was reviewed in the *International Journal of Ethics* (what would later become *Ethics*) by A. Gifford in 1907. Here he drives home the importance of the work, stating, "This book reveals a theory of ethics at work, ethical rules in operation. . . . [P]articularly noteworthy is the avowed and fulfilled purpose of avoiding 'sentimentalism' and the usual 'sugar-coated moral stories.'"⁶⁸ Gifford's comment is important in two respects. First, it underscores the fact that Cabot is engaging in ethical theory, the kind of philosophical project that deserves a review in *Ethics*. Second, *Everyday Ethics* reflectively avoids the repetition of the "feminine" ethical norm of the turn of the century, namely "sentimentalism," by drawing heavily on the lived experience of individuals and on the analytic rigor of Cabot's philosophical instructors.

Cabot and her peers like Mary Parker Follett were committed to both the flesh and blood reality of ethics and the theories that emerged from the fledgling discipline of professional philosophy. For these women, there was no either-or between praxis and theory. This twofold commitment led them to generate novel and important ethical writings that have, unfortunately, been forgotten by an age that has become distracted either by the mundane and all-consuming affairs of the every day or by the esoteric and all-consuming affairs of the academy.

CABOT AND FOLLETT ON SELF-CREATION, POWER, AND POLITICAL WHOLENESS[69]

It is not wholly accurate to say that the thinking of Mary Parker Follett constitutes a "forgotten movement" in American intellectual life. It is more appropriate to say that it has been forgotten by professional philosophers who seem to have ignored Follett on the same grounds that they dismiss Cabot—because both of these author's thought might have some traction in the mundane affairs of politics and business. Scholars of management theory, such as Peter Drucker and Joan Tonn, on the other hand, focus on Follet's work for precisely this reason. Drucker's introduction to *Prophet of Management* (1995) outlines the way in which Follett's progressive and feminist sensibilities might be made operational in a workplace setting.[70] Tonn's *Mary Parker Follett: Creating Democracy, Transforming Management* (2003) provides a sophisticated biographical supplement to this study. Here I try to briefly situate Follett's thinking in the wider context of early American philosophy and draw them into dialogue with Cabot's work on unity, growth, and loyalty. Working during the Progressive movement of the early 1900s, Follett demonstrated an abiding interest in social reform and the development of a more participatory democracy in the United States. In line with this interest, she inherited the belief of Cabot and other Cambridge intellectuals that the truths of philosophy were to be judged by their ability to reform and transform the lives of individuals and their communities. Cabot and Follett were fast friends at Radcliffe, worked together as teachers and reformers in the Roxbury neighborhood of Boston, and corresponded extensively in the years between 1920 and 1933.[71]

In Follett we find a thinker who continually strives to integrate the themes of American pragmatism and German Idealism in order to understand the experience of women, laborers, and racial minorities in the Roxbury neighborhoods of Boston beginning in 1901. These themes also serve as the lens through which she interprets the events surrounding the conflict and resolution of World War I. It is this integration of theory and practice that defines Follett's "Community as a Process," published in 1919, and *Creative Experience*, published five years later.[72] In *Creative Experience*, Follett extends Cabot's intuitions concerning growth and unity along social and political lines.

This work more directly addresses the creative interactions of individuals through the ongoing process of circular relations as it inheres in a community. Follett claims that an individual should never, in her words "be seen as a *ding-an-sich*," as a thing in itself, but rather as something that is emerging in and through the relations of the community.[73] This is also to say that there is neither an individual prior to the formation of a community, nor is there is there an individual who completely autonomously chooses its loyalties and commitments. Follett suggests that individuals, and perhaps most pointedly women, are always already thrown into a social situation and must creatively work their way through the relations that they inherit. Indeed, she takes issue with Royce and her fellow pluralists on the grounds they suggest that an individual must freely choose his or her community. Follett states:

> This individual is a myth. The problem with pluralism is not its pluralism, but that it is based on a non-existent individual. But Royce, who was not a pluralist, would have us choose a cause to be loyal to. Life is knit more closely than that![74]

Expanding on this point, Follett echoes Cabot, stating, "The truth is that the self is always weaving itself out of its relations."[75] We ought to remember that Cabot's portrayal of the person of integrity resonates with this remark to the extent that this person achieves unity only through the warp and woof of her purposes and commitments. It will become clear in the forthcoming discussion that this "weaving," a pointedly feminine activity, is a circular activity that seeks to overcome the historical opposition between the unity of the community and the growth of the individual as it lays the groundwork for a type of political pluralism.

Follett's insight concerning self-creation sets the stage for the discussion of human relations as it is developed in her writings in the early 1920s. She writes that "community is a creative process. It is creative because it is the process of integrating."[76] Follett's understanding of ideal group dynamics stands apart from a standard understanding of consensus formation, compromise, or political unity. She explains that "to integrate is not to absorb, melt, fuse or reconcile in the so-called Hegelian sense. The creative power of the individual appears not when one wish dominates others, but when all wishes unite in a working whole."[77] For Follett, integration connotes a type of unity, but perhaps more important, "integration ought to be considered a type of qualitative adjustment" which is reminiscent of Cabot's understanding of growth.[78] Along these lines, Follett suggests that genuine democratic institutions must seek the *novel creation* of a general will through the intermingling of individual citizens who continually aim to integrate their distinct purposes.

If the community is a creative process, it seems reasonable to ask what exactly is created in this type of integration. Follett responds with a fourfold answer: the by-products of this creativity are personality, purpose, will, and loyalty. To say that community creates personality is not to merely say that individuals always find themselves as persons in a community. Instead, it is to say that the project of self-creation is bound up with the process of community formation. "A man expands," Follett writes, "as his will expands. A man's individuality stops where his power of collective willing stops. If he cannot will beyond his trade union than we must write on his tombstone, 'This was a trade union man.'"[79] Three important points ought to be underscored in this passage.

First, the growth of individual personality is continually and recursively defined by the collective will with which it identifies. This dynamic process is what Follett terms "circular response" and might be understood in the following way. A person's relationship with her environment creates a change in that person. This alteration affects the purposes that one actively pursues, which in turn mediates the response of the environment or the people found therein. It should be noted that circular response is not simply a kind of mechanical feedback, but a process that involves community and individual in a continual evolution. Follett's rendering is a thickening of William James's rather thin claim in the *Principles of Psychology* that "Not only the people but the places and things I know enlarge my Self in a sort of metaphoric social way."[80]

Second, Follett is attempting to revise the modern conception of the individual will that Robert Frost once described as the freedom of being bold. She does so by reminding us of our communal relations that quietly underpin our creative powers and so-called bold freedoms. Follett recognizes that this reminder resonates with the works of James and Royce. For example, she notes that "James brought to popular recognition the truth that since man is a complex of experiences there are many selves in each one."[81] Similarly, for Follett, creative power is found not in singular autonomy (after all, Follett insisted that such autonomy is the stuff of myth) but in the processes of complex relationships. Follett is perhaps the first American thinker to argue that power is, and ought to be conceived as, a "power-with" rather than a "power-over." In so doing, she anticipates the writing of Simone de Beauvoir, Hannah Arendt, and Gloria Anzaldua in suggesting that violence is antithetical to power insofar as violence seeks to destroy relationships.

Third, and most importantly in reference to our earlier discussion of wholeness and growth, is Follett's suggestion that the project of self-creation is ongoing and transcendent in Cabot's sense of the word; it is creative in that it rejects the irrelevant and develops the new. Follett inherits her mentor's sentiment that the "art of living is becoming other people." For Follett the process of community is one that continually seeks deeper and wider integration of various interests. "Power-over" can be achieved in a sort of determinate fashion when one person or group attains total domination over another. "Power-with," however, tends to look beyond itself—discovering and creating relationships that exceed the expectations of its actors. Matthew Shapiro recently elaborated on the transcendent character of circular response, writing that, "Under the right conditions, sustained circular response via dialogue in the pursuit of common goals—which may also evolve as the process continues—will tend to produce unforeseen solutions that fulfill and/or transcend the initial goals of the participants."[82] In *Creative Experience*, Follett indicates that the truth of circular response is one that women have both understood and embodied. She calls it a "pregnant truth," one that fosters the *wholeness* of a certain *creative* relationship.[83] This is a helpful point since it aims to describe a social unity that, in Cabot's words, "welcomes rather than repels" the idea of growth.

These brief comments concerning the mature work of Mary Parker Follett should serve as a type of promissory note, a promise that even the early works of Ella Lyman Cabot resonate closely with forward-looking thoughts of women and men working in the twilight of classical American philosophy. Cabot's early work anticipates and, in some cases, inspires writers who earn their fame in the 1920s, just as American philosophy entered its final years.

CONCLUSION—POWER AND THE FRIENDSHIP OF THE FORGOTTEN

In saying that the self is relational, we tend to forget to say what these relations *mean*. In the midst of theorizing about the unity and growth of the social sphere, there is an unfortunate tendency to overlook the persons who enact the processes of community. In short, it is all too easy to neglect the emotional aspect of "power-with" and the personal sentiment of community. In sifting through these forgotten movements of American philosophy, I found this personal sentiment in a folder of tan letters, the crispness of which belied the time it had remained untouched. On January 23, 1932, Ella Lyman Cabot wrote to a frustrated Mary Parker Follett:

> Dearest Mary,
> I fully understand the need to have one's life-work recognized as real—as a needed contribution to one's time and world. Your writing is so clearly hungered for. You ought not to doubt its virtue for a minute. It is so sound and permanent in its principles and so closely linked to the needs of this age.[84]

Thirty-two years earlier, Cabot closed her talk on "Wholeness in its Relation to Growth" with a section on true friendship. In doing so, she suggests that in our search for creative unity, we need look no further than to those cherished friendships that make our lives meaningful. Cabot's interaction with Royce and her letters to Follett seem to demonstrate this point. The intimate relationship between these individuals is obvious. It is the personal integration to which Cabot and Follett refer in their description of community as a process. This integration, however, does not coalesce in a type of static unity. Instead, intimacy finds its complement in growth, in the willingness to take risks that might give birth to new meaning.

Cabot encourages her younger counterpart to avoid self-doubt, to extend her intellectual pursuits, to persevere in her project of self-growth. It is not mere coincidence that this project of self-growth aims at meaningful participation in a wider intellectual community. Today, we stand as this community and may have the opportunity to inherit these women's purposes concerning unity and growth. With this in mind, we might return to the quotation that opened this chapter with new eyes. Cabot states that, "We need the past, every bit of it, for the sake of our future. . . . [W]e need all we can digest." The works of Cabot and Follett are integral parts of our past and may help sustain us in our roles as American philosophers. Today, our digestion is undoubtedly strong enough for this sustenance.

NOTES

1. Portions of this chapter first appeared in John Kaag, "Women and Forgotten Movements in American Philosophy: The Work of Ella Lyman Cabot and Mary Parker Follett," *Transactions of the Charles S. Peirce Society* 44, no. 1 (2008): 134–57.

2. A 139/322v.

3. Joseph Blau, *Men and Movements in American Philosophy* (New York: Prentice Hall, 1952).

4. Blau, *Men and Movements*, v.

5. Charlene Haddock Seigfried, *Pragmatism and Feminism: Reweaving the Social Fabric* (Chicago: University of Chicago Press, 1998).

6. Judy Whipps, "Jane Addams's Social Thought as a Model for a Pragmatist-Feminist Communitarianism," *Hypatia* 19, no. 3 (2004). Marilyn Fischer, *On Addams* (Belmont: Wadsworth, 2003).

7. Dorothy Rogers, *America's First Women Philosophers* (New York: Continuum Press, 2005).

8. Scott Pratt, *Native Pragmatism: Rethinking the Roots of American Philosophy* (Bloomington: University of Indiana Press, 2002).

9. Erin McKenna, *The Task of Utopia: A Pragmatist and Feminist Perspective* (Lanham, MD: Rowman & Littlefield, 2001).

10. In the "Supplemental Essay" in *The World and the Individual*, Royce pulls back from his willingness to develop the concepts of individual creativity and growth when he suggests that no matter what activity an individual takes, it "come[s] in eternity freely to our home" in the Absolute. Josiah Royce, *The World and the Individual* (New York: Dover, 1959), 374.

11. In Royce's 1899–1900 seminar in twentieth-century philosophy, Cabot wrote extensively on the concepts of unity and purpose, receiving the highest grade in the class (an A), higher than fellow student R. Robbins (who received a B). See Harvard Archives UAIII.15.28. *Yearly Returns 1889–1900*. In Royce's class notes, dated 1902, we find repeated references to the work of Ella and Richard Cabot and their interest in the concepts of unity and growth. This is most apparent in Royce's notes taken on a presentation that E. L. Cabot gives in 1902 on growth and purpose of the natural world: "Mrs. Cabot discussed the element of novelty of growth. . . . [N]ovelty is everywhere in growth, not just at the outset. . . . Evolution has not gotten rid of novelty." These comments are found in the Harvard University Archives. HUG 1755. Box 101. Folder 14. p. 162.

12. Cited in John Clendenning, *The Life and Thought of Josiah Royce* (Nashville: Vanderbilt University Press, 1999), 286.

13. The fact that Royce consults both Ella and Richard Cabot while developing the "Lusitania Address" in 1916 attests to the degree to which Royce trusted their opinion. See *Josiah Royce—Letters*, ed. John Clendenning (Chicago: University of Chicago Press, 1970), 649.

14. A 39/320v. "Philosophical reflections on God, Josiah Royce, etc. 1892."

15. This aspect of Royce's thought is underscored by numerous individuals. See Frank Oppenheim, *Royce's Voyage Down Under: A Journey of the Mind* (Lexington: University of Kentucky, 1980), 17. John McDermott, *The Basic Writings of Josiah Royce*, 2 vols. (Chicago: University of Chicago Press, 1969), and "Josiah Royce's Philosophy of Community—the Danger of the Lost Individual," in *The Philosophy of Possibility: Experience as Philosophy of Culture* (New York: Fordham University Press, 2007). Jacquelyn Ann Kegley, *Genuine Individuals and Genuine Communities* (Nashville: Vanderbilt University Press, 1997). Douglas Anderson, "Royce, Philosophy and Wandering," *Philosophy Americana: Making Philosophy at Home in American Culture* (New York: Fordham University Press, 2006), 33–49. Mat Foust, "Tragedy and the Sorrow of Finitude: Reflections on Sin and Death in the Philosophy of Josiah Royce," *The Pluralist* 2, no. 2 (2007): 106–15.

16. Foust, "Tragedy and the Sorrow of Finitude," 106–15.

17. This is reflected in an early note to Royce, drafted June 28, 1889, in which Cabot praises Royce's *Religious Aspects of Philosophy* (1885) but comments that "the first half [Book I] could be considerably improved" and that many people did not grasp the significance of Book II, which led her "to think that it is not written as clearly as it can be." A 139/319. "Draft of letter from ELC to JR, 1889."

18. A 139/319. "Draft of letter from ELC to JR, 1889."

19. John McDermott, The Basic Writings of Josiah Royce. 2 vol. (Chicago: University of Chicago Press, 1969), and "Josiah Royce's Philosophy of Community—the Danger of the Lost Individual," in The Philosophy of Possibility: Experience as Philosophy of Culture (New York: Fordham University Press, 2007).

20. A 139/320.

21. A 139/320. Italics mine.

22. Douglas Anderson, *Philosophy Americana: Making Philosophy at Home in American Culture* (New York: Fordham University Press, 2008).

23. This approach to manuscripts, one that allows the form and tone of the material to teach philosophical lessons of community and loyalty, is exemplified by Oppenheim's work on the Royce-Mason letters. See Frank Oppenheim, "Royce's Practice of Genuine Loyalty," Transactions of the Charles S. Peirce Society 41, no. 1 (2005): 47–63.

24. For James's comments on Royce after his presentation of the Chicago School materials, see James's Letter to F. C. S. Schiller, dated November 15, 1903. bMS AM 1092.9, #3702.

25. HUG 1755. Box 73. "Introductory Remarks to the Philosophical Conference of 1903."

26. HUG 1755. Box 73. "Introductory Remarks to the Philosophical Conference of 1903."

27. Peirce writes to Royce concerning the *World and the Individual* in May of 1902: "The way I should put what seems to me the most important lesson of your first volume is that purpose and opinion are merely inseparable aspects of the same thing. Only in one case the purposive character is prominent in another the cognitive character. That being fully understood, something like your theory of reality follows as a corollary." See CSP L 385.

28. MS 284.

29. A 139/320. "Philosophical reflections on God, Josiah Royce, etc. 1892."

30. A 139/320. "Philosophical reflections on God, Josiah Royce, etc. 1892."

31. A 139/320. "Philosophical reflections on God, Josiah Royce, etc. 1892."

32. A 139/320. "Philosophical reflections on God, Josiah Royce, etc. 1892."

33. Cited in Peter Ochs, *Peirce, Pragmatism and the Logic of Scripture* (New York: Cambridge University Press, 1998), 162.

34. HUG 1755. Box 125. Folder 6. "The Work of the Truth Seeker ca. 1878–1882." p. 13.

35. HUG 1755. Box 125. Folder 6. "The Work of the Truth Seeker ca. 1878–1882." p. 13.

36. HUG 1755. Box 125. Folder 6. "The Work of the Truth Seeker ca. 1878–1882." p. 13. Cabot's remarks might be understood in the context of Josiah Royce's courses throughout the 1890s. In an early reflection of 1879 that is uncannily similar to Cabot's comment on the integration of the past, present, and future, Royce writes: "Every man lives in a present, and contemplates a past and future. In this consists his whole life. The future and past are shadows both, the present is the only real. Yet in the contemplation of the shadows is the real wholly occupied; and without the shadows this real has for us neither life nor value. No more universal fact of consciousness can be mentioned than this fact, which therefore deserves a more honorable place in Philosophy than has been accorded to it. For it is in view of this that all men may be said to be in some sense Idealists." HUG 1755. Box 126. Folder 1. p. 123. Again, in his *Spirit of Modern Philosophy* (1892), which Cabot reads in the year of 1893, Royce writes that the processes of evolution take place in the finite world, in a segment of time that interrupts the swath of eternity. This segment is the "present" and constitutes the world in which humans, like all organisms, live and grow. See Josiah Royce, *Spirit of Modern Philosophy* (New York: Houghton Mifflin, 1893), 300–20.

37. A 139/322v. "Growth I and II, 1899, 1901."

38. A 139/322v. "Growth I and II, 1899, 1901."

39. Josiah Royce, *Josiah Royce—Basic Writings*, vol. 1, ed. John McDermott (Chicago: University of Chicago Press, 1969), 605.

40. A 139/319. "Draft of letter from ELC to JR, 1889."

41. A 139/324.

42. A 139/324.

43. A 139/324.

44. Royce observes Cabot's dismissal of the quantitative approach to unity in his 1902 notebooks. HUG 1755. Box 101. Folder 14. p. 162.

45. A 139/322v. While this discussion cannot address this issue in detail, it is worth noting that Cabot's rendering of newness may resonate with Charles Sanders Peirce's desire, expressed in 1906, to revise his doctrine of tychism, the doctrine of Absolute chance. In the "Prolegomena to an Apology of Pragmatism," Peirce writes: "I intend, as soon as I can command the requisite leisure from pot-boiling, to revise my tychistic hypothesis. I still believe that the universe is constantly receiving excessively minute accessions of variety; but instead of supposing, as I formerly did, that these are causeless [chances], I think there is sufficient ground for supposing that they are due to psychical action upon matter. . . . [A]t present, the psychical researchers have certainly cast serious doubt on our old materialist theory without

instituting any progressive method of research into the problem. In this situation, a happy working hypothesis might prove of the utmost service. It would be a pity that the human race should go down to its grave, to which it is visible drawing near, without [addressing] its principle problem." In line with this sentiment, Cabot suggests that novelty and variation are not the outcome of causeless chance but the creation of "psychical" or purposive events that appeal to an ideal. See *Collected Papers of C. S. Peirce*. Harvard University. Houghton Library. MS 292.

46. *Collected Papers of C. S. Peirce*. Harvard University. Houghton Library. MS 292.
47. *Collected Papers of C. S. Peirce*. Harvard University. Houghton Library. MS 292.
48. Royce makes several references to music in explaining the dynamic and nature of the Absolute. These references appear in *The Spirit of Modern Philosophy* (1892), *The Conception of God* (1897), *Studies of Good and Evil* (1898), and *The World and the Individual* (1901). It is unlikely that Cabot is the sole motivating factor in Royce's use of the metaphor of music, but it does indicate a deep similarity in their respective works.
49. MS A 139/324. "Notes re: growth, 1901–1902; paper, "The Relation of Chance to Purpose in Invention," 1902.
50. MS A 139/324.
51. MS A 139/324.
52. Josiah Royce, *The World and the Individual*, vol. 1 (New York: Dover Press, 1959), 22.
53. Royce, *The World and the Individual*, 1:22.
54. Royce, *The World and the Individual*, 1:22.
55. Royce, *The World and the Individual*, 1:22. It is important to note that Cabot's rendering of the process of Wholeness implies an aspect of rejection that stands in contrast to the general belief that metaphysical "wholes" are all inclusive. Cabot explains that wholeness rejects only a certain class of ideas, a class that she terms "the irrelevant."
56. Royce, *The World and the Individual*, 1:22.
57. Royce, *The World and the Individual*, 1:22.
58. John Clendenning, *The Life and Thought of Josiah Royce* (Nashville: Vanderbilt University Press, 1999), 284.
59. Josiah Royce, *The Philosophy of Loyalty* (Nashville: Vanderbilt University Press, 1995), 75.
60. MS A 139/320v. "Philosophical reflections on God, Josiah Royce, etc. 1892."
61. Ella Lyman Cabot, *Everyday Ethics* (New York: Henry Holt and Co., 1907), 33. It is worth noting that Cabot suggests that understanding the transcendent nature of purpose is the first step in understanding the fact that "sympathy is intricately bound up with interest" and purpose. Cabot, *Everyday Ethics*, 190.
62. Cabot, *Everyday Ethics*, 70.
63. Cabot, *Everyday Ethics*, 70.
64. Cabot, *Everyday Ethics*, 191.
65. Cabot, *Everyday Ethics*, 191. In the passage that precedes the quoted statement, Cabot does reference Royce's *Religious Aspects of Philosophy* and suggests that it leads to the practical ethical consequences that she outlines in her 1906 book.
66. Cabot cites James's *Principles of Psychology* in a section "My Self Consists in all with which I am Identified." See Cabot, *Everyday Ethics*, 177.
67. Josiah Royce, *The Letters of Josiah Royce*, ed. John Clendenning (Chicago: University of Chicago Press, 1970), 249.
68. A. Gifford, "Review of *Everyday Ethics*," *Ethics* 17 (1907): 509.
69. A biographical note may help in framing the forthcoming discussion. Mary Parker Follett was born on 3 September 1868 in Quincy, Massachusetts. She was educated first at the Thayer Academy and, four years after graduating, attended Radcliffe College, where she earned her BA with distinction. Her philosophical interests and training were in the tradition of German Idealism, but she was also attracted to William James's pluralism. As Evelyn Burg notes, Follett's work resonates closely with G. H. Mead's work in philosophy and sociology. The lineage between Follett and Josiah Royce can be traced through Ella Lyman Cabot but also through Anna Boynston Thompson, Follett's teacher in secondary school. Thompson was Royce's student. Follett comments that Thompson first exposed her to philosophy and

particularly German Idealism. During her lifetime, Follett worked principally as a social worker consultant and was the author of numerous books on human relations, government, and management. Follett lived in England for the last five years of her life and died on 18 December 1933 in Boston.

70. Peter Drucker, *Mary Parker Follett: Prophet of Management*, ed. Pauline Graham (New York: Beard Publishing, 1995).

71. A 139/117. "Mary Follett, 1927–1933."

72. Mary Parker Follett, *Creative Experience* (New York: Longman, Green and Co., 1924).

73. Mary Parker Follett, "Community Is a Process," *Philosophical Review* 28 (1919): 576.

74. Follett, "Community Is a Process," 580.

75. Follett, "Community Is a Process," 586.

76. Follett, "Community Is a Process," 576.

77. Follett, "Community Is a Process," 576.

78. Mary Parker Follett, *Creative Experience* (New York: Longman, Green and Co., 1924), 163.

79. Follett, *Creative Experience*, 163.

80. William James, *Principles of Psychology*, vol. 1 (New York: Dover Publications, 1950), 313.

81. Mary Parker Follett, *The New State: Group Organization, the Solution of Popular Government* (State College: Penn State University Press, 1998), 3.

82. Matthew Shapiro, "Evolutionary Democracy: The Philosophy of Mary Parker Follett," *World Futures* 59 (2003): 587.

83. Mary Parker Follett, *Creative Experience* (New York: Longman, Green and Co., 1924), 63.

84. MS A 139/117. "Mary Follett, 1927–1933."

Chapter Three

Ella Lyman Cabot's Chance: The Nature of Contingency in the American Philosophical Tradition[1]

To understand Dante is, at once, to comprehend the inner workings of ancient Greece and Rome. As the Cabots read the *Divine Comedy* in the early 1890s, they became acquainted with the mythological, literary, and philosophical figures of Western antiquity, coming to know Virgil, Homer, and Achilles in turn. In the fourth circle of the Inferno, Ella Lyman Cabot happened across a character that would figure centrally in her thinking and writing: Fortuna, the Roman goddess of chance occurrences and opportunities. This fateful meeting between Cabot and Fortuna changed the course of Cabot's philosophical life. Much of her writing takes up this meeting explicitly, highlighting and explaining the relationship between contingency and human opportunity.

Any attempt to understand the goddess Fortuna would have led Cabot back to the religious life of ancient Greece, the origin of many Roman myths. She would have discovered that as ancient Greece entered its Golden Age (450–280 BC) its religious landscape began to shift. This shifting occurred very literally "by chance." It shifted by chance not in the sense of changing randomly, but rather in the development of the creation of novel votive practices dedicated to Chance (Tyche) as a deified abstraction. Tyche was the predecessor of the Roman Fortuna. Citizens began to appeal to Tyche in the attempt to explain and negotiate the spontaneous events that seemed to emerge in public and personal histories. These practices also reflected the belief that a particular orientation to chance and possibility could affect the ways in which people grew and flourished in their everyday lives.

As American pragmatism came into its own in the late 1800s, the philosophical investigation, if not the religious veneration, of Tyche had a meaningful resurgence. Literary critics, social theorists, and scientists sought to counteract the determinism and material reductionism of the last stages of the scientific revolution by harkening back to the ancient conception of chance. Ella Lyman Cabot joined thinkers such as Charles Sanders Peirce in contributing to this resurgence. Peirce, appropriating the Greek understanding of chance phenomena in his "pragmaticism," expanded this understanding in his concept of tychism, his doctrine of "absolute chance."

It is interesting to note that Peirce, like Cabot, came to think about the concept of chance by way of the ancients. Peirce, however, unlike Cabot, regards Tyche as a metaphysical concept of ancient philosophy, rather than as a practical concept of ancient life. He traces his tychism to Aristotle's metaphysical observation that things come into existence in variety of ways, one of which is by chance.[2] Cabot recognizes this metaphysical fact, but then turns to the relationship between this fact and ethics, to the way that contingency opens the door for human opportunity and creativity. In order to reveal this juxtaposition between Peirce and Cabot, this chapter undertakes three related objectives. First, it examines Peirce's indebtedness to the Aristotle, a project that has already been undertaken in some detail in the work of Max Fisch, Carl Hausman, and Douglas Anderson.[3] Second, it investigates Peirce's 1906 suggestion that his doctrine of tychism might be reworked in order to expose the relation between chance and purposiveness. Finally, instead of exploring this suggestion in terms of Peirce's later works on semiotics—a worthwhile project unto itself—I have opted to examine Cabot's work that seems to grapple with similar issues and remains largely, if not fully, untouched by the philosophic mainstream.

This chapter, therefore, focuses on Cabot's "The Relation of Chance to Purpose in Invention," written in 1902, and *Everyday Ethics* (1906). These writings center on the place of chance in nature and human conduct. Her 1902 paper, written as a graduate student in Royce's twentieth century seminar, is an important contribution to the American philosophical canon for at least two reasons. First, it seems to attempt a revision of tychism that is made along the lines that Peirce sketches in the early years of the twentieth century. Here, Cabot provides a sustained reflection on the issues of contingency and growth that occupied her male contemporaries. The fact this piece is written four years before Peirce makes his 1906 suggestion concerning chance and purpose is particularly intriguing. Cabot's work complements and helps to unpack Peirce's *Monist* articles written in the 1890s. Second, while the paper has Roycean undertones, Cabot was not looking to Royce on the issues of contingency and purpose. While at first glance, it may appear that Cabot holds the Roycean position that chance is an illusion produced by an individual's limited perspective, Cabot maintains that chance is real, beneficial, and underpins the possibility of human creativity.[4]

At this point, a brief orienting comment seems warranted. As Anderson and others have noted, Royce and Peirce appear to have parted company on the issue of pure chance. Peirce holds that chance is a real and active force; Royce does not. It is also well known that the disagreements between Royce and William James turned precisely on whether possibility and chance were cosmologically and ontologically real. This time, James is the Thrasymachus character, insisting that contingency undermines the steady progress of inquiry; Royce seems to maintain a more deterministic bearing. Cabot's work clears a sort of middle ground between these two positions. Most of her graduate studies survey the fertile space between random contingency and determinacy, the space where she claimed that creativity and imagination seem to reside. In creating this middle position, instead of mimicking any of the aforementioned thinkers, Cabot proposes an original stance that is most akin to Emerson's work in "Fate" and "Quotation and Originality." In effect, Cabot seems to encourage thinkers such as Peirce and Royce to stop their cosmological squabbling, reminds them of their intellectual roots, and at the same time reframes the discourse surrounding chance events in order to focus on issues of human opportunity and creativity. While Cabot seems relatively unaware of Peirce's work, her writing allows us to extend his tychistic hypothesis in new and interesting directions, while reconnecting this hypothesis to the wider field of American thought.

THE ROOT OF PEIRCE'S TYCHISM: ARISTOTLE'S *PHYSICS B*

The term "tychism" appears twenty-five times in Peirce's collected papers, most notably in his *Monist* series published in the early 1890s. However, the concept of chance—and the epistemic and ontological indeterminacy that it implies—defines Peirce's earlier work as well. Peirce's early interest in indeterminism appears in his 1866 Lowell lectures and was enriched during his sustained study of quantified logic throughout the 1870s.[5] This study led Peirce to the belief that the laws of the human mind, and the laws of nature more generally, operate in a hypothetical fashion. These laws could not be defined in absolute terms and that variation itself defined what he would later term the "law of mind."[6] "The Doctrine of Chances," written in the winter of 1878, stands as a succinct articulation of Peirce's early position on the importance and ubiquity of probabilistic events. It presents a discussion on the chance of nonrepeatable events, a discussion that Hilary Putnam would later term "Peirce's puzzle."[7] In the 1890s, however, Peirce distances himself from the conception of chance as mere probability or as being accurately approached by way of quantitative frequency. This realization comes on the heels of a related assertion that Peirce makes throughout the 1880s, namely that abduction, the spontaneous process of hypothesis formation, should be regarded as being distinct from the probabilistic inference of induction. Along these lines, Peirce's later writings do not present tyche as being described as chaos, randomness, or probability, but rather identifies chance as the quality of nonrepeatable and novel occurrences that occur regularly but not axiomatically. In his early works, the seeds of tychism were sown. Peirce turned to the history of philosophy in the cultivation of these seeds, so it seems reasonable to make a similar turn in our study. It is important to note that Peirce excavated these seeds of chance from his studies of Aristotle. This is an intellectual legacy that Cabot also inherited, but also revised in light of her belief that contingency was of vital importance to human creativity and ethical life. Returning to the archaic understanding of tyche will therefore shed light on the place and definition of the phenomenon of chance in American philosophy.

As Peirce observes in the "Doctrine of Necessity Examined," Aristotle's understanding of tyche is developed as a response to both the causal and noncausal strains of determinism that defined the work of the atomists who preceded him. Aristotle considers noncausal determinism in *Interpretatione* 9 and the causal form in both *Physics* II 4 and *Metaphysics* II 3. It is fairly obvious that he takes this position to be ill-conceived when he asks in the *Physics* not whether *all* coming-into-being is necessarily caused, but instead if *any* of it is. This being said, Aristotle insists that coming-into-being necessitates a kind of cause. In his attempt to explain this coming-into-being, however, he is not led to a cause that can be exhaustively defined or one that fully accounts for a given effect outcome. Instead he is led to a cause that is, by his own definition, "obscure" and "hidden." He is led to chance. At first glance, Aristotle's development of tyche might appear to be a type of afterthought to his "theory of the four causes" in *Physics B*. Instead, I contend it is the *conclusion* to his four causes, a conclusion that makes this theory interestingly and uniquely problematic. Chance throws this theory into question for Aristotle states that no particular cause could account for the emergence of chance, but that "it is manifest that luck or chance is (still) something."[8] Aristotle restates the odd tension of chance. On the one hand, "in view of all of this, luck is something indefinite and not revealed to man and there is a sense in which nothing would seem to happen by chance."[9] On the other hand, "chance events are among the things that are produced for the sake of something."[10] As this final passage indicates, chance events are both real and causally important, but not causally final. (That is, chance events are *not* produced for their "results.")

To elaborate on this final point, chance events may be produced for the sake of something, but they are *not* produced for the sake of something intended prior to production. Indeed, as Pascal Massie recently writes in his commentary on the *Physics*, chance events are characterized by the unruly, the exceptional, and the disorderly.[11] As Massie notes, any attempt to address chance by way of prediction, by an attempt to calculate the "frequency of chances," will be frustrated by chance's unexpected quality. These observations border on the prosaic, but set the stage for an important move made by Aristotle, and eventually, by Peirce and Cabot.

Chance events are unexpected, but produced for the sake of something. This "something" appears *as if* it were intended by the purposes of an agent, but the odd character of chance insists that this was not, and could not have possibly been, the case. Aristotle gives the example of digging in one's garden and happening upon a buried treasure, a treasure that actively emerges as if it was intended to be found. The intentions of the gardener, however, could not have seized upon the cache before its discovery. Instead, its discovery stands as an encounter with an unforeseen opportunity, with the field of possibility that is partially—or more often, *predominately*—obscured from our sight. In this case, what is primary is not only the action of the gardener, but the action of the treasure chest, offering itself up to be discovered. Chance events may stand counter to the purposes of a given agent, but do emerge in the nexus of possible purposes between an agent and the world at large. This is a point that resounds in two distinct registers in the works of Peirce and Cabot.[12] In "Design and Chance" (1882) Peirce "questions whether it is exactly true" that "every event has a cause," writing, "may it not be that chance, in the Aristotelian sense, mere absence of cause, has to be admitted as having some place in the universe."[13] Elaborating on this sentiment in the 1898 Cambridge lectures, Peirce states that the world "lives and moves and has its BEING in a logic of event."[14] This logic and life of the world is one in which chance occurrences do, in fact, happen with an almost stunning regularity. The world shows itself to us in any number of unexpected ways. In the words of Epicurus, the universe itself "swerves" without warning. Peirce is making a metaphysical point that he believes points toward an epistemic fact, namely that the difficulty of human knowing is to negotiate and make sense of the emergence of chance in our experience. Cabot agrees, but puts a slightly different spin on the "swerve" of world. The contingency that defines the logic and life of the world is not to be mastered or explained, but rather is to be understood as the locus of human creativity. It is in the confrontation with the unexpected that human opportunity and growth is realized. Indeed, an extension of Aristotle's gardening example exposes this.

The appearance of the treasure ruptures or cuts into the gardener's usual task. This chance event disrupts an established routine, but also sets the stage for future courses of action on the part of the gardener. Once the treasure appears, the gardener is called to respond to this appearance, is called to make a choice. She may choose to ignore the treasure and rebury it; she may dig it up and give it away; she may take leave of her work as a gardener and establish herself as a wealthy landowner. In any event, the gardener's choices are irreparably altered by the emergence of the treasure—chance sets the stage for novel modes of inquiry, investigation and action. In short, chance provides and underscores the phenomenon of genuine growth in its encounter with the field of possibility.

THE DEVELOPMENT OF TYCHISM—DISCOVERING THE ROLE OF AGENCY

While tychism emerges in Peirce's early work, it is clear that he had yet to grasp the ontological and epistemological import of this doctrine of absolute chance. In other words, he did not, immediately, realize the opportunity that chance affords. For example, in his earlier years, he explores, and then rejects, two less radical understandings of chance that try to attribute chance to either "human ignorance (as Hobbes had) or to the coincidence of thoroughly regulated actions."[15] It was only in 1882 that he brought to bear his concept of tychism, or genuine chance, on the problem of determinism, asserting that spontaneity was a real and motivating force in the evolution of the universe and in the growth and variation of law itself. Peirce makes this assertion in opposition to the work of the modern day Democrituses and Leucippuses he faced—namely, the Spencerian and Darwinian evolutionists in Cambridge. He insists that these scholars, while concentrating on determinate facts and laws of evolutions, overlooked the agential force of tyche upon which variation and adaptation depend. I will show in the coming section that Cabot voices similar views concerning the prevailing evolutionary theories of the day. Peirce writes that it "appears to me that chance is the essential agency upon which the whole process [of evolution] depends."[16] As Turley and Fisch explain, chance, as rendered by Aristotle and Peirce, can account for the four main pitfalls that continually befuddle determinists: the phenomenon of growth, the increase of diversity, the existence of regularity, and the continuous processes of consciousness.[17] The work of Cosculluela and others addresses these four points in detail.[18] My discussion will extend this work, but will focus primarily on the relationship between tychism and Peirce's understanding of purpose and creativity. Cabot describes in detail a point that Peirce is slow to address in his published writing, namely that the problem of determinism is not merely a metaphysical one, but rather an ethical one, the solution of which demands a reframing of the concepts of will and agency.

Peirce does, eventually, recognize the relationship between agency and tychism, but this recognition seems to have been delayed by his insistence that philosophy ought to be systematic in nature and that philosophers ought to hold off discussing the intricacies of ethics until their philosophies addressed the broader underlying metaphysical issues. Along these lines, many commentators point to tychism as an important wellspring of the evolutionary cosmology that defines Peirce's thought after 1886. This interpretation seems appropriate since Peirce himself indicates that his attempt to develop an account of diversity, evolution, and continuity stems from his initial investigations of the nature of chance. In 1906, in a lecture to the National Academy of Science, Peirce reflected on the role that tychism played in his thinking on the nature of continuity, suggesting that synechism, his notion of evolutionary continuity, is "the synthesis of tychism and pragmatism."[19] At first glance, this synthesis seems to fit nicely with Darwin's belief that evolution could be largely explained by way of the synthesis of two factors: the random variability of mutation and the pressure of selection exerted on the phenotypic consequences of these mutations. Peirce, however, unlike Darwin, suggests that a full description of evolution ought to concentrate not on random variability, but the variability of spontaneous agency. This may seem to be a minor distinction, but it is a distinction that becomes more dramatic and more decisive in Peirce's later writings on tychism.

In the "Doctrine of Necessity Examined," the second article of his *Monist* series, Peirce begins to develop his mature model of tychism as a response to a train of thought that he terms "necessitarianism."[20] According to the "necessitarian," nature operates by way of mechanistic rules that could, at least ideally, be exhaustively defined. Peirce, however, suggests that "growth and developing complexity, which appears to be universal" cannot be understood by means of necessary laws.[21] Similarly, he states that "variety itself, beyond comparison the most obtrusive character of the universe: no mechanism can account for this."[22] Instead he proposes, and begins to demonstrate by his earlier studies of mathematical probability, that such phenomena can only be explained by way of chance. Here, Peirce writes that he attributes these phenomena "altogether to chance, it is true, but to chance in the form of spontaneity that is to some degree regular."[23]

It is clear that Peirce understands chance in the sense of emerging as a type of purposive spontaneous action. In his description of chance, he writes that there "in nature is probably 'some agency' by which complexity and diversity is increased."[24] Hausman is quite good on this point when he writes that this agency ought to be considered the "originative condition that is in some sense responsible for its own action."[25] At first glance, the relation between chance and agency remains unclear. Peirce addresses this ambiguity, however, in a comment made in 1906 in his unpublished "Prolegomena to an Apology for Pragmatism." He writes:

> I intend, as soon as I can command the requisite leisure from pot-boiling, to revise my tychistic hypothesis. I still believe that the universe is constantly receiving excessively minute accessions of variety; but instead of supposing, as I formerly did, that these are causeless (chances), I think there is sufficient ground for supposing that they are due to psychical action upon matter. . . . [A]t present, the psychical researchers have certainly cast serious doubt on our old materialist theory without instituting any progressive method of research into the problem. In this situation, a happy working hypothesis might prove of the utmost service. It would be a pity that the human race should go down to its grave, to which it is visible drawing near, without (addressing) its principle problem.[26]

In this passage, Peirce makes explicit the way in which chance might be considered the visible outcome of psychical action. This suggestion is significant for it not only recasts the concept of chance, but suggests that we reconsider the continuity of matter and mind. Peirce foreshadows this move when he claims that, "chance is but the outward aspect of that which within itself is feeling."[27]

The vital connection between psychical life and material processes is brought to the fore in Peirce's description of the "regularity" of tyche; Peirce is going to insist that chance does not imply sheer randomness, but rather gives birth to a type of order that emerges provisionally in the midst of phenomena. He repeatedly relies on his studies of variation in Darwinian evolution to suggest that spontaneous acts can beget provisional order. For Peirce, tyche motivates the order of nature, an order that interestingly reflects the spontaneity and adaptation that had been historically reserved for descriptions of the human mind. Just as the habits of the human mind are occasionally overcome and revised by the generation of new hypotheses, the laws of nature are occasionally violated by a novel occurrence that provides the possibility of growth and adaptation. In regard to Peirce's epistemological claims, scholars such as Hausman suggest that Peirce's acknowledgment of tychism in the world coincided with his conviction that chance must also play a vital role in any theory of human knowledge and the growth of the natural world.[28] Knowledge, and the natural processes by which it arises, develops by hypothetical leaps and bounds rather than by the direction of preestablished axioms and laws. Moving deeper into this analysis of Peirce's treatment of chance, deeper into the metaphysical twists and turns, it is worthwhile to remember that this analysis is meant to be given as a backdrop for Cabot's work on the nature and significance of contingency. We will see that her work on chance is neither highly technical nor performed in the service of a grand philosophical system. In effect, her work brings chance back to the practical concerns of the everyday. This is not to say that Cabot disagrees with Peirce on the place of contingency in ontology; rather she seems to suggest that more work is needed in order to show how chance, in terms of metaphysical contingency, is related to chance, in terms of human opportunity.

The contrast between Peirce the theoretician and Cabot the practitioner is reflected in the way that Peirce's investigation of chance phenomena draws him further into study of mathematics and speculative philosophy. In Peirce's words, chance is "a mathematical term to express with accuracy the characteristics of freedom and spontaneity."[29] In this sense, the principle of tychism draws Peirce to rethink the natural world in terms of a type of idealism that he had hitherto dismissed out of hand. He admits this point in "The Law of Mind" when he writes:

> I have begun by showing that *tychism* must give birth to an evolutionary cosmology, in which all the regularities of nature and of mind are regarded as products of growth, and to a Schelling-fashioned idealism which holds matter to be mere specialized and partially deadened mind.[30]

In this article Peirce elaborates, commenting that his interest in tychism per se must, at least for the time being, be put aside in order to pursue the evolutionary idealism that his investigation of chance and spontaneity has revealed. While tychism sets the stage for his later work, Peirce explicitly shifts his focus away from absolute chance toward the principle of synechism and true continuity as described in the "Law of Mind." He justifies this move in the last article of the *Monist* series, "Evolutionary Love," when he explains that synechism in fact encompasses the principle of pure chance, or more accurately put, tychism is a degenerate form of synechism.[31]

To say that Peirce shifts his focus from the topic of spontaneous agency as the defining element of tychism to the character of phenomenological continuity as the characteristic of synechism may misconstrue the development of his writing. Perhaps it would be more appropriate to say that, in his investigation of tychism as "some type of agency," he discovers one of the continuous threads that unifies the psychical-physical world. In this sense, he does not abandon one topic for another, but rather comes to realize the implications of the topic of tychism that had long occupied his attention. In one stroke, tychism entails synechism, Peirce's doctrine of continuity, and agapism, his description of evolutionary love.[32]

To elaborate on these points, it seems wise to return to the passage from his 1906 "Apology to Pragmatism." Here Peirce suggests that chance occurrences—occurrences that characterize every aspect of the universe—

might be understood as emerging in the interaction of psychical and physical actions. To reframe chance along these lines is at once to reconsider the purposive actions by which diversity and complexity are increased, that is to say, to reconsider the agency that animates our natural and mental lives. According to Peirce, this task of understanding chance agency stands for the human race as "its principle problem."[33] Peirce, however, makes only partial attempts to explain *why* the question of chance might be significant. I believe that Cabot provides precisely this explanation, in a form that is both compelling and highly accessible.

In taking up this principle problem—the problem that emerges from his study of chance events—Peirce merely alludes to the fact that we do not only investigate "our own" agency, but also the agency and purposiveness of the world at large. Additionally, he begins to explore the conditions by which individuals maintain fruitful relations with the chance spontaneity of the world. This is the point that Cabot will extend in her works. As she underscores, this is not some abstract problem but an immediate and pressing issue of how human beings are to act rightly and meaningfully in psychical–physical circumstances. And they are ever changing: we are continually confronted by the newness and growth that emerge in our immediate situations and in our wider communities. Peirce seems to suggest, but not state explicitly, that we forego the *chance* of acting rightly precisely at the point that we disregard, or simply overlook, the novelty that we encounter. In such cases, our habits and conventions are out of kilter with our surroundings and lead us further from the harmonious growth that only our encounters with novelty can afford.

CHANCE ENCOUNTERS: CABOT ON CONTINGENCY AND PURPOSE

I did not intend to write any of this. As mentioned earlier, it chanced one summer that I was sifting through a box of notes taken by Josiah Royce during the late 1890s. My purpose at the time was quite clear: I intended to write about the concepts of the imagination and contingency as they were developed in the writings of the fathers of American philosophy. In the process of this inquiry, however, I began to notice things that were outside the scope of my project. More accurately, I noticed a name that continued to emerge in the course of my archival work, a name that was unfamiliar to my given purposes: "Mrs. Cabot."

In his seminars of 1901 and 1902, Royce had repeatedly referenced this individual and her work on growth and chance events.[34] In the *Philosophy of Loyalty* and the *Problem of Christianity* he thanks her for helping to develop his projects. My encounter with this unknown figure in American philosophy caused my former project to take a dramatic turn. Indeed, I never got around to finishing my original project. Some might say, with a certain amount of disgust, that I "got distracted." Perhaps this is true. I would, however, suggest that the distraction and disruption caused by chance encounters can lead to innovation and original work. Indeed, it seems pointedly Peircean to suggest that one's musings ought to hold some sway over the lockstep rules that often govern philosophical pursuits; musement, according to Peirce is the free play involved in sustaining chance encounters. I would later find out that Cabot herself had voiced this opinion in 1899:

> It's a rule of the game that on penalty of death no one shall use uniform phrases or acts save for the task of a new construction. We tend forever to slip into the ease and luxury of our old accustomed ways. A stranger disturbs our peace. We do not see that in the ruffling caused by the interruption may be our opportunity. For the stranger has a message be he a seer or a fool. . . . [E]veryday is a reconstruction period. If I can only work in my particular armchair or niche I am in so far making a story shell—acquiring moral arterial sclerosis. Not that I can instantly and by myself assimilate the difficulty, but that the sources of strength are in the reach of many.[35]

In addressing the work of Cabot, a virtual stranger to most us, we allow ourselves to enter a type of "reconstruction period"—the reconstruction of American philosophy. Cabot herself seems aware of the opportunity that the interruption of chance phenomena can afford. She suggests that distraction may lead us to make original contributions, but that it need not lead us away from our guiding plans and purposes. It only takes a bit of insight to see how creative and improvisational enterprises might lead us back to enrich and enliven our original intentions. I hope that my treatment of Ella Lyman Cabot's work reflects this. I believe that her work on chance and invention helps us revisit and refresh our understanding of Peirce's tychism in a meaningful way. Additionally, by highlighting a figure whose work has been excluded from the field of American thought, we have the chance to revisit and renew our understanding of the canon as a whole.

In "The Relation of Chance to Purpose in Invention" (1902), Cabot opens her reflection by stating that it is her intent to define the three principal terms of her title. She begins by stating that "[c]hance is the encounter of factors outside of our plans with our special end."[36] Next, she addresses purpose, admitting that the term is a slippery one and that there is the temptation, and perhaps even an honest reason, to broaden the term beyond the realm of mere human pursuits. She writes that, "I know of course, that there is and can be no fixed moment in the growth of an individual at which purpose begins and it is rooted in what is less definite, but to keep myself to a standard of clearness, I shall say that an individual has a purpose when he has a deliberate plan of action."³⁷ Cabot's account of chance and purpose seem, at least initially, to mirror Josiah Royce's reflections in *The World and the Individual*. Royce continues to maintain that contingency is an illusion produced by our perspectives as finite individuals. Additionally, and I would argue more importantly, this led Royce to adhere to a particular kind of philosophical practice that eschewed inductive and experimental approaches. Throughout *The World and the Individual*, he indicates that the goal of philosophy is see through this illusion, to tear down the pesky veil of the accidental, in order to see with rational clearness the World, and ultimately God. This objective was to be achieved largely through a particular form of philosophical dialectic that relied heavily on deductive methods. Royce had not strayed too far from his position expressed in *The Spirit of Modern Philosophy*, namely that chance occurrences, not criminals, are the true devils of life. It is chance that disrupts our world and in so doing, gives rise to skepticism and pessimism.³⁸ On this point, Cabot will diverge from Royce's position in several significant respects. The similarities between Cabot and Royce, however, are on full display when she writes:

> The question at once arises what is chance? In the first place it does not involve lawlessness. All effects in Nature, however complicated have causes and hence there is no chance in the outer world. Again, all human actions are determined by ends and there is no chance in the world of man though here, as in any complicated natural event, the difficulty of tracing intricate relations may give the appearance of a lack of motive or cause. There is no accident either in the world of nature or of thought, but what we call chance is always the encounter of factors of which our plans are unaware with our own end.³⁹

We might assume, quite safely, that these views coincide with Royce's insistence that nature be lawful and causally explicable. I am inclined to suggest that in this section Cabot is taking her cues not only from Royce, but also from Emerson in his claim that, "Fate then is a name for facts not yet passed under the fire of thought—for causes which are unpenetrated."⁴⁰ Cabot was attracted to Emerson's work as a teenager, and his essays written in the early 1860s would remain touchstones for her throughout her life. To recognize this intellectual history will grant us to explore a more fruitful interpretation of Cabot's work on the topics of chance and creativity.

For Royce and Peirce, the statement that chance is a name for causes that remain unpenetrated is raises the following question: could the causes of nature, in this case, be ideally and exhaustively penetrated? Both approach this question through a detailed and exhausting investigation of logic—Peirce in his logic of relations and Royce in his development of system Σ. For Emerson and Cabot, however, this question prompts a slightly different response. In Emerson's words, "the question of the times," and here he suggests that this is also the question of fate and chance, "resolved itself into a practical question of the conduct of life. How shall I live?"[41] Cabot's treatment of chance is similarly practical and will take its heading from these remarks. After asserting that fate is the name for unexplained causes, Emerson asserts that some causes will *always remain* beyond the realm of the intellect: "Providence has a wild, rough and incalculable road to its end, and it is no use to try to white wash its huge, mixed instrumentalities, or to dress up that terrific benefactor in a clean shirt and white neckcloth of a student in divinity."[42] This road is "incalculable to its end" in the sense that nature always extends beyond the maps employed to negotiate its confusing intersections, switchbacks and very *longue duree*. This does not, however, mean that we are fated to be perpetually and thoroughly lost, only that our plans and explanations will remain partial and provisional. Cabot will agree with Emerson on this point.

Cabot's friendship with, and tutelage under, James Elliot Cabot allowed her a rare familiarity with Emerson's written work, and also with the oral history that circulated from 1860s to the 1890s concerning Emerson's many lectures. Today, scholars often forget that hundreds of his lectures were given but never transcribed. Indeed, American philosophy was originally conveyed by word of mouth, at dinner tables and summer camps located in the rural reaches of New England. One of Emerson's forgotten lectures that affected the course of American thought was given on May 20, 1870. It was titled "The Metres of Mind—the Law of Mind" and was the thirteenth lecture of the "Natural History of the Intellect" series that Emerson gave as a set of University Lectures at Harvard in that year. In many respects this was the first graduate seminar given at Harvard. This "gem of a graduate program," as it has been called, is important in our current discussion concerning the role of chance and contingency in the American philosophical tradition. It is also important in the way that it binds together the various thinkers that we have addressed so far. First, several important figures were invited to give the lectures in 1870, including James Elliot Cabot, Fredric Hedge, Francis Bowen, and a rather young Charles Sanders Peirce. Peirce lectured on the British logicians, but it seems more than likely that he was also privy to Emerson's work in "The Law of Mind." Indeed the most famous of Peirce's *Monist* series articles, written in the early 1890s, shares Emerson's title and makes explicit his indebtedness to his Transcendental precursors, mentioning Hedge and Emerson in the article. It is in Peirce's "Law of Mind" (1892) that he makes explicit his argument for tychism, stating that laws of mind and of nature admit a "peculiar arbitrariness and caprice."[43] In an unpublished note for Emerson's lecture, we find a snippet that might have proved formative for Peirce and Cabot in their desire to maintain a place for spontaneity and growth in their respective philosophies. Emerson writes that "the universe and the individual perpetually act and react on each other. Thus all philosophy emerges from nox and chaos, the ground or abyss which

Schelling celebrates. And in every man we require a bit of night, of chaos, of *abgrund* as the spring of a watch turns best on a diamond."[44] Originality emerges from our encounters with the darkness of the unknown and unexpected, which—if we are honest with ourselves and faithful to the dynamism of nature—will never be exhausted.

Both Cabot and Peirce follow Emerson insofar as they insist that every theory concerning the external world will fall short in its ability to anticipate the chaos of nature. Whenever we attempt to articulate the workings of nature, we come up short and fail to account for its complexity and breadth. Whenever we attempt to speak of nature, whether our own human nature or nature on the whole, we find ourselves without words or rather we find that we can always say more. In 1891, Cabot writes to this effect, "[s]peech is but the broken light upon the depth of the unspoken."[45] Turning her attention to Darwin's attempt to describe the patterns of evolution, Cabot notes that the scientist used to complain that his plant specimens did not follow the theoretical rules that he had laid out, exclaiming, "the little beggars are doing exactly what I don't want them to."[46] Cabot suggests that Darwin ought to appreciate this sort of irregularity since it is precisely the deviation from the rule of inherited traits that provides the variability by which adaptive selection operates. Organic life grows and flourishes due to variation, and so too does the development and innovation of the human mind. The fact that "the beggars" defied his expectations was the factor "that led Darwin to [the] truly original discoveries" of natural selection and variation.[47] There may "be no accident either in the world of nature or of thought," but for Cabot accident is actual and causally significant in the encounter *between* nature and thought. This is the region where human purposes arise and grow.

On this note, Cabot provides an assertion and an admonition: "first that chance actually does enter into our purposes and second that when we rigidly exclude chance originality dies."[48] In supporting these positions, Cabot turns our attention not to the deductive proof of some of her teachers, but instead to experimental and aesthetic experience, to demonstrate her point. Emerson and Schelling are clearly close at hand when she writes:

> Is not the starting point of invention the imperfect, the chaotic, the disorderly, rather than the exclusively deliberate and definite? . . . [T]he fact that roots grow only in the dark and that seeds must be buried has wider applications than in the realm of horticulture. It is most often out of the dark unconscious that the greatest thoughts grow and poems written for occasions and deliberately commemorative pictures are usually the least original.[49]

Chance factors break into the birth of purpose "at the starting point of invention." While this aspect of chance interests Cabot, she is particularly impressed by the way in which contingency molds our deliberate purposes even in the latter stages of their development.

Seemingly unaware of Peirce's description of thirdness as generality,[50] Cabot writes that contingency's ability to affect habitual purposes is due "primarily to the fact that every idea or plan we form is vague, it is a frame to hold a thousand different pictures. . . . [T]his looseness of indefiniteness of any plan which might be considered a lack, is the center of radiating opportunity."[51] In her notebooks for the "The Search for the Eternal," written in the same year, the author indicates that the indefiniteness reflected in a particular plan may also lurk at the heart of general laws. Here, butted up against a scribbled copy of Wordsworth's "Mutability," Cabot writes:

> When we say that the Truth or the law holds unchanged in spite of incessant variation in manifestation we are separating form from content. We put the law so far off from this changing manifestations that it cannot be hurt. In so doing, we find that it is too remote to be a source of heat.[52]

Cabot realizes that she is treading dangerous philosophic ground—the chasm of relativism and nihilism gapes below. If, as she suggests, plans ought to be vague, what becomes of definite and meaningful purposes? In more cynical terms, we might ask, "What is the point of having ideas or purposes, if chance is just going to come along and change them?" Cabot keeps her balance in answering these questions by leading us back to her initial definition of chance as occurrences that emerge beyond the scope of our current pursuits. "Without purpose," therefore, "there is no chance and . . . any purpose in proportion to its width and strength changes chance to *my* chance."[53] Here it is obvious that the general questions of fate and chance are to be negotiated only to the extent that they respond to the more pressing particular question of "*my* chance," the personal possibilities of human conduct in relation to developing purposes.

For Cabot and Emerson, the encounter with our natural surroundings, often defined by its emergent and unexpected character, provides a space for chance. More specifically, it creates a clearing for *my* chance—a personal and meaningful opportunity for creative engagement. It is Darwin's sensitivity to factors beyond his current purposes, to chance, that led him to original developments.[54] It is the poet's attunement to external facts—the inspiration of rhyme or nature—that grants her the power of the first word. Issues concerning the wildness and contingency of Providence lead Cabot and Emerson not to a study of logic and cosmology, as in the case of Peirce and Royce, but to a reflection on genius and human creativity, to the question of how we are to live our lives. These thinkers are led to address the realm of human conduct, the place where the dilemma of determinism meaningfully matters.

THE VISION OF THE IMAGINATION: THE CHANCE PROVIDED BY CHANCE

> So women, as most susceptible, are the best index of the coming hour. So the great man, that is the man most imbued with the spirit of the time, is the impressionable man, of a fibre irritable and delicate, like iodine to light. He feels infinitesimal attractions. His mind is righter than others, because he yields to a current so feeble as can be felt only by a needle delicately poised.
> —Ralph Waldo Emerson, "Fate" (1860)

A brief comment needs to be made, not on the topic of pure chance *per se*, but on the human capacity that stands equipped to respond to the chance encounters that Cabot describes. It is a comment that is meant to set the stage for a capacity and gift that deserves special treatment in the coming chapter. In addition to purpose, another capacity is required in order to allow chance to emerge and work its way into our projects. Cabot, along with a host of German Idealists and fellow pragmatists, describe this capacity as the imagination. Cabot's work on the imagination is extensive and, written in the first decade of the 1900s, anticipates much of Dewey's thinking in *Art as Experience* and the *Quest for Certainty*, books that continue to be regarded as American philosophy's most definitive word on the subject. Her prescience is evinced in writings, such as *Everyday Ethics*, that wed ethical action to the creative imagination. The reliance of ethics on the imagination will be pursued in the coming chapter, but a few words are warranted on the relationship between the imagination and chance.

In her 1906 *Everyday Ethics*, Cabot writes that "we define as the imagination as the power to follow the spirit and trend of any fact."[55] When chance facts break into our usual routine, as they invariably do, it is the imagination that allows one to respond to these interruptions as real opportunities. It is the imagination that allows one to take a turn in her thinking that is motivated by a chance encounter. Instead of passively ignoring or actively destroying a chance, the imagination seizes upon the unexpected, and recognizes the possibilities that it affords. Cabot returns to the ancient distinction between *eikasia* and *phantasia* in stating the difference between imagination and mere fancy. She writes that, "imagination seeks and tries further to reveal the dawning truth . . . while fancy is not governed by any such allegiance."[56] Here, the definition of the imagination that Cabot provides as a "dawning truth" is a rendition of *eikasia* that Plato gives in Book 6 and 7 of the *Republic* as an "argument from appearances."[57] *Eikasia* connotes the interplay of purposes and contingent appearances. In her words, "in all that we see we constantly use the imagination. The red wall of my neighbour's house looks solid and hard because my imagination leaps to the conclusion that it is made of brick; but my eyes never see the brick."[58] While the imagination may be operative in all cases of seeing, as Cabot suggests, it is most obviously at play when we encounter and creatively integrate chance appearances, that is, appearances that fall outside the narrow confines of our given domain of inquiry.

She elaborates on the character of imagination as *eikesia* through an everyday example, pointing out that while many people have had "delicious fancies awakened as they dream over a steaming kettle," it was only to an imagination like Watts that the fact of boiling water suggests "new principles and prophetic constructions."[59] In effect, the imagination identifies a chance, personal and meaningful, that is provided by chance encounters experienced in relation to a purpose. It is only through the imagination that chance becomes *my* chance. It seems likely that Cabot is again echoing passages from Emerson's "Fate." Here Emerson comments that inexplicable chance is regarded as the devil until the imaginative genius puts it to good use:

> Steam was, till the other day, the devil which we dreaded. Every pot made by any human had a hole in the cover, to let off the enemy, lest he should lift the pot and the roof, and carry the house away. But Watt and Fulton bethought themselves, that, where was power was not devil, but was God; that it must be availed of and not by any means let off or wasted. [60]

Cabot suggests that the lack of this sort of insight begins to explain not only the systemic dullness of her day, but also its disease. She writes, "[t]he man of little imagination may plod along doing about what is expected of him.... [T]housands of iridescent opportunities open for a moment like a rainbow before him, but he sees only the dust in the road."[61] For this wanderer, the road of life is characterized by an odd, but all too familiar, mix of drudgery and anxiety. Things appear on this road in one of two unsatisfactory ways: as a patterned and boring landscape or as disjointed and chaotic terrain. In both cases, Elbert Hubbard would say that, "life is just one damn thing after another." In both cases, we remain oddly out of touch with our surroundings, displaced and forever not at home.

Cabot suggests that it is only through acts of the imagination that we can make a meaningful home on the road, or more accurately, make this road, with all of its blind curves, our home. "The imagination," she writes, "is the power to be in whatever we touch. It is through imagination that we fill the gaps and out of fragments make a whole."[62] This power keeps us firmly grounded to, and in contact with, the facts that continually confront us. In typical fashion, Cabot employs a mundane example to illustrate an esoteric point. She asks her students to consider the facts that one might find in a newspaper. The newspaper is filled, at least ideally, with descriptions of extraordinary events and unforeseen circumstances—hence being called "the *news*." This teacher makes a list of the headlines from the day and then points out that "each of these items ... may be read with a maximum or a minimum of imagination."[63] When the imagination is fully awake, each of these topics—from a railroad accident, to a sudden heavy gale, to a miners' strike in Wilkes-Barre—have a meaningful bearing on our lives. This meaningful bearing is realized by dwelling with the "news," by being intimately familiar with circumstances as they emerge, and grasping the relations that might exist between these chance events and our current purposes. Cabot, however, reflects on the lethargic imagination of the modern age, stating that "so unimaginative are we that often read the newspaper ... and as we throw it down complain that nothing is in it. There is indeed nothing in it for those who are 'out of it.'"[64]

We need to be careful to distinguish between Cabot's suggestion that we are to be imaginatively involved in the novel occurrences, and the modern tendency to fetishize and mindlessly consume the news. As Samuel Johnson indicates in his *Idler* (1754), there is a tendency for an individual "to loose himself in the croud, filling the vacuities of his mind with the news of the day."[65] This state of mind—or mindlessness—is one of passive occupation and serves to mask the tedium that silently threatens our lives. Thomas Gray criticizes women precisely along these lines, stating that women busy themselves with the news, but fail to engage it as meaningful "business." They "always find something to do," according to Gray, "a variety of inventions and occupations fill up the void."[66] Men, on the other hand, must be imbued with a spirit, or a type of "Genius," to occupy their time. Cabot's comments concerning the imagination respond to Gray's insult on a variety of levels.

Cabot's engagement with the news of everyday affairs relies on two equally important dispositions that contemporary thinkers continue to regard as antithetical ideals. On the one hand, this engagement requires an attunement to events and facts outside our current purposes; we are to remain open to chance events and allow them to have a say in our future. On the other hand, it demands an active participation in these events as they unfold. If chance has a say in our future, it is equally true that we can affect the headline of tomorrow's news. Furthermore, the two-sided disposition that Cabot evokes as the character of the imagination may be regarded as uniquely pragmatic, but its origins lie in the description of the imagination and genius as rendered in the works of Kant, Schiller, and Coleridge. Cabot, in effect, reclaims a particular concept of imaginative genius, or at the very least, underlines the way that women once "passed the time" could now be taken up as a meaningful creative enterprise if one approached novel occurrences in a particular pragmatic fashion.

CONCLUSION

At this point, it may be helpful to survey the path that has been covered to this point. It is interesting to note that most commentators suggest that Peirce's investigation of chance events led him deeper into the metaphysical speculation of his later works. A few of these same scholars note that this turn in his later work also signals a type of late-budding interest in the ethical conduct of human beings; I addressed this cursorily above. As Claudine Tiercelin recently writes, in the later years of Peirce's life, "tychism is . . . linked with ethics and theology."[67] For example, his discussion of musement in 1908 serves as a description of a careful encounter of the self with the dawning of new facts. "Neglected Argument for the Reality of God" outlines a type of musing disposition that, apart from opening an individual to the reality of the Divine, reflects a type of ethical attunement that might be necessary to respond to novel circumstances. Let us remember that in the act of musement we temporarily set aside our self-centered purposes or, at the very least, look beyond their constraining scope. That is also to say that we await the emergence of chance and are willing to claim this chance as our own. I think Tiercelin is right in her evaluation of tychism, but I also know that exposing the relation between Peirce's cosmological understanding of chance and the mundane affairs of everyday ethics is arduous labor. If tychism is linked to ethics, it is, at best, a loose link that requires the strong hands of today's scholars to tighten it.

In the case of Cabot's work, however, there is no such challenge. Her investigation of chance and creativity is, from the outset, steeped in the challenges and opportunities of worldly affairs. Being a woman in the intellectual spheres of Cambridge in the late 1800s, Cabot learned firsthand what some of her male contemporaries only vaguely intuited: that circumstances brought about by chance and fate could be seen as obstacles and nuisances, but equally, as occasions for imaginative insight. I would go so far as to say that Peirce, perennially dissatisfied with his career and life trajectory, could have taken a note from Cabot and applied his intellectual ingenuity in reforming *his* everyday ethic. Instead of retreating to an isolated home in eastern Pennsylvania or into the rarified air of metaphysics, Cabot's writings on chance, opportunity, and imagination lead her back to the life of her community, to her activism, and to rethink the ethical sphere.

Cabot's reading lists, drafted between the ages of nineteen and thirty-three, reflect a consistent interest in Emerson's essays. As mentioned earlier, her thinking on chance and creativity resonates with Emerson's "Fate." This resonance with Emerson can also be heard in her willingness to identify the deadening effects of modernity and to chastise her countrymen and women for their lack of meaningful and creative activity. In an 1899 notebook, she takes her cues from the conclusion of the "American Scholar." She writes:

> Americans are inventive and active minded to an unusual degree, but a fearfully large proportion of the population act passively and mechanically. We are parasites, sucking the life out of the past instead of contributing the new word. We don't earn our salt. We have hardly to learn that nothing is to be accepted passively, but all is to be faced imaginatively, not from a sense of superiority, but of indebtedness, of loyalty.[68]

This type of admonishment, usually interpreted as *mere* social commentary, is rooted in Cabot's philosophical study of chance and contingency. Cabot's is the realization that the study of philosophy in America must lead out into the uncharted territory of human relations, in order to understand the chances that may remain open to individuals and communities. We ought to engage in the discourse surrounding tyche not for the sake of intellectual busyness, but for the sake of creative flourishing in human business. Today, in our less-than-golden age, the religious and philosophical veneration of Tyche is still meant to bring us in touch with Fortune—our fortunes—and to awaken us to the chances that lie beyond our current purposes.

NOTES

1. Portions of this chapter first appeared in John Kaag, "Chance and Creativity: The Nature of Contingency in Classical American Philosophy," *Transactions of the Charles S. Peirce Society* 44, no. 3 (2008): 393–411.
2. "A Guess at the Riddle." CP 6.204.
3. Max Fisch, "Peirce's Arisbe: The Greek Influence in his Later Philosophy" in *Peirce, Semiotics and Pragmatism*, ed. Max Fisch (Bloomington: Indiana University Press, 1986), 227. Carl Hausman, *Charles S. Peirce's Evolutionary Philosophy* (Cambridge: Cambridge University Press, 1993). Douglas Anderson, *Philosophy Americana: Making Philosophy at Home in American Culture* (New York: Fordham University Press, 2006).
4. In *The Spirit of Modern Philosophy* (1892), Royce disparages "brute chance" on the grounds that chance jeopardizes the gains made in human inquiry and disrupts our steadfast faith in law and God. He states that "the true devil is not crime, then but brute chance. For this devil teaches us to doubt and grow cold of heart; he denies God everywhere and in all his creatures, makes our world of action, that was to be spiritual tragedy, too often mere farce before our eyes." Josiah Royce, *The Spirit of Modern Philosophy* (Boston: Houghton Mifflin, 1892), 469. In Royce's later works, especially in *The Problem of Christianity*, he amends his position and alludes to the fact that chance *qua* chance may play a very small role in human growth and progress. He seems to tacitly accept that contingent occurrences, facts that lie outside the habits of nature and the purposes of human beings, may serve as the impetus for our imaginative and creative progress.
5. "1866 Lowell Lectures." CP 2.641.
6. Peirce is occasionally inconsistent when it comes to the degree to which the physical world is determined. As late as 1890, he comments: "The laws of physics know nothing of probabilities; whatever they require at all, they require absolutely and without fail and they are

never disobeyed." (CP 1.390) As Turley and others note, however, Peirce is quick to revise this stance. See Peter Turley, "Peirce on Chance," *Transactions of the Charles S. Peirce Society* 5 (1969): 243–54.

7. "The Doctrine of Chances." CP 2.645–60.
8. 196b15.
9. 197b10–11.
10. 196b33.
11. Pascal Massie, *Contingency, Time and Possibility: An Essay on Aristotle and Duns Scotus* (Lanham, MD: Lexington Books, 2010).
12. "Introduction." CP 5. xxix.
13. MS 875.
14. NEM 4:344.
15. Peter Turley, "Peirce on Chance," *Transactions of the Charles S. Peirce Society* 5 (1969), 244.
16. CP 6.58.
17. Ibid.
18. Victor Cosculluela, "Peirce on Tychism and Determinism," *Transactions of the Charles S. Peirce Society* 28 (1992): 741–54. See also David Dearmont, "A Hint of Empirical Evidence for Peirce's Tychism," *Transactions of the Charles S. Peirce Society* 31 (1995): 193.
19. *The Simplest Mathematics*. CP 4.584.
20. "The Doctrine of Necessity Examined." CP 6.64.
21. "The Doctrine of Necessity Examined." CP 6.64.
22. "The Doctrine of Necessity Examined." CP 6.64.
23. "The Doctrine of Necessity Examined." CP 6.64.
24. CP 5.58.
25. Carl Hausman, *Charles S. Peirce's Evolutionary Philosophy* (Cambridge: Cambridge University Press, 1993), 172.
26. MS 292.
27. CP 6.265.
28. Carl Hausman, *Charles S. Peirce's Evolutionary Philosophy* (Cambridge: Cambridge University Press, 1993), 160–67.
29. CP 6.201.
30. "The Law of Mind." CP 6.102.
31. "Evolutionary Love." CP 6.287.
32. Anderson and Ventimiglia address the relationship between chance and love in detail. See Douglas Anderson, *Philosophy Americana: Making Philosophy at Home in American Culture* (New York: Fordham University Press, 2006), 167–87.
33. MS 292.
34. HUG 1755. Box 101. Folder 14. p. 139.
35. A 139/322v.
36. A 139/324.
37. A 139/324.
38. Royce writes, "The true devil isn't crime, then, but brute chance. For this devil teaches us to doubt and grow cold of heart; he denies God everywhere and in all his creatures, makes our world of action, that was to be a spiritual tragedy, too often a mere farce before our eyes. And to see this farcical aspect of the universe is for the first time to come to a sense of the true gloom of life." Josiah Royce, *The Spirit of Modern Philosophy* (New York: Dover, 1983), 469.
39. Royce, *The Spirit of Modern Philosophy*, 469.
40. Ralph Waldo Emerson, "Fate" in *Ralph Waldo Emerson: A Critical Edition of the Major Works*, ed. Richard Poirier (New York: Oxford University Press, 1990), 358.
41. Emerson, "Fate," 345.
42. Emerson, "Fate," 347.
43. Charles Sanders Peirce, *The Essential Peirce*, vol. 1 (Bloomington: Indiana University Press, 1992), 330.
44. Ralph Waldo Emerson, *The Journals and Miscellaneous Notebooks of Ralph Waldo Emerson* (Cambridge, MA: Harvard University Press, 1971), 223.

45. A 139/320. This quotation is from George Eliot and is found in one of Cabot's notebooks.
46. A 139/320.
47. A 139/320.
48. A 139/324. "Notes re: growth, 1901–1902; paper, "The Relation of Chance to Purpose in Invention," 1902.
49. A 139/324.
50. After publishing the *Monist* series in the early 1890s, Peirce becomes increasingly interested in the character of generality and vagueness in the construction of mediating plans and purposes. See CP 3.338.
51. A 139/324. "Notes re: growth, 1901–1902; paper, "The Relation of Chance to Purpose in Invention," 1902.
52. A 139/373. "ch. 2: Origin and Originality." "ch. 3: The Search for the Eternal."
53. A 139/324.
54. In fragments titled, "The Search for the Eternal," Cabot reasserts the ubiquity, not of chance, but of change. This is an interesting passage since Shelley's "Ozymandius" is often interpreted as an ode to fate and chance. Cabot writes: "In Ozymandius of Egypt, Shelley brings before us irresistible devastating crushing power of time. . . . Nothing besides remains. Change has crept in and leveled the glory of the tyrant. His fortresses and palaces have vanished. But what happened to Ozymandius is happening all around us though only the vast stretches of time have made the complete wreck visible yet it is around everywhere if our eyes were keen enough to see it. All is change Heraclitus said and the thought brings a haunting restlessness, a longing for some firm hold. As Clifford says in his essay 1 on Moral Development, 'If you will carefully consider what it is that you have done most often during this day . . . you have really done nothing else from morning to night but to change your mind.' . . . The incessant change is covered up by its gradualness and by the common habit of ignoring. . . . [I]s there in the last analysis anything that remains permanent through the flow of events, any unity that holds past, present and future together? There have been persistent efforts to answer this question. Efforts often as desperate as struggles of one overboard to save himself, for without something solid to which to hold life is meaningless. If change itself is to have meaning it must be through some standard, some unity by which we compare past and present. One of the commonest types of answer to the question what endures through change is though changes are numerous there remains still something that is which is common to and persistent through all change that may occur. We see everywhere the contrast of the relatively permanent with the more lasting. A great many things indeed appear absolutely permanent until we look at them closely." A 139/373. "ch. 2: Origin and Originality." "ch. 3: The Search for the Eternal."
55. Ella Lyman Cabot, *Everyday Ethics* (New York: Henry Holt and Co., 1910), 204.
56. Cabot, *Everyday Ethics*, 203.
57. Plato, *Republic* 516 c–d.
58. Cabot, *Everyday Ethics*, 203.
59. Cabot, *Everyday Ethics*, 203.
60. Emerson, "Fate," 359.
61. Emerson, "Fate," 212.
62. Emerson, "Fate," 210.
63. Emerson, "Fate," 206.
64. Emerson, "Fate," 206.
65. Samuel Johnson, "The Idler" and "The Adventurer," ed. John Bullitt, vol. 2 of *The Yale Edition of the Works of Samuel Johnson* (New Haven: Yale University Press, 1963), 11.
66. Thomas Gray, *The Correspondence of Thomas Gray*, vol. 2, ed. P. Toynbee (Oxford: Oxford University Press, 1971), 666. Patricia Meyer Spacks provides a very useful account of these passages that explores the relation between activity of the imagination and the state of boredom. Patricia Meyer Spacks, *Boredom: The Literary History of a State of Mind* (Chicago: University of Chicago Press, 1995), 31–59.
67. Claudine Tiercelin, "Peirce on Norms, Evolution, and Knowledge," *Transactions of the Charles S. Peirce Society* 33, no. 1 (1997), 59.

68. A 139/322v. "Growth I and II, 1899, 1901."

Chapter Four

Everyday Ethics: Morality and the Imagination[1]

In 1893, John Dewey published "Teaching Ethics in the High Schools," a short article in *Educational Review* that provided the theoretical grounding for his work in the school systems of Pennsylvania and Illinois in the last two decades of nineteenth century. In describing the ends of ethical training, Dewey revised the rule-driven method of Protestant morality, suggesting that, "the end of the method then, is the formation of *sympathetic imagination for human relations in action*; this is the ideal which is substituted for training in moral rules or for analysis of one's sentiments and attitude in conduct."[2] This article, along with *Outlines for a Critical Theory of Ethics* (1891) and his *Study of Ethics* (1894), suggests that the imagination, rather than an adherence of moral rules, serves as the foundation of ethics. Dewey, however, fails to address this issue in detail until he begins to explore it in his *Ethics* (1908). As Stephen Fesmire's *John Dewey and the Moral Imagination* reveals, Dewey's efforts to draw together aesthetic and moral sensibilities are reflected primarily in his later works, such as *Nature and Human Conduct* (1922), *The Quest for Certainty* (1929), and *Art as Experience* (1933).[3] Ella Lyman Cabot visited Dewey's school in Chicago in 1898. She had just finished attending a series of lectures at Radcliffe College led by Dewey's philosophical colleague, Josiah Royce. It was a short trip, but it may have been long enough for her to reflect upon Dewey's brief comments concerning the imagination and its role in human conduct. Unlike Dewey, it did not take Cabot very long to conceptualize this role: her unpublished work in the early 1900s and her *Everyday Ethics* (1906) takes up the concept of the imagination as a central topic and explains the ways in which it might enable sympathy, loyalty, social open-mindedness, and moral foresight.[4] Conversely, in these works, Cabot argues that, "[s]elfishness, cruelty, shiftlessness, prejudice are due to a lack of imagination."[5] In her *Our Part in the World* (1918), Cabot explains that it is only by virtue of the imagination that we can be in the things we touch.[6] It is only through the imagination that we can transcend our narrow self-definition. Dewey would partially echo this sentiment in *Art as Experience* when he writes that, "our great defect in what passes as morality is its anaesthetic quality."[7] This paper provides an overview of Cabot's ethical writings, highlighting her definition of the imagination, the necessity of the imagination in moral conduct, and her ideas concerning the training of the imagination. It sets this argument against a variety of other rendering of the moral imagination established in the classical American philosophical canon.

Everyday Ethics is an interesting admix of treatise, manifesto, journalistic reflection, and teacher's manual. This is also to say that the structure of this work is oddly Deweyan, or at least evinces the genre to which Dewey also adhered. Cabot's indebtedness to Dewey seems obvious; in notebooks, written in the spring of 1892, she begins to comment on his influence and to evaluate his work. This evaluation, however, is not always flattering. As mentioned in chapter two, she occasionally suggests that Dewey, unlike her longstanding mentor, Josiah Royce, was insensitive to the tragedy and moral strenuousness of life. Indeed, this criticism echoes Royce's review of Dewey's *Outlines of a Critical Theory* (1891), where Royce blames him for maintaining a Pollyanna optimism in the face of the harder, more strenuous questions of ethical theory, especially the problem of evil. This being said, it stands to reason that Cabot's trip to Chicago and her interaction with Dewey and Jane Addams encouraged Cabot to extend her interests in pedagogy and ethical upbringing along pragmatic lines. My intent is not to describe yet another Deweyan student or Roycean apostle, but to explore Cabot's works in order to identify ways in which this neglected figure in the American canon may have anticipated the moves that the "fathers" of American thought would make in their later works. *Everyday Ethics* was published in 1906, two years before Dewey's *Ethics* and more than a decade before he undertakes a sustained study of the imagination as the foundation of virtuous conduct. Cabot's work powerfully underscores the way in which the philosophical cultivation of the imagination can enlighten and enliven particular human situations. It is a neglected piece of philosophy that is valuable in its own right, but also seems important in the way in which it allows us to rethink and reevaluate the development of classical American thought.

This project does not turn exclusively on the question that has come to dominate the field of intellectual history, the question of "who came first?" While this chapter aims to unearth a forgotten root of American philosophy, it does not seek the origin of the idea of the moral imagination nor give priority to one intellectual figure over another. Both Cabot and her male contemporaries can make significant contributions to our understanding of the ethical implications of thinking imaginatively and being imaginative. I am interested in listening for complementarities, identifying common sources of inspiration, and highlighting instructive differences. And there are instructive and dramatic differences between Cabot and her male teachers and peers. In many ways Cabot, like Jane Addams, is more willing to focus on the immediate and pressing needs of her time and society. In her investigation of the moral imagination, she identifies societal problems that Royce is not willing to discuss and does not succumb to the ethical instrumentalism or Pollyanna optimism of which Dewey is often accused.

THE LEGACY OF THE IMAGINATION AS A MORAL FACULTY

Before addressing Cabot and her peers in detail, a few situating remarks are warranted. These American pragmatists, and their intellectual precursors, the New England Transcendentalists, were not the first figures to consider the possibilities for the imaginative insight in ethics. I only suggest that they are the most persistent in their attempt and, on the whole, the most successful. The issues that they raise are as timely as today's current events, but are also as old as Plato and Aristotle. It requires only a slight shift in our angle of vision to catch sight of the long history of the moral imagination. Large swaths of the dialogue of the *Republic* can be boiled down to one question: "What is the relation between art and human conduct?" Similarly, the *Nicomachean Ethics* might be summarized as an exploration of the middle ground between insight and human conduct, a middle ground that Cabot seemed intent to occupy. Cabot was aware that it was also in this fertile ground where the moral imagination began to grow, cultivated by eighteenth century moral theory. She was introduced to this theoretical background primarily through her early reading of T. H. Green. Indeed, reading Green is very much like taking a detailed course in the history of philosophy in which a professor slowly takes a student through the chronology and conceptual spaces of a wide variety of thinkers. In Cabot's copy of *The Works of T. H. Green* (1885), which her father gave her in 1889, she made her way through a detailed account of the relationship between David Hume's writings to those of Immanuel Kant.[8] These thinkers would address the concept of imagination and begin to gesture toward its significance to moral theory. David Hume, in his *Treatise on Human Nature* (1739), noted that the imagination is integral to the extension of moral sentiment, particularly the broadening of sympathetic feeling.[9] Adam Smith—who Cabot did not read through Green, but might have read elsewhere—elaborated on this position in 1761. For Smith, "though our brother is on the rack . . . it is only by the imagination that we can form any conception of what his sensations are. . . . By the imagination, we place ourselves in his situation. We enter as it were into his body."[10] The sympathy theorists of the eighteenth century, however, were unable to go beyond the cursory observations concerning the moral imagination for two specific reasons. The first seems to turn on the issue of moral prescription. While Hume and Smith use imaginative sympathy to provide a detailed account of the psychological origins of moral sentiment, they fail to offer general prescriptions that might *legitimate* moral action. During their time, this sort of legislative ideal was the defining feature of large swaths of moral theory; both authors have been criticized for their failure to provide definite moral standards or the principle of justice.[11] In effect, Hume and Smith tell us how moral feelings arise, namely through the imagination, but at no point are we told when and in what cases we ought to have these feelings, or more importantly, when we are to act on these sentiments. Hume suggests that sympathies might be made normative if one was able to hypothetically assume the position of a just witness, one who objectively observes a social interaction and is able to determine the properness of empathetic feelings. As John Rawls recently notes, this attempt is only partially successful for it does not answer, but only defers, the question of justified moral feeling by the presuming of an ideal onlooker.[12]

The difficulties experienced by Hume and Smith can be traced to a second shortcoming that is largely conceptual. Both of these theorists attempt to identify the *role* of the moral imagination without a cohesive *theory* of the imagination. It is unfortunate that the thinker who began to develop this theory began writing a decade after Smith and was unwilling to place the slippery concept of the empathetic imagination at the heart of his ethics. Immanuel Kant initiates the sustained investigation of the imagination, and it is Kant's writings that initiate Ella Lyman Cabot's thinking on the moral imagination. He reacquaints epistemology and aesthetics with a version of the concept, yet remains reticent to discuss the relationship between morality and the imagination. Regardless of this, Kant's rendering of the imagination proved formative for the American appropriation of the concept as a moral power. In the history of American philosophy, it is safe to say that Hume and Smith were not the thinkers that pragmatists of the nineteenth and twentieth centuries returned to in the development of their "new" philosophies; Smith and Hume were not the thinkers that initiated the pragmatic project. The thinker who came closest to pragmatic thinking was Kant. It was Kant's failed project of unifying empiricism and rationalism that served as the impetus in Peirce's philosophical study and, perhaps more controversially, I believe it is this project that should still occupy the attention of philosophers today. What is significant here is that Kant's critical project was, in large part, occupied with developing a theory of the imagination that directly influenced Cabot's notion of the moral imagination.

In the *Critique of Pure Reason*, Kant identifies the reproductive and productive aspects of the imagination. In its reproductive capacity, the imagination synthesizes the manifold of perceptual experience by gathering different representations together in a single act of cognition. In its productive role, the imagination has two distinct parts to play. First, it lifts the aforementioned synthesis out of the sphere of the merely subjective psychological life and makes collective experience of objects possible. Second, the productive imagination serves a schematizing function that bridges the chasm between sensibility and understanding. Imagination operates in the middle ground between the categories of the understanding and the appearances of sensibility. It is clear in Kant's rendering of the reproductive and productive characteristics of the imagination that this cognitive power is responsible for synthetic and mediating character of human reason, and more specifically determinate judgment.[13]

In the *Critique of Judgment*, Kant expands the scope of the imagination in order to envision its creative roles that are played beyond the boundaries of pure reason. In this treatise on aesthetic judgment, he describes the imagination in its creative sense. Creative imagination plays a role in reflective judgments and in the development of novel meaning. Whereas the imagination is subordinated to the understanding in the first *Critique*, in the third *Critique*'s description of reflective judgment, the creative imagination is productive *and* free from formal constraints.[14] Instead of being bound to the preestablished categories of the understanding, the creative imagination is allowed to play alongside the understanding in ways that allow an artist to negotiate novel occurrences, envision possible aesthetic forms, and produce original works of art. Instead of remaining in lockstep, the creative imagination *harmonizes* with the formal role of the understanding. Kant writes that this type of play demonstrates a "purposeness without any definite purpose [*zweckmassigkeit*]."[15] Kant's contribution here is not insignificant. He has reframed the imagination in a way that makes it a "serious" cognitive ability, not the producer of useless flights of fancy as it was construed by earlier thinkers.

While Kant concedes that certain capacities of the imagination are necessary in the epistemology of the first *Critique* and the aesthetics of the third, he is less willing to think through the moral implications of the concept. Following in the footsteps of Hume and Smith, Kant acknowledges the way in which the imagination grants the possibility of sympathetic extension, but insists that sympathy is generally irrelevant to the practice of ethics. Sympathy can serve an indicative role (it can *point* to ethical standards) but it cannot serve as the grounding for these standards. Kant seeks this grounding elsewhere, in pure practical reason. For Kant, the imagination is still too flighty for the gravity of ethics.

Ultimately, Kant abandons the imagination on the grounds that—despite his reframing of the concept—it remains too unruly to serve as a reliable moral guide. In his *Anthropology*, Kant describes the danger of letting the imagination have its say:

> Imagination runs riot when in the still of the night, we study by lamplight . . . or wander about our room building castles in the air. . . . So the rule of curbing your imagination by going to sleep early is a very useful rule. . . . But women and hypochondriacs (whose trouble usually comes from this very habit) prefer the opposite course.[16]

Here Kant assumes the position that repeatedly defined Victorian literature and the history of philosophy more generally: the imagination is a wild and untamed power that is reflected in the hysteria and hypersensitivity of women, and neither the imagination nor women have a place in responsible ethical life. It seems appropriate, if only slightly ironic, to suggest that a woman philosopher, perhaps suffering from the insomnia that she would call "moral sleeplessness," began to rethink the role of the imagination as the animating force of human conduct and ethical life. For Ella Lyman Cabot, and her fellow American thinkers, the imagination may occasionally "run riot" in our lives, but also makes it possible for us to take up creative endeavors and pursue more sensitive, humane, and just projects.

THE ECHOING OF EMERSON: "BE IMAGINATIVE!"

The Americans' treatment of the imagination as integral to the formation of moral character can be understood as a revision and radical extension of Kant's rendering of the imagination as a mental faculty. The "American imagination," owes its general outline to German transcendental philosophy, but it was defined and refined by the American transcendentalists, led by Ralph Waldo Emerson. Emerson and other thinkers of the 1840s and 1850s—Theodore Parker, Margaret Fuller, Frederic Hedge, James Marsh, and Lydia Maria Child—concentrated their energies on unpacking the various aspects of the imagination and explaining how this mental faculty might be regarded as a moral power. The resonances between Cabot and Dewey on the topic of morality and the imagination ought to be negotiated in light of their shared sources of inspiration. These intellectuals were steeped in the same philosophical water that permeated their thoughts on ethics and the imagination. It was the writings of Emerson that seem to have served as the direct wellspring of their thinking.

The passages from the writings of Cabot and Dewey should, in this case, be regarded as a kind of echo, perhaps the reverberation of Emerson's "Poetry and Imagination." Here, Emerson writes that the imagination is a "second sight" that, as opposed to "common-sense" witnesses the inner and concealed meaning of things. In addressing the imagination's domain, he writes:

> All thinking is analogizing, and 'tis the use of life to learn metonymy. The endless passing of one element into new forms, the incessant metamorphosis, explains the rank which the imagination holds in our catalogue of mental powers. The imagination is the reader of these forms. ... [T]he impressions on the imagination make the great days of life: the book, the landscape, the personality which did not stay on the surface of the eye or ear, but penetrated to the inner sense.[17]

The metonymy of the imagination seeks a harmony by seeing a single sense in a diversity of things. This diversity, however, continues to unfold in "incessant metamorphosis." The imagination connotes a type of harmonic unity, but also diversity and novel forms of growth. Emerson, setting the stage for Cabot and Dewey, suggests that this second sight is not unique to poets, but rather that every person, to varying degree, has the capacity of living lives of poetic meaning. This is the capacity to "bring things alive" in our continuous encounter with a given situation.

The distinction between fancy and the imagination, expressed by Cabot and Dewey, is also a resounding of Emerson who says that, "it is the problem of metaphysics to define the province of Fancy and Imagination. The words are often used, and the things confused."[18] As opposed to the second sight of the imagination, fancy plays on the surface of things with little purpose. Emerson puts the two concepts in stark relief:

> Fancy amuses, imagination expands and exalts us. Imagination uses an organic classification (a classification unique to our dwelling with things themselves). Fancy, joins by accidental resemblances, surprises and amuses the idle, but is silent in the presence of great passion.[19]

I take issue with drawing too hard a line between these terms; it is often difficult to determine the difference between accidental resemblances and the original, and often shockingly novel, relations that the imagination occasionally identifies. This being said, the demarcation is important for these American thinkers. Keeping the imagination out of the "merely fanciful" seems necessary if they are to employ this poetic force as a directing power in moral conduct.

In stating that the "imagination expands and exalts us," Emerson begins to indicate the way in which imaginative insight might serve as the basis of right conduct. Anticipating Cabot's comments concerning the transcendent character of the moral imagination, Emerson writes, "Poetry begins, or all becomes poetry, when we look from the center outward, and are using all as if the mind made it. That only can we see which we are and what we make."[20] Whereas the common sense of everyday life is defined by perceptual narrowness, an exclusive provincialism that circumscribes our care and interest, the poet sees fields of possibility that remain, by definition, beyond the scope of custom and norm. These fields can be viewed only from unique and unexplored vistas, but Emerson is careful never to suggest that the poet's place is one of isolation. This expansive second sight is not realized by an objective and detached observer who peers out of his philosopher window, but by one who is intimately familiar with, or who makes intimately familiar, strange and distant horizons. Emerson concludes, "Poetry and Imagination" with a passage that suggests the moral relevance of his discussion of the imagination, writing, "[e]very man may be, and at some time a man is, lifted to a platform whence he looks beyond to moral and spiritual truth. . . . [T]he poet is rare because he must be exquisitely vital and sympathetic, and at the same time, immovably centered."[21] The poet stands, not as a passive or objective observer on a philosopher's lofty platform, but as a vital and sympathetic actor in the discovery of moral truth. The juxtaposition of sympathy and centeredness, ideals that may seem initially at odds, is one that Emerson wishes us to explore in more detail. Cabot and Dewey respond to this call in their efforts to make the imagination ethical.

MAKING THE IMAGINATION ETHICAL: SYMPATHY AND GROWTH

Cabot and Dewey go beyond the epistemic and aesthetic characterization of the imagination, but their work uses this characterization as a useful point of departure. They both agree with Kant's analysis in the first *Critique* that the imagination is a form of insight that unifies the manifold of appearances. They also agree that the imagination provides a bridge between the field of perceptual sense and that of conceptual sensibility. This is to say that they recognize the imagination's synthesizing and schematizing functions in human thinking. In 1906 Cabot writes that "It is by the imagination that we fill in the gaps and out of fragments make a whole."[22] Here, she echoes Kant's understanding of the reproductive imagination and the transcendental apperception of ideas. Cabot's acquaintance with Kant was developed in Josiah Royce's 1891 seminar on Kant and in her interaction with her future father-in-law, James Elliott Cabot, who was Emerson's literary executor and who published several commentaries on Kant in Margaret Fuller's *Dial*. Looking back on Royce's seminars on Kant (1891) and Growth (1893), Cabot reflects on the formative value of these courses on her ethical theory. After explaining that her entry to moral philosophy at the age of sixteen was through Emerson's "Self-Reliance" and "Divinity School Address," Cabot writes:

> My next great experience was the course on Kant with Royce. He approached religion from such a different angle that it took me a long time to grip the meaning, but his masterly exposition of Kant's powers of thought in tracking the Transcendental Apperception of Ideas, in pointing to knowledge deeper that yet implied individual knowledge, helped me recurrently, as year by year I understood him better.[23]

It was not Kant's categorical imperative, however, but rather his understanding of the imagination as granting the possibility of the unity of apperception that provided the necessary grounding for Cabot's writings in ethics. She elaborates by appropriating his description of the schematizing function of the productive imagination, writing,

> Not only in what we plan, but in all that we see, we use the imagination. The red wall of my neighbor's house looks solid and hard because my imagination leaps to the conclusion that the wall is made of brick. But my eyes never see the brick.[24]

This passage exposes two important points. First, Cabot generally agrees with Kant's understanding of the productive schematizing function of the imagination. Seeing is not a passive process, but one that requires the active use of mind. More specifically, only the imagination has the ability to be continuous both with bare sense perception and with the concept "brick." Second, and more importantly, the passage suggests that this schematizing process may not only be productive in the Kantian sense, but also genuinely creative. The imagination "leaps" to the conclusion, catching sight of the inner meaning that may not be visible in perception alone. Her eyes cannot see the brick, but her imagination does. Cabot's comments resonate with Kant, but also a slew of American thinkers of the late nineteenth century, including Peirce's description of abduction and Dewey's interest in hypothesis formation. In his *Psychology*, a book that Cabot read in the late 1890s, Dewey writes:

> In the perception of an object, as an apple, there are actually present, it will be remembered only a few sensations. All the rest of perception is supplied by the mind. The mind supplies sensations coming from other senses besides those in use; it extends and supplements them; it adds the emphasis of its attention, and

the comment of its emotions; it interprets them. Now all this supplied material may fairly be said to be the work of the imagination. The mind idealizes—that is fills in with its own images—the vacuous and chaotic sensations present.[25]

Both of these American thinkers inherit the Kantian vision of the imagination in its reproductive and productive capacities, but are particularly fascinated by the creative aspect of human cognition, an aspect that Kant leaves largely unexplored until the writing of the *Critique of Aesthetic Judgment*. Neither Dewey nor Cabot will be satisfied to relegate creativity to the realm of the "merely aesthetic."

After outlining the way in which the imagination "fills in" the gaps of perception, Dewey suggests that the "highest form of the imagination, however, is precisely an organ of penetration into the inner meaning of things—meaning not visible to perception or memory, nor reflectively attained by the processes of thinking."[26] The imagination attends to the inner meaning of things but also to the way in which this meaning always points beyond the things themselves. Listening to the opening notes of a familiar piece of music, for example, can point to the meaning and harmony of an entire composition. Listening to these opening notes, thanks to the imagination, conveys a pervasive quality of the work on the whole. In Proustian fashion, the imagination begins in a single bite, in a brief exposure to the emergence of things, but immediately senses the possible associations that accompany this morsel of perception. From a single bite, the imagination can make a world. This is the lesson that we learn from the *Remembrance of Things Past* (1913).[27] Indeed, for an individual such as Proust, born in the same year as Cabot, a bite of experience is never just a bite. Instead, it is a moment in the continuous feast of meaning, feeling, and conception. Every bite of experience is an opportunity to be sustained by the whole of the feast. This point is made explicit in Cabot's 1906 *Everyday Ethics*. Here she comments, as Proust does of his home in Combray, that, "my father's house is not to me what I see with my eyes. The life within comes flashing before me as soon as I speak of it and as I look at its visible outline it glows with a warmth of meaning."[28] The associations established by the imagination are not merely the remembrance of things past, but also an attunement to the possibility of a given moment, to the way in which a moment gives rise to ongoing meaning. The past is not so distant, indeed, it is not even wholly past, but rather glows with warmth in the meaning of the present. Cabot is quite good on this point:

> When we define imagination as the power to follow the spirit and trend of any fact, we begin to see how essential it is to all work, how necessary an ally in moral life. It is a lantern that throws light on the path ahead and keeps us from the double danger of standing still or stumbling. We shall realize this more vividly by following its use in different parts of experience.[29]

This passage points to the creative character of the imagination, but more importantly, claims that the imagination is a "necessary ally of moral life." Cabot's work in 1906 begins to unpack this claim in ways that Dewey would pursue in his later works. While his *Psychology* may have served as the foundation of Cabot's thinking on the imagination, she seems to foresee the moral implications of Dewey's position; she provides a lantern that throws light on the path ahead. In effect, Cabot lights the way for Dewey's *Nature and Human Conduct* and *Art as Experience* by explaining how the imagination might function in human interaction:

> Often my friend begins a sentence and I finish it. If I do this rightly it is because I know my friend. Imagination must always work on the basis of sound knowledge. But not only must my friend know my character,—she must also pay the strictest attention to what I am saying just *now*. We all know those provoking people who complete our half-finished sentences by some interpolation of what we *used* to say, who cannot distinguish our ten-year-old maxim from this our newborn idea. They have memory, but lack imagination. To know what I mean now you must listen to these particular words as I speak them and see where they point. If you are following, you will know that they point somewhere, as all facts do.[30]

Cabot's prose is tailored to a classroom setting in which a teacher would employ *Everyday Ethics* in the development of particular lessons. The pedagogical tone of her writing occasionally masks the philosophical sophistication of her thought. In light of this, several points in this passage deserve special attention. First, Cabot claims that, "imagination must always work on the basis of sound knowledge." Cabot's insistence brings the power of the imagination into contact with the epistemic category of "knowledge," therefore avoiding a mistake made by previous thinkers, namely the mistake of placing the imagination against forms of reason. For Cabot, the imagination keeps knowledge on the move, yet must always attend to the body of information that has been culled from immediate and previous experience. Second, Cabot claims that in personal interactions, the imagination must proceed from the knowledge of "character," the cultivated virtues and dispositions of the friend. This being said, it dwells not in the past, but rather in the "now-ness" of the current situation. It is in this sense that the imagination is attuned to the "new-born idea" rather than to the ten-year-old maxim. Third, Cabot insists that, like any newborn, the idea that the imagination identifies is future directed, always on the way, always becoming. It is the imagination's distinctive ability not only to identify the idea as a *fact*, but also to anticipate the idea as a *purpose* that outlines a future course of action, a novel development, an *end* in sight. Here, we catch a first glimpse of the way in which the imagination is integral to the apprehension of the purposes and ends of others. This fact has been routinely ignored in the continual restatement of Kant's moral ideal, namely that we regard individuals as ends in themselves rather than means. In pragmatic terms, the ability to regard individuals as ends rather than means turns into a practical matter of discerning the purposes and ends for which another individual strives. To regard a person as an end in itself, one must recognize that this person has his or her own ends and purposes. Cabot is very much aware of where she stands in relation to Kant. She notes that without imaginative insight, the ability to apprehend the purposes of others, the ethical imperative that Kant describes remains an empty formalism. In a paper written for Royce in 1900, she writes,

> Take first a type of ethics where the content of ideals is accented exclusively. The code of traditional Sunday school ethics is abstractly universal and therein lies its instability. The children are told to be good, to indefinitely love one another.... [S]omething of the same character is seen in the Kantian code.[31]

Cabot explains that two vital components are left out in both cases. First, neither Kant nor the Sunday school teacher account for the special character of each student. Second, neither aims to foster the capacity to see the inner meaning of the unique individuals that each of us encounter, often at first as strangers, in our daily lives.

Cabot's lesson on the imagination outlines a *particular* method of inquiry and discovery, but also begins to outline a regulative ideal. It is worth noting that ideals remain important for Cabot, but they must be ideals supplemented, and filled out, in the course of human activity. In her earliest writings, dating to the early 1880s, Cabot is especially interested in patterns of growth and the conditions by which personal growth might be fostered. In "*Werden*," a poem written in February, 1883, Cabot plays with the German word for "becoming," and suggests that becoming is an ideal around which a moral life can be centered: "Oh faith, Oh courage strong, / Unspoken and half concealed / To thee of right belong / The highest thing revealed / By 'Werden' to become."[32] In Royce's 1893 seminar entitled "Growth," Cabot was the star pupil, earning the highest marks in a class filled by soon-to-be distinguished thinkers, including William Ernest Hocking and Richard Cabot. In this course, she grappled with a concept that was as vague and knotty as the imagination. Indeed, she saw a close correspondence between these concepts and seemed to realize that these knotty notions—imagination and growth—must be simultaneously unwound in the development of a pragmatic moral system. In her notebooks from this class, Cabot makes clear the connection between the imagination and growth, a connection that would hold here rapt attention for the remainder of her life.

It is worth noting that Cabot practiced what she preached. She was known to her fellow students and friends as a person of growth, one who sought out chances for personal and professional development that ran against the grain of current societal norms. As a woman working among the movers and shakers of the American philosophical tradition, Cabot was remarkably prescient and independent in her thinking. Her interest in growth stemmed as much from her experience as a woman in the late nineteenth century as it did from any more esoteric commitments. Unlike many of her peers, she wrote, taught, and lectured for an income (even though her family fortune would have allowed her to avoid these forms of work). Her desire for personal fulfillment was integrally connected to her wish to contribute to the workings of her community; she was continually involved in the plans and purposes of the Massachusetts General Hospital, the state board of education, and Radcliffe College. She initially refused to marry Richard Cabot on the grounds that this conjugal tie would impede her intellectual and social growth. As we saw above, she concedes to the union only after it was placed in writing that the couple would not have children and would not consummate the marriage. In true pragmatic fashion, the ideal of growth had definite consequences in Cabot's life as a thinker, a woman, and as a social activist. The ideal of growth called for imaginative modes of action.

"MAKE KEEN MY EAR": THE IMAGINATION AND MORAL SENSITIVITY

On February 4, 1889, at the age of twenty-three, Cabot wrote a short poem entitled "Insight." Ada McCormick, Cabot's goddaughter, writes that this poem served as the driving force in all of her works and reflects Cabot's nascent thoughts concerning moral sentiment and the power of sympathy. "Insight" set the stage for her later thinking on the ethical implications of the imagination.

> Make keen my ear, that I may never miss
> One murmur of the voices of the infinite
> That surge from human rapture, need and pain.
> Make clear my eyes that, looking through a rift
> Of clouded sky, I may not lose the star
> Of beauty in a life that seems all sin.
> Make sensitive my touch, that I may know
> E'en through the blackness of unfathomed wrong
> The need and tenderness of human souls
> And thrill responsive to their slightest move.
> And oh! Make strong my heart, and pure and wide
> That touching, seeing, hearing this vast world,

> Insight may find its truest way through love,
> And pity know its deepest help in truth.[33]

This poem highlights Cabot's motivation in undertaking a study of the imagination, and here we come to understand the stakes of Cabot's intellectual pursuit. Her development of the imagination is not an abstruse exercise, meant only to mediate the disagreements, tensions, and fissures of epistemology. Instead, imaginative insight is meant to mediate the disagreements, tensions, and continual vulnerabilities of life. "Insight" *is* imagination: the ability to catch sight of the inner meaning of things. This poem expresses a desire to be intimately "in touch" with one's immediate situation and with the needs of others. It is a desire to associate and to harmonize with the facts of the world. It is a desire that can only be fulfilled by the gift of insight. It is not the physical touch that achieves this association and harmony, just as it is not the eye that sees the red brick. Instead, it is insight, or the imagination, that allows us to cultivate an intimacy with our surroundings. Implicit in this early poem is a sentiment that would dominate Cabot's ethical writings and a challenge that pragmatic ethics continue faces to this very day, namely, that it is profoundly difficult to remain attentive and wide-eyed to the "tenderness of human souls" even in the "blackness of unfathomed wrong."

In a notebook dated 1908, Cabot elaborates on these points, stating that "Imagination is a natural connecting link between ethics and religion, [for] the imagination sees any fact in all its meanings and so, as far as it goes, sees as God sees."[34] This comment resonates closely with Emerson's essays of 1844 and 1847, and she seems to intentionally bring it to a Transcendental point. Through the aperture of the imagination, the sight of a primrose is never just a primrose. Instead, she writes that,

> it *means* botany, of something good for a cow to eat, means a poem, means beauty, means color, means a power to transform to Burbank, means laughter to a gleeful child, means industry to a florist, means the coming of spring, means a brave precursor of summer, means the light of the past in sudden memory or the call of the future.[35]

Let us pause on these words for a short time. Do they simply stand as the purple prose of a woman who longed for a bygone Victorian era? Perhaps, but it may also be the case that such an accusation demonstrates something significant about our own time. Could it not be that cynicism, arguably the defining characteristic of the modern day, cannot stomach the idea of the imagination? *Why has it become so distasteful for a primrose to mean so much?* Cabot suggests that the growth of human life depends on the plurality of meanings that the imagination explores. In William James's words, the imagination "thickens" things up.[36] This is not simply a matter of enriching personal experience, which could be viewed as a shallow and isolating bourgeois pursuit. For Cabot, the imagination thickens things up in the sense that it gives things—oftentimes small things—substance and significance. Insight grants us the possibility of establishing an ethical and aesthetic regard for those people, places, things, and ideas that are often overlooked in the routine of daily life. Cabot routinely demonstrates her points with examples drawn from her experience with children (not her own) to highlight the way that the imagination can enliven the deadening routine of the every day. In a journal in the late 1890s, she describes a summer afternoon with her young students and the rapturous joy of a four-year-old who had lined up and counted a row of three cherries in her outstretched hand. Cabot writes: "And again I knew that we are dull, stupid, and blasphemous not to see the overwhelming joy of three cherries all in a row between our fingers."[37] It is only through our imaginative attunement that the ordinary can be realized as aesthetically rapturous, and the mundane can be regarded as sacred.

Cabot claimed that her exposure to Emerson's writing, as well as the personal experience of losing her sister to tuberculosis at an early age, encouraged her to think through the value of existential sensitivity and imaginative awareness. She comments that while she learned a great deal from Royce's treatment of Kant's system, she had already cultivated the sense of moral insight that Royce would begin to offer students at Harvard in the 1890s. In 1907, she describes her own development, writing, "I was much farther ahead still on the ethical side than I was on the metaphysical however, having swallowed eagerly Royce's insight doctrine which seemed akin to me."[38] As her poem "Insight" indicates, Cabot was already on her way to Royce's description of moral and religious attunement: the ability to discern the discontinuities of a given situation, interpret the meaning of these discontinuities, and respond in moments of active mediation.

A significant difference between Cabot and her male teachers, however, needs to be underscored. Both Royce and Emerson often seem to regard connectivity, the Transcendental continuity of things in the world, as a type of law, or at the very least, a postulate that underpins their respective philosophies. Cabot balks at this understanding of continuity, stating in 1902 that, "the eternal law in Emerson's starlit writing is felt by many to be cold and aloof. It is unmoved for no better reason than it avoids the hot frictions of reality. . . . [T]he law of justice, the rules of logic do not nourish us until they are brought into living relation with experience."[39] For Cabot, continuity and connection ought not to be regarded as a postulate, but rather as an insight or hypothesis that is to be tested in the course of pragmatic inquiry. Her experience in Royce's Radcliffe-Harvard seminars between 1894 and 1904 led her to a similar position. At this point, Royce's thinking had not taken the turn toward the concrete ethical issues of everyday life that would define his later writing in the *Philosophy of Loyalty* (1908) and the *Problem of*

Christianity (1913). In the *Philosophy of Loyalty*, Royce thanks Cabot for her contributions to his writing, but in the same year, Cabot commented that Royce had not gone far enough in developing the practical applications of his philosophy of loyalty. In describing her aims for the coming years she writes that she wants to "translate Royce into popular and convincing language and to pull together the best material on the experience of ethics and religion."[40] This remark seems to indicate Cabot regarded Royce's intellectual project as a traditionally philosophical one, that is to say, as a project that remained largely detached from the world of practical affairs.

In the summer of 1912, Cabot left for Royce's California. The Cabots had both been invited to give a series of lectures on ethics at Berkley University. On this trip Ella Lyman Cabot writes to Royce from San Francisco, concerning the *Sources of Religious Insight*, published earlier that year. Her letter is revealing in several significant respects. First, it reveals the abiding similarities between the two thinkers on the topic of insight. Second, it provides Cabot's interpretation of Royce's late ethics, underscoring the way that she would like to see Royce apply his ethical theory. Third, and perhaps most importantly, it exposes the fact that Cabot sees herself as anticipating some of Royce's thinking on moral insight and the imagination. Cabot writes:

> Many a time I have thanked you silently (and a little I hope in my way of living) for your noble *Sources of Religious Insight*. . . . Let me tell you some of the things I was especially stirred by. . . . I think your rich definition of insight, a word that has been especially dear to me since I was 14 and that seems all the richer in your account of the personal sources from which it flows. . . . I also love the way in which you've kept the normal human character linked eternally with the mystical superhuman nature of religion. . . . I was especially grateful that you spoke of the slow growth of the qualities (of insight) that blossom in visible heroism, grateful in part because I can immediately take its message into my ethical teaching.[41]

Cabot, however, would like Royce to go further, suggesting that he might notice the way in which insight—described by Emerson and Thoreau—is cultivated in the uncanny face of nature. By the time that the *Sources of Religious Insight* was published, Royce had lost both his son Christopher and his dear friend William James. In light of this, he was more than willing to empathize with fellow human beings, but he failed to notice the way that the imagination might draw one into proximity with nature more broadly. Cabot, on the other hand, observes that, "In your book I've missed the insight that comes from our brothers the trees, and thrushes, and anemones."[42] Wildness challenges and trains the imagination, heightening awareness and driving home the importance of sensitivity to one's surroundings, even, and especially, those surroundings that seem most foreign to us. In addition to this point, Cabot also seems dissatisfied by the fact that Royce does not offer practical examples of insight for students (not fellow professional philosophers) and lessons on the cultivation of the moral imagination.

In contrast, *Everyday Ethics* (1906) hammers away at the rough and dangerous edges of ethical life, attempting to smooth out the jagged bits of American moral conduct at the turn of the century. There were jagged bits: xenophobia, racism, sexism, and all the other ethical byproducts of American imperialism. In addressing these byproducts, Cabot introduces the imagination as the cognitive process that reveals the inner lives of persons such that they can be regarded as moral agents rather than as tokens, types, or stereotypes. The imagination, in this case, functions as the practical means of fostering ethical regard for others. The appendix to *Everyday Ethics* consists of a series of exercises for students that allow them to exercise their moral imagination. At the end of these exercises, Cabot instructs the students to explain how moral failures, typical of nineteenth century Americans, are at once the failure of the imagination. She writes: "Show that it is a lack of imagination which makes people stare at a deformed woman, call Italians "dagoes," or poorer children "muckers," and injure property that is not theirs."[43] This little assignment, spelled out in the harsh vernacular of the time, reveals the extent to which Cabot was willing and able to "translate Royce into popular and convincing language." Cabot ties Royce's interests in race relations and applied ethics, occasionally evinced in *California* (1886), *Religious Aspects of Philosophy* (1888), and the *Fugitive Essays* (published posthumously in 1920), to the insight born of the imagination. In so doing, she suggests that it is within our capacity to see others not as aliens or strangers that can be discounted, but as unique individuals who deserve our respect and care. Indeed, she interprets *The Religious Aspects of Philosophy* along these lines in *Everyday Ethics*, writing that,

> Prof. Josiah Royce in a stirring chapter in "The Religious Aspects of Philosophy" says that all selfishness is due to illusion. It is only through sympathy [grounded in the moral imagination] that we reach the truth, . . . realize things and people as they are, see and feel them as real, not as masks or shadows.[44]

CONCLUSION: "RESERVE" AND THE DANGERS OF THE IMAGINATION

In the winter of 1889, Cabot penned "Insight," but also "Reserve." When read together—as one might read Emerson's "Self-Reliance" and "Compensation" or "Fate" and "Power"—they expose both the possibility and the limitations of the moral imagination. Cabot opens "Reserve" with a claim that seems to be a challenge to the power of insight: "We live alone, thoughts that are deepest drawn / and purest in our inner consciousness / Abide undreamed by the common throng."[45] To "reserve" is to keep one's thoughts, feelings, and affairs to oneself. A "reserve" is something held back, set aside, and kept in hiding. "Reserve" is a type of reticence, an unwillingness or inability to disclose those hidden parts of ourselves. Reserve has its purposes, although they are purposes that remain, at least for the time being, in the dark. It lays in wait for possible or probable demands and then, only occasionally, emerges with unforeseen strength. No amount of insight can discern or exhaust this most personal of hidden stockpiles. As Jane Austen notes, "There is safety in reserve but no attraction. One cannot love a reserved person."[46] Cabot seems to echo at least one aspect of this Victorian remark, namely that there remains something unknowable, and hence something unlovable, at the heart of human individuality. In this light, she maintains that we ought not to overstate the power of the sympathetic imagination.

To be reserved is to refuse the possibility of sympathetic extension. Living and thinking on the cusp between Victorian womanhood and modern American feminism, this philosopher is still well aware that women were encouraged, *indeed expected*, to exhibit a type of moral sensitivity to the plight of others. Women were expected to be forever "in touch" with the world at large. This idea was at the core of nineteenth-century sentimentalism. Being "in touch," however, has its drawbacks. The sentimental expectations placed on women resulted in a receptive hyperawareness that often constituted a form of psychological abuse. In 1889, on the brink of adulthood, Cabot reflects on this:

> Men meet in business on an impersonal basis; girls have to keep a perpetual cruse of tenderness to oil the jarring tempers. And because she needs to be more alive to the feelings of others a girl is more quick to be hurt, more sensitive. Is it strange that girls are more subject to moods than men?[47]

Imaginative sympathy makes one *tender*, both in the sense of establishing profound care but also in the sense of rubbing raw. By regarding the imagination as a core ideal of moral philosophy, one runs the risk of being overwhelmed and paralyzed by the ethical demands of others that are felt in immediate empathetic relation.[48] One also runs a risk that will be addressed more fully in the coming chapter: the risk of sacrificing self-respect and self-concern in an effort to achieve sympathetic extension. Cabot seems painfully aware of both of these risks, risks that seem to have encouraged her to flee the social demands of Boston at the turn of the century.

In a lecture that Royce gives to the School of Education at Boston University in January of 1898, a lecture that Ella Lyman Cabot could have easily attended, he begins by stating that the lecture's "importance lies in tracing the beginning of the social life to a 'love of imitation of the alter' as operating when seeded by a social-contrast effect. [The] relation between ego and alter is the fundamental social relation."[49] Cabot largely agrees with Royce. This being said, she seems more inclined to describe imagination, rather than imitation, as the foundation of empathy. She also recognizes the dangerous implications of regarding the "relation between ego and alter" as the "fundamental social relation." The danger rests in losing one's own sense of self-possession in the empathetic extension with the "alter"; this point will become clear in Cabot's emphasis on the necessity of self-expression.

After Cabot's death in 1934, Evelyn Whitehead, the wife of Alfred North Whitehead, noted that Cabot's involvement with social and political projects had coincided with her withdrawal from the interpersonal life of upper-middle-class Bostonians. Cabot remained, in large part, hidden from the gossip, probing eyes, and subtle demands of neighbors and friends. Cabot's self-imposed isolation could be attributed to two related factors. First, it seems that imaginative insight can be a constructive force only when an individual has the ability to freely respond to this insight by means of deliberative action, action that presumably seeks to answer the perceived ethical call of another. Women at the turn of the century were expected to remain sensitive to the plight of others, but were often barred access to the outlets through which social and political reform could be enacted. In short, they exposed themselves by way of imaginative insight, were rubbed raw by a harsh reality, and were then forbidden to affect change in a world that cried for action. Here, it seems worthwhile to return to the passage from 1889 in which she writes,

> A girl's life is indefinitely harder than a man's in some ways. His sacrifices hard though they are, are only for some end he really believes better, while hers are often the bearing of the loss of helpful and joy-giving intercourse with nothing in her life to take its place.[50]

Lyman describes the imaginative sensitivity, inactivity, and domestic confinement that was prescribed as the "rest cure" for a nervous disposition. This "cure" was prescribed, to a greater or lesser extent, to all women during this time; indeed, sensitivity and passivity were the genteel norms of Lyman's day. Imposed rest, the inactive lifestyle of a "privileged" Victorian woman, caused "psychological bedsores" which were the result of imaginative receptivity and exacerbated by prohibition against meaningful and ameliorative engagement. Cabot is well aware of this and identifies it in

Royce's work in the mid-1890s. On a letter written from Royce to Richard Cabot, dated July 30, 1895, Ella Lyman Cabot writes that, "Royce's point that pessimism comes from *passive* sympathy is very important."[51]

Cabot's occasional flight from the affairs of the world may be traced to her desire to shield herself from the danger of the imagination, the pain that often accompanies insight. Isolation, however, can be a result not only of the dangers of the moral imagination, but also its limitations. At pivotal moments, we are temporarily, or permanently, unable to engage our surroundings. Instead, we experience ourselves as being radically detached from the ebb and flow of experience. In the face of unfamiliar occurrences and uncanny sights, individuals often fail to grasp the inner purpose of other individuals and foreign situations. Cabot was raised in the Boston Brahmin culture of the nineteenth century, yet she was academically trained by classical American pragmatists who believed that thoughts must have traction in the harsh world of human conduct. She was simultaneously drawn to, and disgusted by, social and political realities that demanded thoughtful attention. In this respect, she provides an interesting and instructive case study for many of today's academics who have enjoyed some sort of privilege—economic, social, or cultural—while sensing some obligation to translate their studies into concrete human activity.

In October of 1907, Cabot returned to Chicago, this time to visit Jane Addams's Hull House. Her reflection on this experience sheds light on the obstacles to the moral imagination and the way that sympathetic insight might be limited by particular modes of habituation. She writes:

> Beauty liberates me as if it opened up channels damned by the accumulation of the weeds of triviality of misunderstanding and weariness, and let the real leaping spirit of me flow outward toward the sea. Ugliness makes me lonely unless I stifle the sight of it by preoccupation or find somewhere in it a cranny of beautifying human character. This loneliness, born of incongruity, is again, I think, the damning of the channel. I am solitary because I am shut away from the largest life I am capable of holding.
>
> Why does ugliness shut me in? I think it is because it puts before me grimly, disproportionately, the means to an end, not the end known through, illumined by, the means. One hurries by it conscious of the dust, noise and fatigue necessary to attain one's end. But a railroad station may be beautiful if in the architect's mind, and in his embodiment of his thought was held the conception of a railroad station as an entrance to a city, a foreshadowing, a welcome, an introduction to what the city may bring.[52]

Far from the clean and familiar walls of Radcliffe College, the institution she helped found, Cabot experiences the "loneliness born of incongruity," the sense of being out of place. Being out of place describes the scattered, often sickeningly chaotic, scenes of poverty in Chicago, but also describes Cabot's relationship to these scenes. Ugliness, as the apprehension of a disjointed and unfamiliar situation, makes Cabot, herself, feel something of the uncanniness and alienation that she witnesses. "The ugly" is not merely something "out there" in the world, but also the experience of the gulf between an individual and a world that grants it no access. The social isolation that Cabot describes is caused by the inability to envision the ends and purposes of the individuals who frequented Hull House.

Her comments once again suggest that it is the imagination that allows one to enact the Kantian maxim that one is to foster a moral attitude that regards individuals as ends rather than mere means. In most cases, we experience people in action, the middle of things, in the midst of their personal pursuits. To see the inner meaning of their actions, we must imagine the ends that they are seeking, just as Cabot suggests that her friend must "listen to these particular words as I speak them and see where they point." This is not to be confused with projecting our interests, aims and ideals on the actions of another. Instead, one is to remain attentive to the actions of *another* in order to catch sight of *another's* purpose or end. As Cabot states in *Everyday Ethics*, "Sympathy is then the power of making any situation become alive through us by realizing it *as it is*."[53] This type of insightful realization is difficult to cultivate and, as Cabot and Dewey both note, must be practiced and honed through the dramatic rehearsal of particular situations and the continual feedback of a lived situation.

There is, however, some value in the failure of the moral imagination, or, more accurately, in the recognition of this failure. Cabot seems to overlook this at times, and maintains her search for sympathetic access to the problematic situation of others. Cabot's quest seems to aim at a symmetric moral relationship, described by William James as the realization that the universe is not an impersonal and ugly "It" but a pervasive and personal "Thou."[54] In *Twenty Years at Hull House*, Jane Addams takes an alternative approach to moral relations, occasionally emphasizing an asymmetric relationship in which individual difference cannot be fully overcome by way of the imagination. Addams praises the etchings of Albrecht Durer (1471–1528) not for finding and presenting the "cranny of beautifying human character" that Cabot seeks in the midst of an ugly world, but rather for his willingness to present ugliness *as* ugliness. In Addams's words,

> I was chiefly appealed to by his unwillingness to lend himself to a smooth and cultivated view of life, by his determination to record its frustrations and even the hideous forms which darken the day for our human imagination and to ignore no human complication.[55]

The imagination is challenged by hideous forms and the darkest scenes of our social and political reality. There is, however, hope in the darkness for, as Addams insists in a subsequent passage, Durer's etchings are "surcharged with pity." This seems right, for these images call for sympathetic insight, a type of moral recompense that remains outstanding.

The brilliance of Durer's realism, like that of Courbet's *The Stone Breakers* (1849) and Millet's *The Gleaners* (finished in 1857 and one of Cabot's favorite paintings), is that it represents, literally "shows again," the appearance of ugliness. In his etchings, Durer "sites" the unsightly, giving the uncanny a place to show itself. These appearances, often pushed out of sight in everyday life, remain disturbingly present in Durer's work, for they are made available while simultaneously evading the comprehension of understanding and imaginative insight. His work stands as both a challenge and a reminder: it challenges us to exercise our powers of imagination in the face of sights that appear unfamiliar, and it reminds us that the work of the imagination is never something done or fully accomplished.

NOTES

1. Portions of this chapter first appeared in John Kaag, "Everyday Ethics: Morality and the Imagination in Classical American Thought," *Transactions of the Charles S. Peirce Society* 46, no. 3 (2010): 364–85.
2. John Dewey, *The Early Works of John Dewey, 1882–1898*, vol. 4, ed. Jo Ann Boydston (Carbondale: Southern Illinois University Press, 1984), 57.
3. Steven Fesmire, *John Dewey and the Moral Imagination: Pragmatism in Ethics* (Bloomington: University of Indiana Press, 2003).
4. Cabot's exposure to Dewey's early ethics is documented in the correspondence between Ella Lyman and Richard Cabot (who was also in Royce's classes in the late 1880s). In the summer of 1891, Richard spent several weeks at the Putnam camp in the Keene Valley. Dewey visits this camp, and Richard and he speak about *Outlines of a Critical Theory of Ethics* (1891). At Richard's recommendation, Ella Lyman reads this book in the same season and discusses it with Royce at length. She reports back to Richard: "Mr. Royce speaks very highly of Dewey's Ethics." Ella Lyman Cabot Collection. Schlesinger Library. Radcliffe Institute for Advanced Study. Harvard University. A 139/32.
5. Ella Lyman Cabot, *Everyday Ethics* (New York: Henry Holt and Co., 1906), 397.
6. Ella Lyman Cabot, *Our Part in the World* (Boston: Beacon Press, 1918), 126–29.
7. John Dewey, *The Later Works of John Dewey, 1925–1953*, vol. 10, ed. Jo Ann Boydson (Carbondale: Southern Illinois University Press, 1990), 46.
8. This book was recovered in a barn of the William Ernest Hock Estate in Madison, New Hampshire. It is inscribed "Ella Lyman. From Papa. December 25, 1889."
9. David Hume, *A Treatise of Human Nature*, 1739, ed. E. Selby Bigge (Oxford: Clarendon Press, 1968), 574–75.
10. Adam Smith, *Theory of Moral Sentiments* (London: Henry Bohn, 1853), 323–24.
11. David Gauthier is one of the more recent scholars to make this argument. David Gauthier, *Morals by Agreement* (Oxford: Clarendon Press, 1986), 237–39.
12. John Rawls, *Lectures on the History of Moral Philosophy* (Cambridge, MA: Harvard University Press, 2000), 93.

13. Immanuel Kant, *The Critique of Pure Reason*, trans. J. Bernard (New York: Haffner Press, 1970), B 138.
14. Immanuel Kant, *The Critique of Judgment*, trans. J. Bernard (New York: Haffner Press, 1951), sec. 17.
15. Kant, *The Critique of Judgment*, sec. 17.
16. Immanuel Kant, *Anthropology from a Pragmatic Point of View*, trans. Mary Gregor (The Hague: Martinus Nijoff, 1974), 39.
17. Ralph Waldo Emerson, *Ralph Waldo Emerson: A Critical Edition of the Major Works*, ed. R. Poirier (Oxford: Oxford University Press, 1990), 445.
18. Emerson, *Ralph Waldo Emerson*, 445.
19. Emerson, *Ralph Waldo Emerson*, 451.
20. Emerson, *Ralph Waldo Emerson*, 457.
21. Ralph Waldo Emerson, "Poetry and Imagination," in *The Complete Prose Works of Ralph Waldo Emerson* (New York: Kessinger Publishing, 2006), 509.
22. Cabot, *Everyday Ethics*, 202.
23. A 139/278V. "April–July 1908; includes diary entries 1910, 1914."
24. Cabot, *Everyday Ethics*, 203.
25. John Dewey, *Psychology* (New York: Kessinger Publishing, 2005/1886), 193.
26. Dewey, *Psychology*, 195.
27. Marcel Proust, *Remembrance of Things Past* (New York: Wordsworth, 2006).
28. Cabot, *Everyday Ethics*, 203.
29. Cabot, *Everyday Ethics*, 204.
30. Cabot, *Everyday Ethics*, 204.
31. A 139/370. "Individuality."
32. A 139/311–17. "Poetry."
33. A 139/311–17. "Poetry."
34. A 139/278. "April–July 1908; includes diary entries 1910, 1914."
35. A 139/278. "April–July 1908; includes diary entries 1910, 1914."
36. William James, *A Pluralistic Universe* (New York: Longman, Green and Co., 1909), 136.
37. James, *A Pluralistic Universe*, 136. In a very early passage (1891), Cabot writes about the relation between imagination and realization, that is the ability to see the inner meaning of things, commenting that the workings of society seem so devoid of this power of seeing: "What a vast thing realization is and how little we attain it in anything. Society is almost purposely blind." A 139/230.
38. A 139/230.
39. A 139/373. "ch. 2: Origin and Originality." "ch. 3: The Search for the Eternal."
40. A 139/279. "May–July 1908; includes diary entries, 1894, 1909–1910."
41. HUG 1755. Box 121. "Letters from R. and E. L. Cabot."
42. Richard Cabot comments that Ella Lyman Cabot would call animals people and suggest that a failure to regard animal interests as real is a failure of human imagination. See transcript between Richard Cabot and Ada McCormick from August 1936. HUG 4255.80. Box 1. "Various Subjects (32 pp.)."
43. Cabot, *Everyday Ethics*, 397.
44. Cabot, *Everyday Ethics*, 191.
45. A 139/311–17. "Poetry."
46. Jane Austen, *Emma: A Novel* (J. Bartley, 1841), 180.
47. A 139/214. "June–Sept. 1889."
48. In 1901, Cabot develops a paper for Royce's twentieth-century philosophy seminar that describes the necessity of, and the possibility of, being overwhelmed by the experience of sympathy, writing: "'Not alms but a friend,' the Associated Charities takes as its motto, but to be a real friend demands both a wide and a thorough and concentrated knowledge of everything in the world! We are usually satisfied with less, but in so far as we are loyal to the ideal of friendship we cannot be. I cannot be the best friend without understanding at first hand all that my friend cares for. A stupendous task, but only the beginning of my mission. The true friend not only must share his friend's life, but must open him to all other interests that enrich and

broaden him. To be a perfect friend to a single man you must love and sympathize with all men and the whole world of interests. No one is insane enough to try to do this all at once; it would defeat its own end as effectually as the attempt would do to gain a year's growth by eating a year's food at one meal." One might notice the interesting correspondence between Cabot's comment and Royce's conception of "loyalty to loyalty" as developed in his later works. A 139/373.

49. HUG 1755. Box 69. "Lecture III."
50. A 139/243.
51. A 139/346.
52. A 139/346.
53. Cabot, *Everyday Ethics*, 193. Italics mine.
54. William James, *Varieties of Religious Experience* (New York: Longmans, Green and Co., 1911), 44.
55. Jane Addams, *Twenty Years at Hull House* (Chicago: Macmillan Company, 1911), 75.

Chapter Five

"How Does It Feel to Be a Problem?": Women in American Thought

THE SUBJECTION OF WOMEN

When John Stuart Mill published *The Subjection of Women* in 1869, he anticipated its reception by writing that, "In every respect the burthen is hard on those who attack an almost universal opinion. They must be very fortunate as well as unusually capable if they obtain a hearing at all."[1] Mill was right. His argument for gender equality ran counter to the prevailing and very limiting roles that women were expected to assume in the Victorian era, roles that had acquired the status of almost universal opinion. While Mill's earlier work in logic, epistemology, and the philosophy of science was both well received and critically engaged with by classical American philosophers, *The Subjection of Women* was slow to receive a formal hearing. Peirce, for example, grappled with Mill's rendering of induction throughout the late 1860s and early 1870s, but largely ignores his social and political thought. Even when this position was given a hearing, what was heard in the American interpretations of *The Subjection of Women* often, and surprisingly, neglected or rejected the pointed feminist rationale that the work expressed. Along these lines, when William James reviewed the book in the August of 1869, he was unable to agree with Mill's stance that the dispositions of men and women could change in light of cultural and educational reform. This comes as no huge surprise since James remained closely wed to the belief held by his father, Henry, and by Peirce's father, Benjamin—namely that women were spiritually and intellectually inferior to men and were, on those grounds, to remain outside the walls of academia. James's pragmatic anti-essentialism was rarely extended to an analysis of gender and race. While he was bothered, in principle, by the prospect of gender quality—since it disrupts the natural dispositions of the sexes—James (ever the true pragmatist) seemed more troubled by the practical implications that this equality might have on the affairs of domestic life. He does not seem particularly disturbed by the problem of gender inequality, and he only rarely imagines what it might feel like to embody this problem. Instead, what disturbed James about Mill's feminist claim was that it stood to upset the tenuous balance between the sexes and destroy traditional matrimonial relations that continued to be the keystone of culture in nineteenth century New England.

Along these lines, James writes that what is most jarring in *The Subjection of Women* is its "thorough hostility to the typical sentimental ideal of the personal intercourse of man and wife."[2] According to Mill, this sentimental relationship was defined by the morality of subjection, most notably by the character of generosity and chivalry. Mill argued that this moral code, one that maintained the subjection of women, was to be overcome in a morality of justice in which men and women would be given equal access to educational and political resources. This equality was to form the basis of any acceptable ideal of marriage, one that looked more like a friendship between peers than the asymmetric arrangement that characterized gender relations in the Victorian era. In the circle of Cambridge pragmatism, this sort of relationship was still a rarity, but it was the kind that Ella Lyman consciously pursued in the early 1890s as she considered marriage.

In opposition to the likes of Mill and Lyman, James held that the "representative American" male was not ready to submit to the radical views of gender equality. While such representatives were hesitant to express the opinion, James stated that, "the wife his heart more or less craves is at bottom a dependent being."[3] The "natural" ambition and strenuousness of manhood sought a respite in marriage, a type of necessary rest that was provided by the comfort and submissiveness of the opposite gender. James writes:

> In a word, the elements of security and repose are essential to his ideal; and the question is, Are they easily attainable without some feeling of dependence on the woman's side—without her relying on him to be her mediator with the external world,—without his activity overlapping hers and surrounding it on almost every side, so that he makes as it were the atmosphere in which she lives?[4]

For James, this question was to be answered in the negative. This being said, it seems unwise to automatically assume that this early statement should be regarded as James's definitive statement on gender. After all, at the turn of the century, he and Josiah Royce wrote on behalf of Mary Whiton Calkins's petition to receive a degree from Harvard. Her petition failed, however, and James, *on the whole*, failed to support progressive sociopolitical views. This is brought out at some length in Charlene Haddock Seigfried's *Pragmatism and Feminism*.[5] In 1905, in his memorial to Thomas Davidson, James remained puzzled by Davidson's belief that women ought to be regarded as philosophical peers. Referring to Davidson's tendency to take on female students in the study of classics and philosophy, James writes that, "Naturally a man who is willing, as he was, to be a prophet, always finds some women who are willing to be disciples."[6] Obviously, the subjection of women in the household mirrored a broader cultural expectation that women were to remain at the feet of the prophetic male intellectual. As Seigfried notes, James was under the impression that women were naturally more intellectually fragile than men, a fact that accounted for their submissive nature and pointed to the necessity of chivalry and paternalism. Along these lines, James expressed surprise that the female students in Davidson's class could be treated "without accommodation," that is to say with the same hardnosed criticism that male students were used to receiving in the philosophy seminars. Oddly enough, these women did not go to pieces in the face of Davidson's intellectual cross-examinations.

James's comments reflected the general sentiment of many American thinkers of his time, that women lacked the agency, flexibility, and durability to do the work of men. To the extent that the Western philosophical canon had been dominated and defined by the work of men, it followed that women would be slow to gain a foothold in this most manly of disciplines. Despite its legacy of Emersonian iconoclasm and nonconformity, the golden age of American philosophy (1880–1910) fit snuggly and happily into the gender stereotypes of the day. This is also to say that women such as Ella Lyman Cabot, individuals who stood to be real contributors to this philosophical tradition, simply *did not* fit. The distinct ways that she handled her intellectual marginalization sheds light not only on the challenges faced by women philosophers at the turn of the century, but reframes the relationship between human agency, work, and mental health that are touted as being the centerpieces of the American pragmatic movement.

PHILOSOPHY OR "SASSIETY"

> It is ridiculous to say that no woman can work. I know that you except me, but I don't mean that. It hurts every time you lump them in one class anyway. They do splendid work in all grades, from magnificent housecleaning up to the infinitely harder saving of souls. Miss Morse can work, your mother can work, my mother can do the very highest personal work and magnificent executive work; Miss Smith can work; Mrs. Kidder can work; Mrs. Charles Homans has wonderful working power, Mrs. Evans, Mrs. Whitman, and myriad of girls and women in ways too subtle to tell in facts just yet. Don't ever underestimate

women; you owe a full half of your power to their patient delicate work in making you understand. —Letter from Ella Lyman to Richard Cabot, March 9, 1892[7]

In the midst of their six-year courtship Ella Lyman repeatedly reminded Richard Cabot that women "have wonderful working power" and need to exercise this power in order to maintain mental health. He seems to have needed a bit of a reminder. Lyman's comments throughout the 1890s suggest that the prevalence of physical weakness, "nervous prostration," and hysteria in women could be traced to a cultural atmosphere that stifled their creative impulses and barred them access to a variety occupational outlets. The corridors of professional philosophy, for example, were off limits to Lyman. Charlotte Perkins Gilman makes a similar point in her "Yellow Wallpaper" (1892) and *Women and Economics* (1898). However, the differences between these women are stark. Cabot remained in a celibate marriage for nearly forty years, would never identify herself as a feminist, and would work for most of her life in the midst of the cultural establishment of New England. Gilman, after giving birth to her first child, separated from her husband, fled to the West coast, and self-consciously assumed the banner of American feminism at the turn of the century. One abiding similarity, however, emerges in an analysis of these women's lives and writings. For both of these thinkers, the cultural expectations of womanhood impeded their ability to do scholarly work, a fact that was often interpreted as an innate weakness of mind and character. This interpretation only heightened the sense of impediment for these women and produced the "nervousness" that would be pathologized as hysteria at the turn of the century.

Before Cabot attended the Kant-Hegel course that Royce gave in the spring of 1891, a course that she would later cite as being one of the formative moments in her intellectual life, she wondered if such a venture was appropriate for a woman of her time. She posed the question to Richard, who answers in reference to Lyman's earlier experience in George Herbert Palmer's course on ethics (1890):

> As far as I notice, your ideas are not much changed by anything you have studied in philosophy: you have found out historically what various people thought; but your ideas of duty, of God and the universe were too clear before to admit of your feeling any real doubt of the outcome of your work, and I doubt that if any new conceptions were born to you in the course. You do not see things any decidedly different color since the winter. I think one studies philosophy either for a new and truer attitude towards life or in order to teach it. Palmer made the world look new to me and Royce changed it again and so like Plato I wanted to drag all the blind men into the light, but when they appear to have been born with eyes open to the truths I labor to get, I doubt if they had better study philosophy. If you want my opinion yes or no as to going on in philosophy I should say no. The fact that you doubt it, added to the above

considerations, lead me to this. I never felt the least doubt after I had tasted philosophy that I could get the same elixir nowhere else. I learn little from "sassiety." You learn much.[8]

Cabot's assessment of Lyman's prospects in philosophy turn on several related themes that need to be addressed. His comments may suggest that Lyman's treatment of philosophy remained superficial, that the ideas that she has encountered did not affect her conception of selfhood or of the universe at large. Even at this early point in her development, such a claim seems to be unfounded. Lyman's comments on Emerson's Essays, Oliver Wendell Holmes's *Common Law* (1881), and T. H. Green's *Ethics* (first published in *Mind* in the early 1880s) indicate that these works had a lasting effect on her thinking. This being said, it does stand to reason that the intellectual transformation that Lyman undergoes in the early 1890s is largely a private one and must be understood in light of her poem "Reserve" that underscores the fact that many women during this time were forced to take their personal cultivation as a solitary task. The hidden character of Lyman's intellectual maturation allowed her future husband to confuse her reserve for superficiality and, likewise, Lyman's ambivalence concerning philosophy for a lack of commitment.

Ambivalence stems from the prefix "both" (*ambi-*) and the Latin verb "to be strong" (*valere*). Being ambivalent is often characterized by either an unwillingness and inability to decide between options, or an apathy that pervades one's thinking about two options. At best these characterizations understate, and at worst misconstrue, the meaning of the word. To be ambivalent is to be simultaneously compelled and repelled by the same object of concern, to be torn by two mutually exclusive impulses. One can only be ambivalent if she feels strongly the pull of these impulses. Ella Lyman was ambivalent precisely to the extent that she was both *already* committed to philosophy and fully aware of the dangers that that commitment entailed. This fact seems to be lost on Richard Cabot who, instead of encouraging Lyman to work through this existential and cultural tension, encourages her to abandon the commitment to philosophy in order to overcome this ambivalence.

Additionally, Cabot appears to assume that her hesitancy concerning philosophy is a function of the way that Lyman "learn(s) much from . . . sassiety" and therefore does not need the formal training of philosophy. It is difficult to read this comment in a positive light. In the late 1880s, "sassiety" was a term used to deride and satirize the "high society" of the late Victorian era. By virtue of her socioeconomic status, the young Lyman was firmly fixed in this society. "Sassiety," a slang word drawn from urban diction of the time, was meant to connote the shallow mindlessness of high society practices. The statement that Cabot could learn nothing from these practices is an implicit criticism of Lyman for her supposedly feminine ability to glean meaning from them. Instead of her pursuing philosophy, Cabot recommends an alternative course of action for Lyman in 1891:

> Why don't you settle yourself down to creative writing, writing for publication? Write essays on favorite authors, try your hand at a novel or short story, or a study of some social problem. I believe that would teach you more than any Annex [philosophy] course and more use to us all. Perhaps you and Mabel could take Peabody's Social Reforms course and work up something together. Or prepare yourself to teach Pol. Economy which girls need so sorely to be taught.[9]

Having been raised in a traditional Victorian home and being steered clear of philosophy by her husband-to-be, Ella Lyman Cabot continued to doubt her intellectual abilities, internalizing her culture's prohibition against women philosophers. In moments of self-doubt she wrote in 1908 that, "I never had a speculative nature. Seeds perhaps fell into the soil, but they took a long time to germinate. They never sprang holey up in the proper way or died out in despair."[10] This comment might be read in light of another American thinker whose "seeds" never had the chance to germinate. In 1856, Anna Lowell wrote *Seed Grains of Thought*, a book of quotations from poetry and philosophy that revealed her philosophical interests but also the culturally-encouraged tendency for women of the time to speak through the words of men. It was this Cambridge neighbor who gave Peirce his first copy of Schiller's *Aesthetic Letters*, the same woman who he would describe as an "angel" who guided him to his theory of abductive inference. The flourishing of women in American philosophy was a lengthy process (indeed, it continues to this day) but for Ella Lyman Cabot these seeds eventually grew into original thought. Unlike Anna Lowell, she managed to cultivate a unique shoot of American philosophy.

Let us return to Richard Cabot's suggestion to Lyman that she avoid taking more philosophy courses. To give Cabot credit, his suggestion that Lyman study Political Economy instead of philosophy stands in marked contrast to the standard answer to the question of women's intellectual work. Throughout the 1880s women who pursued intellectual projects, such as Lyman and Charlotte Perkins Gilman, expressed the nervousness born of conflicting cultural impulses. In response, family members and medical professionals encouraged Gilman to abandon her literary work altogether. At this point in the history of mental health, Weir Mitchell's "rest cure" held sway as the common response to the budding diagnosis of hysteria and "nervous prostration" which medical experts used to describe the behavior of an increasing number of women intellectuals at the turn of the century. Patients who presented with nervous symptoms—restlessness, paralysis, reclusiveness, and an inability to perform domestic tasks—were treated with bed rest, massage, and restricted mental activity. Gilman describes the treatment, writing:

> I was put in bed and kept there. I was fed, bathed, rubbed, and responded with the vigorous body of twenty-six. As far as he could see there was nothing the matter with me, so after a month of this agreeable treatment he sent me home, with this prescription: Live as domestic a life as possible. Have your child with you all the time. (be it remarked that if I did but dress the baby it left me shaking and crying—certainly far from a healthy companionship for her, to say nothing of the effect on me). Lie down an hour after each meal. Have but two hours intellectual life a day. And never touch a pen, brush or pencil as long as you live. . . . I went home, followed those directions rigidly for months and came perilously near to losing my mind.[11]

Implicit in the rest cure is the assumption that the natural and culturally suitable locus of femininity is in the home. This position was in fact tacitly expressed by Mill and other feminists in the mid-nineteenth century. He suggests that women will not only tend toward domestic work, but ought to do so:

> The common arrangement, but which the man earns the income and the wife superintends the domestic expenditure, seems to me in general the most suitable division of labour between the two persons. . . . In an otherwise just state of things, it is not . . . I think, a desirable custom, that the wife should contribute by her labour to the income of the family.[12]

In light of this comment, the scholarly labor that Ella Lyman Cabot undertook was unique in two respects. First, her efforts would eventually be in the fields of ethics and civics, fields that straddled her desire to work in philosophy and the cultural expectation that she would restrict her interest to more mundane areas such as political economy. Second, while Lyman would never have to worry about a family income, she did, unlike many of her female peers, receive paychecks for her teaching ethics at Salem Normal School and Pine Manor College.

Both of these points reflect the fact that Ella Lyman Cabot hoped to maintain ownership of her intellectual projects and personal interests. Cabot managed her family fortune and salary to great effect, investing in stocks and bonds, a practice that most women avoided at the turn of the century. Her efforts eventually resulted in the formation of the Ella Lyman Cabot Trust, a large granting institution in the Northeast United States. Today, the mission statement of the Trust continues to shed light on Cabot's interests and the obstacles she faced in pursuing them, emphasizing the importance of self-expression and autonomy in action. The grants that the Trust supports aid individuals at critical points in their lives in the development of projects which have "personal significance to them and, at the same time, show some promise of making a contribution to other people. A project must be strategic and in some way unique for the individual, a turning point perhaps, and not a part of his or her routine professional or occupational efforts."[13] Cabot understood firsthand that "professional or occupational efforts," often assigned to individuals due to socioeconomic status and gender norms, were rarely the way to encourage the flourishing of individual interests. Indeed, these occupational efforts often ran against the hidden callings of individuals, those unique vocations that could be facilitated only by freeing these individuals from the norms and customs of their daily lives.

She comments on the subjection of women in her *Everyday Ethics*, noting the moral and psychological importance of freely chosen interests. Interestingly, this reflection could have arisen during her honeymoon in Tuscany a decade earlier, for she writes:

> In Italy one sees women harnessed to carts and taking the place of horses. They do it poorly for they are not adapted to it; a horse or a donkey would do it better. But there is something in our feeling of surprise and pain at seeing them harnessed that goes far deeper than the sense that the work is cruelly hard. We feel that these women are treated like slaves, that they are not serving their own ends and so are not living a human life.[14]

The subjection of women could take many forms. Being tied to the Victorian institutions of marriage and domestic life may appear less violent than being bound to a cart and forced to pull it. The basic structure of subjection, however, remained consistent. Ella Lyman Cabot observed that in both cases women were not "serving their own ends," a situation that led to a profound form of cognitive dissonance and dis-ease. It was not sufficient for women to employ their "wonderful working power" in any *given* project (such as pulling a cart or directing family life), but rather women were to be free to designate which projects they were interested in undertaking. This point would be decisive in her understanding of the "work cure" for nervous prostration.

THE CABOTS' "WORK CURE"

> Work cure is the best of all psychotherapy, in my opinion. . . . As well might we expect a patient to recover without food as to recover without work. . . . The sound man needs work to keep him sound, but the nervous invalid has an even greater need of work to draw him out of his isolation, and to stop the miseries of doubt and self-scrutiny, to win back self-respect and the support of fellowship. —Richard Cabot, "The Work Cure," *Psychotherapy*, 1909[15]

Richard Cabot eventually listened to Ella Lyman when she said that women have a "wonderful working power." While the rest cure was a standard treatment of hysteria at the turn of the century, it was, by no means, the only game in town. At the encouragement of his partner, Richard Cabot slowly developed and received wide acclaim for a "work cure" which prescribed a regimen of mental and physical exercises that were meant to relieve the symptoms of nervous prostration and chronic anxiety. It is very likely that Cabot has women in mind when he juxtaposes "the sound man" with the "nervous invalid." By 1909, Richard Cabot seems to have gotten the message that Lyman conveyed in the 1890s: women could work and must work if they are to remain psychologically sound. This being said, his development of the work cure is still lacking in several important respects that can be seen in the light of Ella Lyman Cabot's contemporaneous writings on the subject of mental health.

The rationale behind Richard Cabot's work cure can be traced to several sources. By the mid-1890s, Cambridge was abuzz with the ideas of James's *Principles of Psychology* that affirmed the positive feedback loop between physical activity and mental health. Fighting depression since puberty had taught James that embodying the purposive activities of "healthy-mindedness" could contribute to the feeling of psychological stability. In his chapter on the emotions, James instructs the depressive to "smooth the brow, brighten the eye, contract the dorsal rather than the ventral aspect of the frame and speak in a major key."[16] In short, he directs the patient to *do something*: to stand up straight and to carry themselves into a public space with confidence. In so doing, a man, according to James, could be instilled with fellow-feeling and good cheer. It is worth noting that James does occasionally apply his psychological findings to the lives of women who suffer from culturally imposed inhibition. In his *Talks to Teachers*, a series of lectures with which Ella Lyman Cabot was intimately familiar, James writes:

> Consider, for example, the effects of a well-toned motor-apparatus, nervous and muscular, on our general personal self-consciousness, the sense of elasticity and efficiency that results. They tell us that in Norway the life of the women has lately been entirely revolutionized by the new order of muscular feelings with which the use of the ski, or long snow-shoes, as a sport for both sexes, has made the women acquainted. Fifteen years ago the Norwegian women were even more than the women of other lands votaries of the old-fashioned ideal of femininity, "the domestic angel," the "gentle and refining influence" sort of thing. Now these sedentary fireside tabby-cats of Norway have been trained, they say, by the snow-shoes into lithe and audacious creatures, for whom no night is too dark or height too giddy, and who are not only saying good-bye to the traditional feminine pallor and delicacy of constitution, but actually taking the lead in every educational and social reform. I cannot but think that the tennis and tramping and skating habits and

the bicycle-craze which are so rapidly extending among our dear sisters and daughters in this country are going also to lead to a sounder and heartier moral tone, which will send its tonic breath through all our American life.[17]

But this willingness to consider women's interests is the exception for James, rather than the rule. Ella Lyman Cabot, far more so than James does in his *Psychology*, extends his psychological findings to the women of their day. Richard Cabot wrote out of the American pragmatic tradition, but his writing and theorizing was more directly affected by his interactions with his wife, who was more than happy to translate James's *Psychology* into actionable feminist principles. After reading James in the early 1890s, Lyman writes that, "Having purposes, concrete and widely embracing, gives poise, cheer, bearing and eagerness to life. In its deepest meaning, a purpose is a creed."[18]

During this time, she was also exploring John Dewey's early ethical thought. In addition to fixing her attention on the topic of the moral imagination, she resonates closely with Dewey's sense that moral life remains empty unless it is filled with moral activity that seeks to change the world at large. In March of 1892, she underscores the way that interests and purposes serve as the basis of moral character. More importantly, she recognizes the way that Dewey might speak directly to her character as a woman who struggled to undertake meaningful intellectual projects in an inhibiting culture: "Dewey's statement of the close relation of character and conduct brings home to me forcibly tonight the need of insisting on conduct in myself."[19] For Ella Lyman Cabot, one was not to claim a purpose in a merely sentimental or purely intellectual sense, but rather, and always, *have* a purpose in a practical and emotional sense when it is enacted.

These points serve as the basis of *Everyday Ethics*, a book that is particularly remarkable when one recognizes the obstacles that the author faced in realizing her own purposes as an intellectual at the turn of the century. It is for this reason that this book has served as a touchstone in the current study of Ella Lyman Cabot's philosophy. In her chapter entitled, "Interests as Life Givers and Life Savers," she writes that, "unrooted interest inevitably withers and . . . the roots of interest grow only by thorough, persistent work."[20] Many women of Cabot's time would have understood firsthand that to have an interest that was not "worked out" was to frustrate the most life-giving of human tendencies. Additionally, Cabot explains that the common conception that her female peers were devoid of meaningful interests was also a function of the fact that their activities were so dramatically restricted when she writes that, "without work no interest can permanently live, and the test of interest is the readiness to work."[21] This comment begins to flesh out the mutuality of action and belief that is the hallmark of American pragmatic thought. For example, in this passage Cabot comes very close to William James's position in the "Will to Believe" and the "Dilemma of Determinism," where he suggests that willfully enacting certain beliefs (those that cannot be established through empirical justification) makes them true in the process. It should be noted that James's position is only defensible in situations where the beliefs cannot be directly corroborated by facts, and, more importantly in this case, when one has the ability to act upon these belief. This second point would not obtain for the beliefs of individuals whose purposes and pursuits were stifled by external constraints.

While James wrestled with the metaphysical issue of free will, Cabot was deeply concerned about more practical topics, namely the freedom of women in the social and political sphere. In the midst of his intellectual gymnastics, James suggests, "our first act of freedom, if we are free, ought in all inward propriety to be to affirm that we are free."[22] Cabot amends this performative proof in order to place gender equality on a new footing, insisting that the question of women's abilities could only be answered when they committed themselves wholly to their beliefs in the form of personal and practical activities. In 1906, she writes:

> When we are doing any important work we must forget all else. There is a half-heartedness fatal to the efficiency in the work of anyone whose whole attention is not on it. We are like motormen, steering through crowded streets and bound to go ahead; if our attention wanders from the work in hand . . . we are unworthy of our post. In planning we live in the past and future, but in action we must live in the present.[23]

This full-fledged commitment to ideals was difficult to maintain for individuals who felt torn between the duties of domesticity and "society" and the vocations to which they were called. Even after the publication of *Everyday Ethics*, Cabot struggled to maintain her mental health, often commenting on the "restlessness" that defined her days. Along these lines, she asks a question that almost answers itself: "Where does this restlessness come from? Perhaps two distinct causes: lack of definite work and the too great effect that other people have on me."[24]

For Cabot, ideals and interests were never in short supply; it was the appropriate outlets to pursue these ideals that were difficult to find. She reflects on this, noting the difference between the nervousness suffered by many of her peers and her own psychological disposition. She writes that, "Restlessness in general may spring from a deeper source of having no high ideals or satisfying conceptions of duty, or the dependence on pleasure and external sources of meaning, but I do not think that is the case with me."[25] For Cabot, what was needed were not ideals in the abstract, but the time, energy, and freedom to pursue these high ideals and satisfying conceptions *in concreto*. Her goddaughter, Ada McCormick, would comment on the way in which Ella Lyman Cabot was frequently distracted from her academic work in religion and philosophy. Oftentimes she was distracted by Richard Cabot's almost feverish attempts to encourage her to work in *other* fields. McCormick writes that, "except for philosophy and religion, the meat she loved, it sometimes made her a little breathless to play accompaniments on the piano and to keep up with all the interests that she and her husband shared.... People criticized his way with her, for protecting her too much and for hustling her too much."[26] In principle, Richard Cabot would have known the distinction between mere "hustling" and a "work cure" that could bring relief to patients. He notes that working for the sake of working could quickly devolve into drudgery that only exacerbated feelings of psychological dis-ease. This being said, in practice, he often forgets that the work of the patient needs to be self-motivated.

Beginning in 1906, Richard Cabot began to speak and publish on the character of the work cure. In this year Cabot spoke to the Colorado Medical Society, suggesting that a physician, instead of encouraging a patient to rest ought to, "'speed her up,' teach the patient to live harder, faster, faster, more intensely, or with some better reason for his activities."[27] In her biography of Mary Parker Follett, Joan Tonn highlights this passage, noting the curious way in which Cabot used both the male and female pronouns. She explains that Cabot is intentionally drawing attention to the fact that nervous prostration was generally considered to be a uniquely feminine disorder. This may be the case, but there seems to be more to his comment. Cabot's instruction to "speed her up" indicates that it is the physician's responsibility to drive and direct the patient's work. The agency and choice in the work cure comes not from the patient (often a woman) but from the expert practitioner (often a man) who "winds up" the patient and sets her off in a productive direction. While it may *appear* that the patient has adopted an active physical regimen of productive work, it is in fact only the case that she has been motivated, as a type of wind-up toy or tool, by a doctor who "knows best." In this active treatment, the passivity of the patient is masked, but not addressed in any meaningful way.

In 1908, Richard Cabot summarizes his finding on the work cure in the journal *Psychotherapy*, suggesting that the prescribed work should have the following three characteristics.[28] First, the work was already to be in progress and be swift-moving so that a patient could set herself into its current and be carried along. Second, the work should have practical effect, whether in the form of remuneration or in the concrete change it makes to the patient's community. Finally, it should afford companionship with others who are healthy and happy in the employment of the task. What is notably missing in the description of this work is that it should be the outcome of a freely chosen purpose and interest. Work is only made one's own if it the outcome of a unique and emotionally laden interest: if one *chooses* this work. This comes home to us when we attend to Ella Lyman Cabot's journals from the same year, records of the success and shortcomings of the work cure. She expands on the two cures that might address the symptoms of hysteria and restlessness: "First, of course, definite work, not necessarily harder work, but more planned."[29] The planning, anticipation and execution of a task seems to separate drudgery, which is performed in accord with another's plan, from meaningful and inspiring work. This statement is merely a reiteration of her comments in *Everyday Ethics* and her personal letters to Richard Cabot in the prior decade. At this point, however, she adds a second cure that tends to be missed by the male physicians of her day: "Second the cure is greater self-control. The power I mean of relentlessly putting away from my thoughts anything that is not helping me to think. *A more absolute sense of the relative value of other's advice and criticism.*"[30] Cabot is here using self-control in the sense of self-possession, the ability to differentiate one's life and interests from another.

There are two thrusts of this type of psychological differentiation. First, one must be able to filter and limit the incoming influences from her surroundings. Second, healthy differentiation involves being authentically "there" amidst others without retreating into the "reserve" to which Cabot often refers. Being able to fulfill these two guidelines of personal individuation allows an individual to be free while, at the same time, interacting with her environment. These passages are wholly in line with Cabot's philosophical studies with Royce and her acquaintance with Kant's moral theory. Kant states that while "I can indeed be constrained by others to perform actions that are directed as a means to an end, I can never be constrained by others to have an end: only I myself can make something my end."[31] Throughout her adult life, Cabot received an abundance of advice and criticism from Richard Cabot who continually, if not unerringly, attempted to drive her into any number of causes and intellectual projects. Ella Lyman Cabot's comments, written at the same time that Richard was receiving notoriety for his "work cure," reflects the fact that "keeping her moving" in the name of a cure was, at least in part, counterproductive insofar as it robbed this individual of the sense of free agency and freely chosen purpose that might have given her sustained relief.

ELLA LYMAN CABOT ON THE DUTY OF SELF-EXPRESSION

In the early years of the twentieth century, as she struggled with the collective effects of neurasthenia and patriarchy, Ella Lyman Cabot voices a question concerning freely chosen work that remains unanswered in contemporary feminist scholarship: "In how far is direct self-expression a duty?"[32] It is a question far from strictly academic. To what extent am I obligated to exercise my free agency? It is a question that must be answered by women—and all individuals—in their everyday affairs. It is a question that is meant to be answered by those individuals who suffer from oppression, whose desires have been deformed by a dominant mindset, and whose autonomy is jeopardized by cultural and physical constraints. Cabot's response to this question is prescient and telling. Cabot suggests that the fact that the autonomy of certain individuals may be curtailed and jeopardized does not free them from the duty of self-expression.

At first glance, this "duty of self-expression" may appear as a contradiction in terms in two ways. First, there is the concern that the requirements of duty will often run counter to the freedom of self-expression. By the turn of the century, Cabot had been thoroughly exposed to Kant's moral theory through Royce and Palmer, and she understood that true ethical duties are not to be heteronomously imposed, but rather given to oneself. That is to say that the duty of self-expression is a duty to, and for, oneself. In expressing one's autonomy, one is not fulfilling a duty to God or country, but to the most inviolable part of being a unique human being: human autonomy. Second, and perhaps more problematically, there is the concern that a duty of self-expression is misplaced in the case of individuals who may not be able to fully fulfill this duty due to social or personal constraints. Is an oppressed individual morally culpable for not attempting to free themselves? Without "blaming the victim," Cabot is quite forceful in her assessment: "Women let themselves be under the dominance of all kinds of fear. Fear of ridicule, of the sight of suffering, of the sound of their own voices . . . such cowardice is demoralizing and not to be tolerated."[33] Like some contemporary theorists, she seems to believe that this duty of self-expression is *especially* important in the case of individuals who experience oppression.[34] Indeed, attempting to fulfill this duty, which often translates into resisting forms of patriarchy or sexism, may increase their sense of self-control and freedom. This is not to say that Cabot downplays the difficulty of self-expression. She writes:

> It is hard and I think not natural to me; many people pour out themselves on all occasions and always want a confidant and adviser. I try my cases and fight my battles alone, though with the indirect help from people that I observe and understand. . . . With a person like Susie [Cabot] to whom spontaneous confidence is natural it is beautiful and does constant good, but I have to force inarticulate words through a voice controlled lest its feeling should overcome it, and my natural tendency is to fly away alone to my room or play in the dark. I believe that this is at least partly wrong and it is going to make people misunderstand me.[35]

Cabot's position suggests that the intuitive responses to oppression or inhibition—"to fly away alone to my room or play in the dark"—may in fact perpetuate the cycles of injustice. Doing so, is "partly wrong" because it gives the impression that the oppressed individual desires seclusion and would rather retreat into a remote playroom than freely engage the problems that she faces. In fact, the oppressed often retreat in order to protect some last shard of self-regard from a threatening world. This, however, was rarely grasped by onlookers of the late Victorian period, and many people did misunderstand Cabot as being passive and somewhat infantile in her desire for isolation. Well aware of this misunderstanding, Cabot asserts that she will overcome the problems of autonomy and self-expression "not as I tried before by cutting off my inner life, but by greater outward expression."[36]

It may be tempting to pigeonhole Cabot's personal writings as the musings of a conflicted woman that ought to be regarded as mere social commentary. This interpretation is partially accurate. They are the musings of a conflicted woman. But they are also the stuff of American philosophy. If philosophy, according to Hegel, is the elevation of culture to the level of thought, Cabot's personal writings represent philosophy *written by women* at the turn of the century. The culture that was raised to the level of thought was, in Cabot's writing, a subtly repressive one, one that demanded that the history of philosophy be recast and reworked to address new and unique challenges. Her discussion of the duty of self-expression should be understood along these lines.

Here, Cabot attempts to reframe a principle of the Kantian moral philosophy at the service of feminist projects. Significantly, she recognizes that self-expression is a type of Kantian imperfect duty, one that can be meaningfully pursued, but only partially or provisionally fulfilled. Kant describes at length the imperfect duty to oneself of cultivating one's individual talents and endowments. In the first formulation of the categorical imperative in the *Groundwork of the Metaphysics of Morals*, Kant outlines a type of duty that cannot be fully realized nor constantly pursued. This being said, such duties do possess normative strength and ought to help guide our actions. In the second formulation in the *Groundwork*, he argues that the effort to pursue our ends and the ends of others, to foster our natural and personal talents and those of others, constitutes this sort of imperfect duty. There are, undoubtedly, obstacles to performing these duties that will occasionally, or even often, force us to amend our plans for their pursuit. This fact, however, does not cut short the process of self-cultivation. Cabot puts this point in stark relief when she writes: "To 'recognize your limitations' is a misleading phrase. I have no absolute limitation, no direction in which I am shut off from growth. The knowledge of the barrier helps me to knock it down."[37] The pursuit of the duty of self-expression is forever incomplete and frequently obstructed by the suggestions and prohibitions of others. These "barriers" that often characterized the subjection of women were not to be recognized in the sense of being accepted, but recognized as the first step of overcoming them. Attempting to overcome them stood, and continues to stand, as a moral obligation for autonomous individuals who face oppression. If we are to recognize anything in the sense of acceptance, it is not our limitations, but rather our own proclivities and capacities. As Cabot suggests, "[w]hat I think we ought to recognize is our nature, and what way it can do the best work and which work is the best for it."[38] This comment amounts to a feminizing of Kant's statement that, "Man has a duty to himself to cultivate his natural powers . . . as a means to all sorts of ends. Man owes it to himself not to leave idle and as it were, rusting away the natural predispositions and capacities that his reason can someday use."[39] Indeed, Cabot is applying a wide swath of moral theory that includes the virtue ethics of Aristotle, the confessional reflections of Augustine, and the Pauline ethic of the New Testament to her situation as a woman at the turn of the century. While most figures from the Western philosophical tradition restrict their analysis to male self-cultivation and moral perfection, Cabot insisted that this imperfect duty was to serve as the basis of moral life for women as well. For Cabot, following Kant and Aristotle, the appeal to "our own nature" in the process of self-cultivation is not an appeal to the outmoded teleological conception of "human nature," but rather an acknowledgement of the obligation that we have to ourselves as particular individuals possessing unique capacities.

In his discussion of the duty to foster our natural endowments, Kant leaves open several conceptual gaps that commentators since Hegel have attempted to fill. First, the duty to enact and cultivate our natural talents seems opaque to the extent that it remains unclear exactly which ones ought to take priority in our daily affairs. Choosing one set of talents seems to necessarily preclude the development of others. As Kant states in the Introduction to the *Metaphysics of Morals*, "The variety of circumstances which men may encounter makes quite optional the choice of the kind of occupation for which one should cultivate his talent."[40] Second, and more problematically, it is not clear in Kant's account how we are to weigh the cultivation of our natural talents against the moral duty of helping others. Cabot is very aware of both of these difficulties. In her classes with Royce, she returns to the hard fact faced by all human beings, namely that the choice and selection of particular interests necessarily involves the negation and elimination of others. More notably for the current discussion, Cabot constantly weighs the explicit price and opportunity costs of cultivating her own talents. In a journal written on December 27, 1908, she picks up where Kant's discussion of imperfect duties to oneself leaves off. She is deeply concerned about the manner in which her self-cultivation might disturb the people to whom she feels a moral obligation. She writes:

> Self-knowledge, self-control and self-realization—these I seek. What dangers do I run toward myself and others in this course of conduct? It is the ever-recurring question. The criticisms that people make on us and on our actions in general give usually an inaccurate but still a valuable picture of ourselves as in the world. But the real criticism can come only from ourselves; it must be constant and searching, not blinded by partiality or self-deception. It must be based on pure love of truth and never imagine it has solved the whole problem. The watchword of life is awake thou that sleepest![41]

Cabot, like Kant, insists that the response to a duty of virtue, in this case the cultivation of one's own perfection, is a task that is ongoing. In fact, the duty is only lost or disobeyed when one assumes, mistakenly, that she has fulfilled its mandate.

In the above passages Cabot is also wrestling with a rather difficult issue that will come to define much of the feminist ethical theory of the twentieth century. Throughout her discussions of the moral imagination, discussed in chapter four, Cabot occasionally seems to prioritize sympathy over self-expression. In so doing, she is working squarely in a field that would later be described as the "ethics of care." As Dorothy Rogers has noted, many women who grew up in the culture of sentiment and entered the field of philosophy in the late nineteenth century addressed altruism as a philosophical concept prior to the treatment of "care" in the 1970s and 1980s. Rogers outlines the way in which Marrietta Kies and Lucia Ames Mead extended the history of philosophy in order to fashion theories of altruism.[42] In the above passage, however, Cabot does not restate these theories, but rather points to some of the dangers implicit in sacrificing one's autonomy to the interests of others. These dangers have been fleshed out to a great extent more recently. According to Nel Noddings and Carol Gilligan, this particular ethic, associated almost exclusively with the acculturation of women, encourages individuals to value care and social affiliation over autonomy and self-realization.[43] Subsequent feminist thinkers have taken alternative perspectives on this issue. Care ethicists such as Noddings and Gilligan hold that the role of the caretaker is to be revalued, embraced, and appreciated. But, as we will see, other subsequent feminist thinkers have been more reticent here, suggesting that while there are clearly valuable lessons to be learned in adopting the "care perspective," there is also always a danger that social roles defined primarily by sympathy and care-giving might inhibit the personal growth of women. As her early poem "Reserve" reflects, at an early age Cabot was aware of the dangers of sympathetic insight, and as she matures as a thinker, her concerns take on a pointedly philosophical flavor.

Jean Hampton has developed the most recent, and I would argue, most compelling, argument against an ethic of thoroughgoing self-sacrifice.[44] Her argument turns on three points, all of which resonate closely with Cabot's ethical thought. First, Hampton interrogates the motivations behind calling self-sacrifice "moral." She suggests that caregivers provide useful services to members of their community; and at the turn of the century most of these caregivers gave valuable resources to their male spouses. What better way, Hampton asks, to maintain this power dynamic than to call subordinated women "moral saints?" In this case, altruistic individuals are at risk of becoming "prey" (to use Hobbes's words) of self-interested counterparts. Second, Hampton argues, in a Kantian vein, that individuals who respect the legitimate needs of others have a similar obligation to recognize and respond to the needs of themselves. Finally, she echoes both Cabot and Kant in stating that one's duties to perfect oneself, or to develop a meaningful personality, might run counter to self-denial or extreme forms of altruism.

Anticipating this recent work, Cabot states quite clearly that ethical life is initiated not in the wholesale sacrifice of the self in sympathetic activity, but in the self-possession and self-realization of the individual who freely engages with her surroundings. Along with Kant, Cabot understands that if one's moral value is wholly tied to an ability to help others, this individual can be quickly and easily reduced to a mere means used at the service of others' ends. This is a tenuous point, but it should be noted that Cabot does not suggest that self-realization is contingent upon the subjection of others, but only that moral life is *equally* a matter of self-respect and the respect of others as ends in themselves. It is a tenuous point to the extent that moral life involves a balancing act between autonomy and differentiation on the one hand and empathy and self-sacrifice on the other. This equilibrium is never wholly achieved, but rather continually sought in the course of self-reflection and interaction. According to Cabot, in attempting to maintain this balance one should never imagine it has solved the whole problem since imperfect duties, by definition, are not to be decisively fulfilled. What is decisive, however, is Cabot's insistence that meaningful work must be freely chosen by an individual who has accessed "her own nature" and decided what project might be best suited to her capabilities. This is a significant departure from the standard work cure that her husband develops, a departure motivated largely by her study of the history of philosophy.

ALTRUISM, AUTONOMY, AND SELFHOOD

In the *Critique of Practical Reason*, Kant outlines the dangers of an ethic of care that sacrifices selfhood in the name of the moral obligation to others or altruism. He describes the attempts of a sailor to save his crew from a shipwreck while facing extreme danger to his own wellbeing. Kant claims that while most people would deem this action as being morally meritorious, there is a sense in which our "esteem for it would be greatly decreased by the concept of duty to himself, which in this case seems to suffer a great infringement."[45] Kant's comment suggests that selfless action, while morally laudable, always risks the functional core of moral life, namely the core of autonomy that makes an ethical life possible. Throughout *Everyday Ethics*, Cabot concentrates on the pursuit of the moral stability between autonomy and altruism. She does so in a pointedly Kantian fashion, drawing heavily from the course that she took from Royce in the early 1890s. This philosophical legacy is easy to overlook in a book whose language and style is tailored for the ethical training of adolescents, but the distinct flavor of Kant's moral theory and his antinomies comes through as Cabot resolves the moral contradictions that seem to arise between autonomy and altruism. These antinomies are seen in the following long passage from *Everyday Ethics*:

> Self-centered is a term of reproach, yet self-reliance is a duty. Self-seeking again is a sign of narrowness, but self-possession is all important. But can you possess anything you do not seek? Self-complacency we all scorn, but self-respect is an important virtue. Self-sacrifice is as we have seen essential to all good life, yet surely self-preservation is a duty. Self-consciousness is interesting because in ordinary usage it is a defect; to a philosopher it is the central characteristic of man. Tennyson writes: "Self-reverence, self-knowledge, self-control. These alone lead life to sovereign power." But Christ said: "If any man will come after me let him deny himself." ... In these words and lines we see man's struggle in thought crystallized in language. Our very words as we pick them out dried and pressed into a dictionary show that people now insist on the virtue of denying yourself, again on the duty of relying on yourself, here on the sin of being self-centered and there on the necessity of self-respect, without fully seeing that the one little four-lettered word [the "self"] is twisted and tortured as we throw it about.[46]

Cabot suggests that a reformulation of the concept of selfhood might begin to mediate the paradoxes that she outlines above and the tension that Kant identifies between self-respect and the care for others.

In the subsequent passages from *Everyday Ethics*, Cabot undertakes this reformulation by drawing from the writings of her philosophy instructors who become the fathers of classical American thought. From Royce, she cites the story of the highway robber from the *Religious Aspects of Philosophy* (1888), a book that is obviously influenced by Royce's extensive study of Kant and Hegel. In this story, the robber's selfish intent of stealing a victim's purse is reversed when the would-be victim draws a pistol on the criminal and forces him to return to town at gunpoint. Under duress, the robber becomes much more interested in altruistic behavior, hoping that the man who is now holding the gun will have mercy on him. Following Royce, Cabot notes that this transition from selfish to selfless interests cannot be regarded as moral since it is motivated by external factors. Moral activity in general, and altruism more particularly, presupposes a free choice made by an individual engaged in a particular social context. And in Cabot's words, "no one can be selfish or unselfish unless he acts of his own accord."[47] From this conclusion, she draws another, namely that in selfless altruistic activity, a self must always be operative as legislator and actor. She looks to Royce for this restatement of the relationship between autonomy and morality, but Royce does not go far enough for Cabot in the reformulation of selfhood.

Therefore, after addressing the *Religious Aspect of Philosophy*, Cabot turns to William James's account of the self in the *Principles of Psychology* in order to explore how it might shed more light on the tension between a moral care for others and self-respect. She inquires about the exact nature of the self that chooses its course in moral life: "What really is ourself?"[48] In response, she turns to the section in the *Psychology* where James states that, "our fame, our children, the work of our hands, may be as dear to us as our bodies are and arouse the same feelings, the same acts of reprisal if attacked."[49] The self that James and Cabot envision is, by its very nature, relational. The social relations to which an individual is loyal are not merely additive, but constitutive of the self. If this conception of selfhood holds, Cabot writes, "we cannot limit ourselves to our bodies or to our brain, we must reach out to include as ourself all that we love, all with which we can identify ourselves, that is, our interests."[50] It should be noted that emphasizing the relational nature of the self is not to necessarily affirm a thoroughgoing ethics of care; indeed, the dangers associated with the ethics of care are mitigated if the relations that constitute the self are freely chosen. Cabot seems in agreement with Jean Hampton's recent assertion that "service to others is morally acceptable when it arises from an authentically defined preference, interest, or project undertaken by one who pursues her legitimate needs as a human being and who accepts a Kantian conception of human value."[51]

In returning to the earlier discussion of the work cure, what was lacking in Richard Cabot's formulation of the cure was the way that it overlooked how the development of authentically defined interests might provide the basis of a meaningful moral life for a patient suffering from hysteria or neurasthenia. There are two sides to this type of interest. On the one hand, Ella Lyman Cabot holds that an interest is necessarily personal and unique. Interests are always "my" interests, or always held as dear by some individual. On the other hand, interests always open out into a world that demands our attention. Cabot reflects on this fact, stating that interests should be "more than mine"—in other words, interests should be other oriented.[52] This two-sided description of an interest has wider philosophical implications for, as Cabot writes in an unpublished paper entitled "Individuality," "In an interest then we see the universal and the particular aspects not in opposition but in necessary unity of relation and interaction."[53] An interest is universal in the sense that it necessarily opens out into other realms of inquiry, while at the same time it is an interest only to the extent that it is *interesting* to the particular individual. Just as James and Dewey encourage us to reconstruct experience in an effort to overcome the longstanding squabbles in the history—between the one and the many, the collective and the individual, between permanence and flux—Cabot's account of interest aims to overcome the opposition between the particular and the universal.

At the very least, Cabot believes that she has begun to unwind the knot of autonomy and altruism that has troubled so many thinkers in the Western tradition. The concept of an interest has two sides that speak to dual obligation to others and to oneself. She expands on this point, writing:

> We reach here an important conclusion: *If all we love is ourself, the separation between doing things for ourselves that doing things for others whom we love is broken down.* It was an unreal distinction though it looked firm in the distance, and it crumbles when we really come up against it. There is no one who lives wholly in his narrow shell, shutting out the entire world of people and pursuits.[54]

Dwelling on Cabot's conclusion involves addressing the double *entendre* that resides at its core and the double meaning of the term "interest." She believes that the dichotomy of altruism and autonomy breaks down in the statement that "all we love is ourselves." In one sense, this statement is the mantra of ethical egoism, the position that results from an inflated sense of autonomy and self-expression. Seen in this light, the statement could be rephrased as "the only thing I love is my self and my interests." As Cabot reaches middle age, she returns to the importance of self-respect in the formation of ethical character. As an ethical agent, one must realize the worth of oneself as an autonomous being in order to *freely* recognize and respond to the needs of others.

The realization of our own intrinsic worth as moral agents, however, is never divorced from the social interactions in which we find ourselves. It is not the case, according to Cabot, that we "get a hold of ourselves" as moral agents *and then* engage in sympathetic activity. While self-regard is a precondition of moral activity, it is not, practically speaking, temporally prior to our activity with others. This brings us to the second way of reading the phrase that, "all we love is ourselves." While it might be interpreted as calling for a thoroughgoing egoism, the phrase is also simultaneously a statement of the self's profound relatedness. "All we love is ourselves" is another way of summarizing James's work on the social self in which he states that selfhood is nothing save the meaningful and ethical relations that are formed between selves. These relations are formed in many ways, but a willingness to give of oneself for the sake of others seems to be a common characteristic of most of the relationships that sediment the self. In this respect, Cabot's comment could be reframed in the following manner: "I am only a self to the extent that I am concerned for others and have interests in the world." While summarizing James's work, Cabot's conclusion is unique to the extent that she seeks to translate the pragmatic conception of selfhood into explicitly ethical language, grappling with the question of maintaining the freedom of the will while exercising it in the care for others. Again, this question is especially apposite for a woman-philosopher at the end of the nineteenth century since the conception of Victorian womanhood was characterized by a woman's ability to provide assistance to a dominant male figure. Unfortunately, this ability to provide services to others often came hand-in-hand with an inability to freely cultivate a sense of meaningful subjectivity. In print, Cabot maintained that the either/or of self-regard and altruism was an unreal distinction. In her personal life, however, Cabot seems to have been frequently torn between the call to act autonomously and a cultural rendering that continued to reduce women to their instrumental value. In short, she was caught between her desire to be a subject and her lived reality as being an objectified woman.

While much of the pragmatic moral theory of her time (developed by James, Dewey, and Addams) emphasized the need for sympathetic insight and concern for others, Cabot is concerned that personal freedom not be sacrificed in the midst of this concern. This being said, it remains unclear whether Cabot was herself able to engage in projects and purposes that were freely chosen. Her life work often seems to cater to the interests of others, most notably her husband and male mentors. Ada McCormick, reflecting on Cabot's life, notes that she "had the curiously feminine quality of being able to help others do work that they could not do themselves."[55] As the acknowledgements from *their* books reveals, Ella Lyman Cabot served as a constant sounding board for Josiah Royce, Richard Cabot, Mary Foote, and Mary Parker Follett. In reviewing Richard Cabot's *Adventures on the Borderlands of Ethics* (1926), a writer from *Time Magazine* writes that in the study of ethics and education, "Dr. Cabot has the experience of his wife, Ella Lyman Cabot, to draw upon as well as his own."[56] A month later, *Time* did a follow-up article on this book. Here the author states, "[t]hose who know Dr. Richard Clarke Cabot feel that he owes considerable of his sociological curiosity to his wife, Ella Lyman Cabot."[57] Perhaps it is in this respect that McCormick writes that, "in this way she wrote many books by proxy."[58] Living by proxy, as the sidekick to other people's purposes, was not always sufficient for this individual. McCormick notes in the 1935 issue of the *Radcliffe Quarterly* that Ella Lyman Cabot, "was not a wholly happy woman," that decisions and work were always a great strain for her. This strain is produced by the dual commitment that Cabot has outlined in her discussion of autonomy and service, a type of double consciousness that is characteristic of subjection.[59]

CONCLUSION: WORKING THROUGH DOUBLE-CONSCIOUSNESS

As Cabot prepared *Everyday Ethics* for publication in the dawning of the new century, another figure in classical American philosophy described the psychological and social tension that is experienced by oppressed individuals. In 1903, W. E. B. Du Bois published the *Souls of Black Folk* in which he describes the "double-consciousness" of African Americans as caught in a state of limbo between freedom and subjugation, between experiencing themselves as autonomous human subjects and sensing their objectification as tools to be used by others.[60] The white majority, according to Du Bois usually glossed over the mental strife of double-consciousness by noting how race relations had improved since the Civil War, how Reconstruction, despite its obvious shortcomings, had made at least some progress in terms of racial equality. Du Bois was not satisfied with this reaction. Instead of glossing over the tension that African Americans experienced, he encouraged his white neighbors (and his teachers like James and Royce) to ask a question that might allow African Americans to speak for themselves: "How does it feel to be a problem?"[61] How does it feel to be caught between freedom and subjection? How does it feel to have your freedom curtailed by the demand to assist others? How does it feel to destroy autonomy in the name of self-sacrifice? How does it feel to have abilities that will never be cultivated? The *Souls of Black Folk* stands as the articulate and unequivocal answer: it does not feel good. More subtly, Du Bois writes, "[i]t is a peculiar sensation, this double-consciousness, this sense of always looking at oneself through the eyes of others, of measuring one's soul by the tape of a world that looks on in amused contempt and pity. One always feels his two-ness."[62]

Margaret Fuller and Lydia Maria Child, two neglected founders of the American philosophical tradition, note that the problem of double-consciousness faced by African Americans in the nineteenth century bears a marked resemblance to the struggle that women faced at the same time. As Iris Marion Young would later note, a woman, like any slave, lives the contradiction of being both subject and object.[63] In *Woman in the Nineteenth Century*, Fuller draws out this comparison: "As the friend of the negro assumes that that one man cannot by right, hold another in bondage, so should the friend of woman assume that man cannot by right lay even well-meant restrictions on woman."[64] Ella Lyman Cabot, writing a generation after Fuller, faces resolutely these "well-meant restrictions on woman," in both her philosophical writings and her personal life. Despite her privileged social standing and race, in virtue of her gender she remains caught in the type of double-consciousness that Du Bois describes. While the formation of her marriage contract with Richard Cabot was explicitly geared to counteract the subjection of women, Ella Lyman Cabot struggled to "work through" the cultural restrictions on many forms of women's work that caused widespread psychological trauma in many of her contemporaries.

Cabot faced the obstacles that women continue to face as they enter the field of philosophy, most notably, the assumption that their skills might be better fitted to other disciplines. This mistaken assumption plagued Cabot's pursuit of meaningful purposes and self-motivated work. As highlighted in *Time*, Cabot was largely responsible for her husband's insights in sociology, a fact that comes to light in the course of this chapter; her insistence that women need to have a freely chosen interest that inspires work anticipates, and dovetails with, Richard Cabot's subsequent development of the work cure. But as we have seen, Richard Cabot often fails to emphasize the need for self-respect that his wife is so keen to underscore. And she does underscore it. Interestingly, her attempts to conceptualize the balance between autonomy and altruism were made by way of the history of philosophy, a field that she freely chose, against the advisement of others. In this respect, her philosophical argument for the importance of interests and purposive work was, in fact, an enactment of her own attempts to carve out a meaningful life project. While these attempts remained only partially successful, it is obvious that Cabot continued to pursue the duty, albeit an imperfect one, of self-realization. She attempts to work through the difficulty of double-consciousness and, in Du Bois's words, to merge her "double self into a better and truer self."[65]

NOTES

1. John Stuart Mill, *The Subjection of Women* (London: Longmans, Greene, Reader and Dyer, 1869), 3.
2. Cited in Gerald Myers, *William James* (New Haven: Yale University Press, 2001), 425.
3. Cited in Myers, *William James*, 426.
4. Cited in Myers, *William James*, 426.
5. Cited in Charlene Haddock Seigfried, *Pragmatism and Feminism: Reweaving the Social Fabric* (Chicago: University of Chicago Press, 1996).
6. Cited in Seigfried, *Pragmatism and Feminism*, 120. Also in William James, "Thomas Davidson: A Knight-Errant of the Intellectual Life," *McClure Magazine* (May 1905).
7. A 139/32.
8. A 139/32.
9. A 139/32.
10. A 139/278V, 1908.
11. Charlotte Perkins Gilman, *The Living of Charlotte Perkins Gilman* (Madison: University of Wisconsin Press, 1995), 96.
12. Mill, *The Subjection of Women*, 87.
13. Ella Lyman Cabot Trust, www.lightstalkers.org/posts/ella-lyman-cabot-trust-personal-grant (accessed April 3, 2011).
14. Ella Lyman Cabot, Everyday Ethics (New York: Henry Holt and Co., 1906), 55.

15. Richard Cabot, "Work Cure—I," *Psychotherapy* 3, no. 1 (1909): 24.
16. William James, *Psychology* (New York: Henry Holt and Co., 1905), 383.
17. William James, *Talks to Teachers on Psychology* (Boston: Holt, 1900), 204.
18. A 139/320.
19. A 139/320. During the same period, Cabot reflects on the active disposition of a creed, often regarded as a static point of religious doctrine. She writes: "Your creed is your life principle and cannot be fully uttered until you have lived your life and found expression for its many sides. . . . But because your creed is your working motive it must be as clear to you as possible." A 139/320.
20. Cabot, *Everyday Ethics*, 138.
21. Cabot, *Everyday Ethics*, 138.
22. William James, "The Dilemma of Determinism," in *The Will to Believe and Other Essays* (New York: Longmans, Green and Co., 1911), 146.
23. Cabot, *Everyday Ethics*, 138.
24. A 139/278V, 1908.
25. A 139/278V, 1908.
26. Richard Clarke Cabot Papers. Harvard University Archives. HUG 4255.80. Box 1. "APM Notes on Cabots." (Fragment)
27. Cited in Joan Tonn, *Mary Parker Follett: Creating Democracy, Transforming Management* (New Haven, CT: Yale University Press, 2003), 196.
28. Richard Cabot, "Work Cure—I," *Psychotherapy* 3, no. 1 (1909), 28.
29. A 139/279v.
30. A 139/279v.
31. Cited in Paul Guyer, *Freedom, Law and Happiness* (Cambridge: Cambridge University Press, 2000), 312.
32. A 139/279v.
33. A 139/320.
34. Robin Dillon, "Kant on Arrogance and Self-Respect," in *Setting the Moral Compass: Essays by Woman Philosophers*, ed. Cheshire Calhoun (New York: Oxford University, 2004), 191–216. See also Carol Hay, "Whether to Ignore Them and Spin," *Hypatia* 20, no. 4 (2005): 94–108, and "The Obligation to Resist Oppression," *Journal of Social Philosophy* 42 (2011): 21–45.
35. A 139/320.
36. A 139/320.
37. A 139/320.
38. A 139/320.
39. Immanuel Kant, *The Doctrine of Virtue*, trans. Mary Gregor as *Metaphysical First Principles of the Doctrine of Virtue* in *The Metaphysics of Morals* (Cambridge: Cambridge University Press, 1991), 444.
40. Kant, *The Doctrine of Virtue*, 392.
41. A 139/279v.
42. Dorothy Rogers, "Before 'Care': Marietta Kies, Lucia Ames Mead, and Feminist Political Theory," *Hypatia* 19, no. 2 (2004): 105–17.
43. See Daryl Koehn, *Rethinking Feminist Care Ethics* (New York: Psychology Press, 1998).
44. Jean Hampton, *The Intrinsic Worth of Persons: Contractarianism in Moral and Political Philosophy* (Cambridge: Cambridge University Press, 2007), 55–58.
45. Immanuel Kant, *Critique of Practical Reason*, trans. Mary Gregor (Cambridge: Cambridge University Press, 1997), 159.
46. Cabot, *Everyday Ethics*, 173–74.
47. Cabot, *Everyday Ethics*, 175.
48. Cabot, *Everyday Ethics*, 177.
49. Cited in Cabot, *Everyday Ethics*, 177. Also in William James, *The Principles of Psychology*, vol. 1 (New York: Macmillan Press, 1890), 291.
50. Cabot, *Everyday Ethics*, 178.

51. Jean Hampton, *The Intrinsic Worth of Persons: Contractarianism in Moral and Political Philosophy* (Cambridge: Cambridge University Press, 2007), 62.
52. Cabot, *Everyday Ethics*, 178.
53. A 139/370.
54. A 139/370.
55. Richard Clarke Cabot Papers. Harvard University Archives. 4255.80. Box 1. "Research Material for Ada McCormick."
56. "Books: Non-Fiction (*Adventures in the Borderland of Ethics*)," in *Time Magazine*, December 27, 1926.
57. "Medicine: Cabot on Ethics," in *Time Magazine*, April 12, 1926.
58. Richard Clarke Cabot Papers. Harvard University Archives. 4255.80. Box 1. "Research Material for Ada McCormick."
59. First cited in Harvard University Archives. Richard Clarke Cabot Papers. HUG 4255.80. Box 1. "Ella Lyman Cabot—by APM."
60. W. E. B. Du Bois, *The Souls of Black Folk* (Chicago: A. C. McClurg and Co., 1907).
61. Du Bois, *The Souls of Black Folk*, 3.
62. Du Bois, *The Souls of Black Folk*, 3.
63. Iris Marion Young, *On Female Bodily Experience* (New York: Oxford University Press, 2005).
64. Cited in Nancy Cott, *No Small Courage: A History of Women in the United States* (New York: Oxford University Press, 2004), 200.
65. Cited in Cott, *No Small Courage*, 200.

Chapter Six

Cabot on Peace Education: Moral Psychology, Ethics, and International Affairs (1906–1930)

On the evening of December 18, 1930, President Herbert Hoover invited a group of forty to the White House for a dinner in honor of Vice President Curtis. To the right of the president sat General Otto Falk, who had earned considerable acclaim in the Spanish American War. To the right of General Falk sat Ella Lyman Cabot, who had, after considerable difficulty, earned a reputation as a social and educational reformer in the early decades of the twentieth century. Cabot's purposes and intellectual projects were inhibited by the cultural norms of the day, but she was eventually successful in situating her work in the burgeoning social progressive movement that took the nation by storm and ushered John Dewey, George Herbert Mead, and Jane Addams, into the public spotlight.

The publishing of *Everyday Ethics* in 1906 coincided with a growing sentiment that conservative ideologies of the past were ill-equipped to handle the difficult realities of the present. The progressives sought to strike a pragmatic balance between conservatism and the radical strains of anarchy and socialism that quickly arose as its counterbalance. Cabot's mature ethics and social-political thought can be understood in light of the progressive attempt to address the corruption of bureaucracy while insisting that government should in fact have a role in facing the social crises that arose in the wake of the Industrial Revolution. According to Cabot and others, the solution to these crises was not a "bigger" government, but a better one— better in the sense of promoting new and more responsive forms of deliberative democracy. At the heart of this ideal democracy were educational practices that might inform and sustain the American public.

As John Dewey states in the *Public and its Problems* (1927), a genuine public comes into being in the face of problematic situations that its members must collectively face. This public is born through the realization of collective interests as a way of avoiding the negative, sometimes disastrous, consequences that occur when members of a society interact without a guiding purpose. Education, according to the progressive political theorists, was meant to prime members of a population to be full-fledged citizens, both in the sense of exercising their individual political freedoms and in embodying an active civic-mindedness. Beginning in the 1830s, in a time that coincided with the birth of classical American philosophy, the civic-mindedness of Americans was closely tied to the project of westward expansion that revealed threats that demanded a unified national response. As this Manifest Destiny was revived in the 1890s, notable early progressives such as Jane Addams tried to clip the wings of imperialism while maintaining a sense of national identity and patriotism. This was no easy task. The difficulty can be traced to several different sources. First, these newer ideals of peace and cooperation, put forward by the likes of Addams in 1907, did not fit with the growth of militarism that accounted for the livelihood of so many across the expanding United States. Second, these ideals appeared "weak" and "feminine" in the face of a sexist culture still dominated by stereotypically "masculine" prerogatives of exploration and conquest. Finally, public intellectuals, such as James, who were enamored by such prerogatives downplayed or wholly ignored peace ideals that might provide an alternative to bellicosity. James and others proposed "moral equivalents of war" that did not provide alternatives to, but only sublimated, the seemingly natural pugnacity of human beings. This is the context in which Ella Lyman Cabot attempted to fashion her educational theory and social-political thought. Cabot is unique to the extent that in her framing of the problems of pacificism, patriotism, and political diversity, she follows James's lead in attempting to salvage some value from the political iconography of the early twentieth century, but she, unlike James, remained faithful to the progressive reform and pacifism of Jane Addams.

This chapter provides a commentary on Cabot's social and political thought as presented in her *Everyday Ethics, Ethics for Children* (1910), *A Course in Citizenship* (1914), and *Our Part in the World* (1918). The train of thought that Cabot follows in these works and which will be outlined in this chapter is the movement from moral psychology, to ethics, and finally, to international affairs. Cabot's early works outline the psychological dispositions that make moral training possible. Her middle works open out into a detailed investigation of ethical training, one based on moral imagination and emulation. The later works investigate the ways that ethical training can be applied in wider communities of interpretation, and specifically, in a budding loyalty to the international community.

MORAL PSYCHOLOGY AND ETHICAL IMITATION

Cabot's ethical pedagogy evinced a pragmatic sensibility—contra the dominant current of ethical theory prior to 1900—that ethical training had to be tailored to particular individuals and that the moral imagination might be used in the anticipation of ethical problems, in the imitation of virtuous and heroic actions, and in the extension of moral obligations. Instruction in the field of ethics was not to begin with principles and maxims, but with lived experience and the psychological dispositions of the student. This approach to ethical training may be regarded as pragmatist in its orientation, but at the turn of the century, it was an idealist who concentrated on developing practical models of ethical behavior that could serve as the basis for emulation. While James may be credited for founding empirical psychology, a very strong case can be made that Josiah Royce founded *moral* psychology in the United States. Royce was a keen student of early social psychology and child development, stating that imitation was integral to human learning and to establishing a moral sense. In his *Talk to Teachers*, James, who is often cited as developing the pragmatic notion of the relational self, noted that it was Royce who was at the forefront of the research on the role of imitation in child development.[1] Indeed, Royce reflected a longstanding interest in the way that our relations with others were not merely additive, but genuinely constitutive of our unique personalities. Additionally, he underscored the way that imitation facilitated a notion of selfhood, explaining how the relational self came into being. In a note made by Cabot after 1896 titled "The Relation between Self-Reliance and Providence," she writes that moral "individuality, as Royce has beautifully shown, [develops] first of all by company with others and trying to imitate them, (*Conception of God*, 278 ff), and from this [we] gradually learn to judge ourselves not by the standard of any other man but by our own ideal."[2] In 1908, following on the heels of these early studies in psychology, Royce noted that the psychology of young children lends itself to the emulation of ethical models, stating that, "[t]here is one contribution which childhood early makes to a possible future loyalty,—a contribution which we sometimes fail to sufficiently take into account. That contribution is the well-known disposition to idealize heroes and adventures, to live an imaginary life, to have ideal comrades, and to dream of possible great enterprises."[3] Royce provides many examples in his later ethical writings in order to give a reader a diverse set of practices that could be extended and imitated in the development of genuine loyalties. This process of emulation was meant to expand the limited loyalties that form a child's conception of selfhood.

Following Royce on this point, Cabot states that ethics must be taught by beginning with the most natural, simplest, ethical tie and then proceed to more complex forms. This is not strictly a Roycean point, but one that is repeatedly expressed in the history of moral theory. In his *Nicomachean Ethics*, Aristotle states that the ethical character of an adult is intimately tied to his or her upbringing as a child. Ethics must begin with *ethos*, or the accustomed, everyday habits of the child in order for a mature ethical sensibility to flourish. For Aristotle, however, there is a problem in beginning ethical training in childhood, for he often suggests that children, stymied by their innate self-centeredness, are unable to understand and respond to ethical lessons. In Aristotle's view, one is either too old or too young for ethical training. This ethical paradox does not arise in the same way for Cabot and her American contemporaries. In the *Philosophy of Loyalty*, Royce states that, "in normal childhood there do indeed appear, in a fragmentary way, forms of conduct which already include a simple, but, so far as it goes, an actual loyalty to the causes the child already understands."[4] Along with Dewey and Royce, Cabot suspects that children have a latent sense of loyalty, narrowly enacted in friendships and familial relationships, a sense that merely needs to be reflected upon and enlarged in later life.

While avoiding the paradox that confronts Aristotle, Royce and Cabot understood that the process of broadening the "natural" and narrow loyalties of the self is extremely difficult. This difficulty stems from the degenerate forms of loyalty that are established in childhood. The loyalties of childhood—to gangs, to friends, to family members, to local communities—are usually exclusive and are often antagonistic to diversity and difference. This is clear to Cabot as she describes the cruel treatment of outsiders by close-knit groups of students. This being said, she encourages teachers to recognize and reshape another type of loyalty that prefigures even the gang mentality. She observes that in the habits of the earliest stage of childhood, children often adopt the causes and loyalties of their caretakers. Cabot maintains that young children are born with an innate sense of helpfulness, and she uses this observation as the point of departure in her course of ethical training. The pleasure that a child finds in helping others is not the pleasure that stems from a self-conscious choice, but rather the enactment of a child's dependence on the caretaker. She observes that ethical differentiation does not occur in this early moment of childhood, stating that, "[i]ndependence of attitude has not usually developed at this age; children are conscious of themselves as assistants in the work of grown-up."[5] This form of loyalty is degenerate in its lack of autonomy, but it is far from being useless. The dependence that a young child feels in relation to its parents and home, while not sufficient to affix moral conscience, can be employed as a type of propaedeutic in ethical training. Cabot believes that it helps to foster a child's appreciation of meaningful work, and that this work serves at least two purposes in moral development. First, in work, "a child sets himself a goal and pursues it against his inclination" to abandon the difficult task.[6] Cabot asserts that a youngster who undertakes this type of active self-control is "showing conscience."[7] Second, to the extent that a child's early purposes and pursuits are usually set in the midst of larger family projects, the youth has the chance to understand her or his individual activity as being recognized by others. Cabot observes that the early exercise of conscience needs to eventually be overcome, since the child's early "conscience is not what is right, but what *we* think is right. It will be years before he accepts a right and a wrong of his own."[8] Moral differentiation occurs later in life when children begin to claim their work as their own. This process can be encouraged, according to Cabot, by teachers and caregivers who begin to recognize the unique talents and proclivities that each student possesses. In *Ethics for Children*, she suggests that teachers "should not be content until we know the strength of each child and have helped him develop it."[9] We might notice the way that this approach to moral training meshes nicely with Cabot's philosophical work on the nature of interests as "life-givers and life-savers." In addressing the particular talents of her students, Cabot is attempting to cultivate a student's ability to claim interests as personally meaningful. While a teacher should encourage the individuation of her students' interests, she is simultaneously charged with connecting these interests to an ever-widening world of responsibility and care.

In developing her ideas on moral psychology, Cabot writes that children who emerge from the earliest years of dependence (their third and fourth years) are naturally attuned to lessons that draw on their budding imagination and their ability to emulate adult behaviors. After dependence, she writes, comes the "dramatic age" in which children begin to imitate their caregivers and play out various forms of social and moral behavior.[10] This is where the models of peace heroes enter the scene. The dramatic rehearsal of particular ethical scenarios prepares children for the high-stakes situations of later life in which they will "act out" moral obligations. At first glance, these rehearsals may appear as childish fantasies: playing doctor, pretending to drive a locomotive, taking on the role of a teacher or storeowner, and assuming the character of mother or father. Cabot, however, holds that this type of imaginative play, enacted repeatedly in a seemingly scripted manner, is in fact an integral part of creating moral habits and is the first step in instilling a genuine sense of moral responsibility. Additionally, Cabot follows Mead and Dewey in her belief that the end of education is not the acquisition of information, but rather the preparation for a meaningful adult life. She suggests that guided play, rather than the passive acquisition of facts, may best prepare students for the activities of being active and responsible citizens. Instead of imposing a regime of memorization and drill, Cabot proposes that teachers allow their students to have a hand in shaping their own education. Having read Emerson's lectures on education from the 1860s, she echoes his sentiment that education lies in respecting the pupil. Good teachers are able to *follow* the imaginative workings of the young pupil, allowing a game of "playing doctor" to slowly transform into a lesson concerning our obligation to ease human suffering. As Emerson instructs: "Respect the child. Wait and see the new product of Nature."[11] To follow the imagination of the child, however, is not to give up a teacher's authority, but rather to reframe the nature of authority. Emerson encourages his audience, saying, "Respect the child, respect him to the end, but also respect yourself. Be the companion of his thought, the friend of his friendship, the lover of his virtue—but no kinsman of his sin."[12] To maintain pedagogical authority is to encourage students to become authors of their own actions and ideas while creating guidelines and examples through which pupils can exercise their freedom. To return to Follett's concept of power described in chapter 2, Emerson encourages us to reframe power as "power with" instead of "power over." Exercising this type of power takes surprising reserves of self-control and courage, willingness to face the unexpected in the classroom. Emersonian pedagogy requires a teacher to have the confidence to guide a child's behavior when necessary, but also the self-assurance that allows child to have her own way. This latter sense of confidence may sound a little odd, but Cabot suspects that many teachers feel threatened by their students' independence and counteract this threat by stifling original thought in their classrooms.

Now we can turn to Cabot's use of ethical exemplars with new eyes. The pedagogy that Transcendentalist and progressive educators advanced, one that aims to foster a type of independence in their students, provides the pedagogical and psychological justification for the extensive use of moral exemplars in Cabot's courses on ethics. The stories and allegories that she provides give her readers particular cases in which ethical principles are expressed in the workings of the every day. Students are meant to regard these examples as being analogous to the situations that they may face in their own personal affairs. The teachers who used *Everyday Ethics* in their classrooms helped students to apply these examples in novel ways that illuminated the unique circumstances of their lives. As mentioned in chapter four, Emerson held that it is the "use of life to learn metonymy"; Cabot extends this position in the field of ethics by emphasizing the role that analogy and imitation plays in informing moral behaviors. In effect, she more closely echoes Royce's unpublished comment in 1893 that,

> Imitation is not merely a third function over above the ordinary functions of the will and of the intellect. I insist that our human intelligence has no existence apart from some sort of intelligent imitative activities. I insist that

the most original of normal men is chiefly original in the selection of things and what people he has chosen to imitate, and in the peculiar and individual coloring that he has been moved to give to his imitations.[13]

Here we find an interesting overlap between Royce and Dewey, who would later underscore the importance of rehearsal and imagination in moral life. While Dewey usually gets credit for this insight, Royce and his students, such as Cabot, were quick to make this point. Cabot is especially prescient in her extensive use of diverse exemplars that might guide American moral sentiment at the turn of the century. As described earlier, Cabot hoped that *Everyday Ethics* would occasion what Royce calls "imitative insights" in the moral realm. While Royce's conception of "imitative insight" plays a key role in Cabot's thinking, what is important for the current discussion is the range and diversity Cabot's choices for the models of moral behavior. Her selection reveals a desire to salvage some moral value from the popular figures of the day—a tactic that is used by James in the "Moral Equivalent of War"—but also a desire to supplement and enrich the standards of heroism to include figures that would have been marginalized due to their gender, ethnicity, and socioeconomic status.

ETHICAL EXEMPLARS—PROBLEMATIC AND HEROIC

In her selection of moral exemplars, Cabot draws heavily from the progressive social activism of her day, especially the work of Addams and Fannie Fern Andrews, leading peace activists of the early 1900s. Cabot coedits *A Course in Citizenship* with Andrews, who had graduated from Radcliffe in 1902 with a degree in psychology and founded the American Peace League in 1908. Having attended The Hague Peace Conferences of 1899 and 1907, Andrews became deeply interested in the structural factors that led to war, concentrating most of her energies on economic equality and social justice. By 1914, the league was the most recognized peace education organization in the United States and Europe. Andrews invited Cabot to edit *A Course on Citizenship* after reading *Everyday Ethics* in 1907. Cabot's *Ethics for Children*, published in 1910, was a precursor to the *Course* and was used as a textbook by many middle schools, especially in the Midwestern United States.

Led by Andrews and Cabot, the authors of the *Course* discussed the importance of what they called peace heroes, a diverse group of individuals that revised the common conceptions of patriotism, national identity, and heroism. The notion of a "peace hero" was first envisioned by Andrew Carnegie, who aimed to provide the financial support to these individuals through the Carnegie Endowment for International Peace; the *Course on*

Citizenship was meant to provide the educational backing by training students to emulate the actions of these exemplars. In so doing, its authors began to answer what they considered "the most important public question before us today," namely "the question of how to develop a class of trained citizens who shall bring into political life such upright devotion and such a high degree of efficient service that our civic life will show the results."[14] The introduction for *The Course on Citizenship* was written by former President William Taft, who believed that the book addressed a related problem, namely the challenge of fostering patriotism in a time of peace. In opening the book, he wrote that it was relatively simple to enflame collective sentiment in a time of civil or foreign war, "but in times of peace this must be done in different ways."[15] One of these ways was embodied in the emulation of virtuous and peaceful exemplars; this emulation stands in dramatic contrast to the positing of general principles of ethical conduct that were supposed to hold in all cases.

Before moving forward, a word of caution needs to be expressed. There are certain problems in pointing to moral exemplars as a means of attuning students to ideal behaviors. The imitation of heroes can expand one's sense of moral obligation and genuine loyalty only in cases when the heroes themselves actually embody these commitments. Cabot's peace heroes were chosen for their pursuit of the ethical ideals that she wished to highlight, yet these heroes' pursuits were occasionally interrupted by ethical shortcomings or complicated by intervening projects that were less than ideal. This may amount to saying that examples of moral behavior, unlike ethical principles, are never perfect. Given this, when a hero falls short of heroic behavior, their shortcomings need to be addressed with clear-eyed determination. Only in this way can models of virtue be instructive, in spite of, or perhaps because of, their complexity: in a sense, they give a reader an idea of the difficulties of maintaining a moral bearing. Cabot encountered some of these problems in *Everyday Ethics*, a work that is strewn with a diverse group of ethical heroes. It falls to us to evaluate the strengths and weaknesses of her models.

One notably weak example is Cecil Rhodes, who Cabot lauds for his ambition and loyalty to a guiding purpose. Rhodes, the English-born diamond magnate of the British South Africa Company, was a motivating force in the colonization of southern Africa. His guiding purpose, as Cabot accurately states, was to spread the Anglo-Saxon civilization to the African continent. His method diverged radically from the peaceful means and cooperative activity that Cabot describes in most of her writings. Rhodes waged ruthless campaigns against the indigenous populations of present-day Zimbabwe and Zambia in establishing Rhodesia. Cabot simply missed this when she writes in *Everyday Ethics* that, "Rhodes could not carry out his great schemes without creative imagination and keen sympathy for men."[16] The military campaigns that Rhodes waged caused thousands of deaths and escalated into the first and second Matebele Wars and set the context for the Boer War (1899–1902). In these military confrontations a small number of British troops leveraged technological advantages in weaponry to defeat a large indigenous population. In the face of the carnage, Rhodes wishes merely that there was more land to annex: "To think of these stars that you see overhead at night, these vast worlds which we can never reach. I would annex the planets if I could; I often think of that. It makes me sad to see them so clear and yet so far."[17] It is difficult, nay, impossible, to interpret Rhodes as demonstrating insight and moral imagination in his political dealings and imperial impulses.

So why was Cabot drawn to a figure like Rhodes? Several factors may have been at play. Classically trained, Oxford educated, and fiercely independent, Rhodes may have reflected a type of personal freedom for which Ella Lyman Cabot secretly longed. Rhodes never married, a fact that he attributed to not having enough time between his industrial and political ambitions. The prioritization of vocational responsibilities over cultural expectations was undoubtedly not lost on Cabot, who had struggled with the decision to marry for similar reasons. Finally, and most likely, Cabot could probably not fully shake the vestiges of Manifest Destiny. If this is the case, Cabot is not alone in her shortcoming. By the turn of the century, the Cabots had grown even closer to their mentor Royce. Richard was regularly a part of the "Sunday circle" that Royce held at his Irving Street house. (The group discussed philosophy in lieu of going to church.) Ella Lyman Cabot, having been granted permission to attend graduate courses in philosophy at Harvard in 1900, attended a huge number of Royce's public lectures in the first decade of the twentieth century. It was during this time that her teacher began to turn his attention to international affairs. It is probable that Royce's thinking on social and political assimilation and imperialism affected Cabot's choice of Cecil Rhodes as an exemplar in *Everyday Ethics*. Many scholars have underscored Royce's dedicated and progressive work on issues of cultural diversity, immigration, race relations, and provincialism.[18] Royce's writing around the turn of the century, however, was not consistent in its tone and often belied an assimilating tendency that aims to place diverse groups at the service of a unifying purpose. It is only his mature thought, reflected in works written after 1908, that places a thick pluralism as a central principle of ethical practice.

In 1900, Royce delivers an address titled "Some Characteristic Tendencies of American Civilization." Given the date, and the fact that parts of this manuscript were published in the *Transactions of the Aberdeen Philosophical Society*, it is likely that Royce gave this talk in the United Kingdom. It is also probable that Royce gave this lecture to a group at Oxford, Rhodes's alma mater and a bastion of Anglo-American imperialism. Evidence for this possibility is not in short supply. His frequent references to, and prioritization of, "Empire" give way to Royce's claim that he regards himself and his audience as "servants of human civilization."[19] He elaborates on this dramatic rendering of the "white man's burden" by stating that this obligation brings Anglo-America together: "near to each other, not only in blood, but in their whole spiritual kinship."[20] This would have warmed the heart of Rhodes (founder of the Rhodes Scholarship) and the rest of the members of an Oxford audience. As he goes on to describe the tendency of the United States to assimilate "our foreigners" and the "strangers upon our shores," Royce observes that conflict often arises between majority practice and minority opinion. He states that this conflict could be seen in the Boer War, a war initiated in response to Rhodes's expansionist policies in South Africa. Through the incorporation or subjugation of indigenous people, Royce hopes that the British Empire, which in truth was on the brink of collapse, could realize a higher unity:

> Your Empire might become not only the protector of alien subjects, but the assimilator of men of kindred blood, and the object of a common loyalty even to those who now perhaps fail to comprehend their true share in your destiny. You have often carried power, protection, and order, into remote regions. May you in the future more and more fully knit together your Empire by the ties of a conscious community of ideas, of interests, and of civilization. May your wars (the wars of African colonization) end in liberty and in future brotherhood.[21]

Royce did express hopes that such wars could be averted, pointing out the tendency of Americans to not fret too much about the influx of foreigners, as long as these immigrants respected and upheld American (Anglo-Saxon) customs. Along these lines, he suggests that the demographic of Chicago was almost too diverse, since he believed there had to be a balance between conflicting cultural practices and an overarching loyalty to common ideals. In the face of this problematic cultural melting pot, Royce believed that the educational system and industrial complex of the Anglo-American civilization could be leveraged in order to encourage assimilation.

In a comment that runs counter to his position on the importance of provincial and local loyalties, Royce stated that, "past unifications of industries leads to both direct and indirect results which certainly tend to the absorption of the foreign peoples, to making them part of *our* system."[22] The possessive tone of Royce's comment echoes Rhodes' tendency to call regions of southern Africa "my country," and it goes against the grain of works such as *The Problem of Christianity* that emphasize toleration in the face of diversity. On the topic of education, Royce reflects a blatantly Eurocentric mindset. He states that Anglo-American tradition has always been based on the realization of humanity through the liberal arts and sciences. This tradition, according to Royce, could be effectively exported to foreign nations through what he calls "the invisible ties of Spirit," a reference to the development of Germanic hegemony by instilling national consciousness through educational practices. At the end of the lecture, Royce indicates that secular cultural missionaries might be used to foster this consciousness in foreign lands since, as he concludes, "[w]here the ideas are, there, in the long run, is the power also."[23] This is an interesting way to conclude a paean to imperialism, for it resonates very closely with Friedrich Holderlin's stanzas: "Where the dangers are, the saving power also."[24] The ideas of Anglo-American imperialism (individual autonomy, equality, freedom, rule of law, and democracy) had and continue to have a certain saving power, yet are dangerous to the extent that they tend to be imposed on foreign communities with little regard to local custom. For this danger to be mitigated, the ideas of national consciousness had to be tempered by the respect for the growing diversity that came hand in hand with the complex immigration patterns that would affect the United States in the dawning century.

While both Royce and Cabot might have flirted with the draw of Anglo-American imperialism at the turn of the century, in their mature thought, they sought alternatives to the models of hegemony that had been put forward by previous generations of Americans. Indeed, in the material that Cabot writes after 1908 there is no sign of Rhodes. After this point, her writings resemble the rest of *Everyday Ethics* where she provides instructive vignettes of moral behavior that evince the pluralism that has become the hallmark of progressive pragmatic thought. In developing her ethical models, Cabot draws from a variety of characters with whom her readers would have been familiar: Dorethea Dix, Clara Barton, Florence Nightingale, and Charles Darwin. In these cases, Cabot's analysis attempted to draw the lives of women into the discussion of moral theory. More significantly, it did not simply restate the stereotypes of women as compassionate and obedient caregivers. In the case of the three women mentioned above, all of whom could be considered caregivers, Cabot suggests that their caring dispositions were underpinned by a clear and strong sense of autonomy and selfhood. "Clara Barton is, everyone would say," Cabot writes, "a remarkably self-reliant woman and we wholly respect her for it."[25] According to Cabot, Florence Nightingale's vocation as a nurse demanded incredible courage, a trait that was often reserved for the men she treated. Cabot's treatment of Dorethea Dix is particularly interesting, for she makes the case that this peace hero shares many characteristics with a well-known male scientist:

> If we turn again to the work of Dorethea Dix we see further points of likeness to that of Darwin. She supplied a more direct and pressing need than he, but she also worked out a new principle of treatment for the insane, that of treating them as sick and in need of rest, nourishment and gentleness instead of as

possessed by demons and needing to be controlled. No special work can be so far reaching as that which evolves a new principle. Darwin and Miss Dix alike sought a new principle, though she worked first to redress immediate crying needs and he first for the slowly enlightening truth. Was either work greater because it required more of the worker? No.[26]

Cabot is clear in speaking directly to young women of her time, providing them a set of exemplars who encourage them to broaden the cultural expectations that often constrained female identity. Dix serves this purpose nicely since Cabot argued that she was courageous, inventive, and original—all characteristics that had been used to describe the masculine engines of history.

Many of the heroes that Cabot selected in *Everyday Ethics* were meant to reverse the effects of the sexism of her time. In addition, several of her exemplars pointedly rejected other everyday customs of late-nineteenth-century America, most dramatically, the customs of slavery and racism. In light of Cabot's commitment to liberal Unitarianism, a tradition that underpinned the American abolition movement, this should come as no real surprise. As she finished the manuscript between 1903 and 1906, Cabot was very much aware of the social and political issues that attended the period of Reconstruction after the Civil War. The Jim Crow laws had been passed in the last decades of the nineteenth century. African Americans were pushed, and fled, into the urban centers in search of work. Race riots began in Wilmington, North Carolina in 1898 and spread to Atlanta by 1906. In the face of this political turmoil, Cabot continued to highlight the actions of Unitarian abolitionists such as Samuel May and Derrit Smith who in 1851 freed Jerry McHenry, an individual who had been imprisoned as a fugitive slave in a Syracuse prison. After providing McHenry safe passage to Canada, these two men turned themselves in to local authorities and stated that they were prepared to "rest their defense upon the unconstitutionality . . . of the Fugitive Slave Law."[27] Cabot drew two important conclusions from this event. First, she observes that heroism did not always coincide with a dominant patriotic or nationalistic sentiment. Second, and just as importantly, she suggests that, "it is by such courageous and open violations of a law held to be wrong, not by evasion and concealment, that moral advance is made."[28] This strain of civil disobedience has a long legacy in the history of classical American thought, and it is clear that in Cabot's moral theory we hear a strand of Thoreau:

> How does it become a man to behave toward this American government today? I answer, that he cannot without disgrace be associated with it. I cannot for an instant recognize that political organization as *my* government which is the *slave's* government also.[29]

This is Cabot's position as well, restated at a time when the United States government again risked mishandling the issue of race. Cabot, however, diverged significantly from her Transcendentalist precursors. Instead of writing about freedom in the *abstract*, in a manner reminiscent of Emerson, Cabot wished to point out those individuals who had fought, and in many cases, died, for freedom in the *concrete*. While she does not blame Emerson for his reticence, she does observe that he did not support the abolitionists in the early 1850s and declines when he is faced with the decision of whether to enlist in the Union Army. In contrast, Cabot focuses on an individual whose response to the decision of enlistment that allows him to assume a unique position in the Civil War: Robert Shaw.

Colonel Shaw was not the type of heroic figure that James described in "The Moral Equivalent of War." He was no Ajax or Achilles, ideals of masculine ambition and strength. In fact, he objected when he received the order to burn and pillage the defenseless city of Darien, Georgia. Cabot chooses Shaw for other reasons. Shaw was the head of the 54th Massachusetts Volunteer Infantry, a regiment of African American soldiers that joined the Union Army in 1863. Shaw himself was not African American; he was white. In many respects, his life as a hero only truly began after his death at Fort Wagner in July of 1863. At this battle, Shaw led his men into the fort and was promptly shot and killed. His body fell over the parapet and he was buried in a mass grave with many of his troops. This burial took on iconic significance for Confederates, who believed that burying a white man with his black troops was a tremendous insult to the Colonel. It took on symbolic meaning for the Union as well; after Shaw's death, his parents announced how proud they were that their son was buried with his comrades in arms. It was a suitable burial for a son who had always believed in social justice and racial equality. Cabot's interest in Shaw is understandable. Theodore Lyman, a close relative of Cabot, had served in General Meade's headquarters on the Potomac and had written extensively about the confrontation and about the meaning of Shaw's life and death.

Ella Lyman Cabot may have been brought up in a household that was dominated by European gentility, but she inherited a strong sense of the American ethos, in all of its conflicting sentiments and hopeful ideals. The fact that she could applaud a character such as Cecil Rhodes and honor ones like Samuel May and Robert Shaw does not mean, or only mean, that her idealism was problematic. It also means that her idealism was problematically American. The tension between American ambition, expressed in the imperialism of the nineteenth and twentieth centuries, and the respect for diversity, expressed in the nation's founding commitment to equality, is one that Cornell West touches on throughout his assessment of American thought and it is one that Cabot continually reflects in her early writings.[30] In her mature thought, she begins to grapple with this possible contradiction, laying out a more unified conception of heroism and national unity.

INSTRUMENTAL IDEALISM: ACTION AND "SUPERIOR IDEALS"

In the preface to *Everyday Ethics*, William Torrey Harris, the St. Louis Hegelian and founder of the *Journal of Speculative Philosophy*, wrote that, "Along . . . this line of ethical theory and practice—which is that chosen by Mrs. Cabot in this book—the somewhat advanced student is called away from the ethical habit to the consideration of the moral grounds of all habit."[31] Following Aristotle and other virtue theorists, Cabot understands the important role that habit serves in the formation of moral character. Indeed, large sections of *Everyday Ethics* are meant to instill certain types of practices in American school children. The development of habits, however, while vitally important in the early stages of moral training, must give way to the active evaluation of moral principles and the inventive application of these principles in the unique circumstances of individuals and their communities. *Hexis*, often translated as "habit" in Aristotle's ethics, actually connotes an active condition of having or holding. What is held up for consideration is a possible course of action that is to be judged and enacted in real time. This is the "consideration of the moral grounds of all principles" to which Harris refers in his preface.

Cabot helps her reader foster this moral reflection through the analysis of famous figures in heroic situations, but also of not-so-famous characters in the midst of their mundane lives. She effectively unearths the principles that underpin everyday action and holds them up for her reader to consider. Additionally, by choosing "everyday folk" as her peace heroes, she hopes to demystify an array of ethical ideals that had to that point been reserved for larger than life stories and mythologies. For example, in her chapter on courage, she focuses on the way that Dorothy Pattison, a English medical reformer, responded to a group of men on a train trip to London. This was not the account of a military hero in the midst of a historic battle, but the account of a gendered battle that was quietly waged on the field of modern European history. Cabot explains how the men had offended Pattison with their language and boisterous behavior. The offense, according to Cabot, was obvious enough that Pattison thought to herself, "What must these men think about a woman who can hear these words and sit by unmoved?"[32] At the risk of personal injury, Pattison stands up to her offenders. "Immediately they dragged her down into her seat with a torrent of oaths, and one of the most violent roared: 'hold your jaw you fool; do you want your face smashed in.'"[33] Cabot writes that they physically held her down between them, until she escaped at the next train stop. Upon leaving a train, a man who had remained relatively quiet in the argument congratulated Pattison for her "pluck" saying, that, "You were right and we were wrong."[34]

Cabot's rendering of this story reveals a belief that civil disobedience can be extended beyond the rebellion against an unjust government, to include the revolt against dominant cultural practices. Pattison's resistance against the behavior of these men makes explicit the abusive character of their behaviors, a character that was overlooked in their everyday practice. It also reveals the way that a woman, often regarded as a subordinate figure in British society, could stand up to a group of larger, and more physically powerful, men. Without her dissension, the abusive language would have continued unabated and been regarded as the acceptable norm. Similarly, without risking herself in her moral revolt, Pattison may have been regarded as an individual who was willing to "take" abuse. After all, she does ask herself what people would think of a woman who could accept this behavior. In vocally objecting to the dominant social setting, Pattison calls these men up short and in so doing risks her own person in the process. Some risks, according to Cabot, are worth taking.

After telling this story, she turns to the words of Reverend Brooks, the Bishop of Boston: "Moral courage consists in the disregard of ordinary fears out of absorbing desire of and devotion to some great superior principle."[35] This quotation comes from Brooks's lecture on courage given on July 7, 1875. James draws from Brooks in his "What Makes Life Significant," agreeing with Brooks and Cabot that moral life must be nourished by "ideal inner springs," ideals that provide consistent guidance through the vicissitudes of daily life.[36] Today's accounts of classical American pragmatism often downplay its religious underpinnings, instead emphasizing the way in which pragmatism stands in contrast to a lockstep belief in religious absolutes. The religious traditions of New England, however, had more to offer than dogmatism. It should not be forgotten that pragmatism grew out of the Calvinist and Unitarian roots of American intellectual life. Religious thinkers such as Reverend Brooks were political activists in their own right, often overlooking points of doctrine and tradition in order to pursue social justice on the frontiers of American society. The pragmatists of Cambridge and Chicago were well aware of this fact. Brooks was a staunch supporter of the normal schools of Northeast, centers of education that aimed to support women and racial minorities at the turn of the century. Brooks's support of the Hampton School in Fort Monroe, Virginia was highlighted in the writings of Booker T. Washington, who was admitted to Hampton in 1872. After the Civil War, Hampton, which was one of the first schools to teach African Americans, was supported by funds from church groups such as Brooks's Boston congregation. The religious idealism of the bishop, Cabot believed, did not run counter to the pragmatic sentiment that virtue had to be world ready and had to enable ameliorative reform in the real world. Indeed, a type of idealism *had* to be operative in order for social reform to maintain its bearings when it was buffeted by countervailing winds.

"Ideal inner springs" tend to run into the stream and current of daily activity. Thoughtful living and social reform depends on the ebb and flow of activity and reflection. This is brought home in the practical story of Pattison and the abusive men. Pattison takes immediate and dramatic action and in so doing effects change, a change in the current social atmosphere and an attitudinal change in the individuals involved. At the same time, Cabot suggests that the courage that Pattison demonstrates arises from ethical reflection and from a loyalty to a broader ideal or "superior principle." The opening segments of Cabot's *Course on Citizenship*, which was to be taught over a six-year period, began by underscoring the good habits that may have already been functional in the lives of young students, but quickly transcended these habits in search of a variety of moral ideals in the unexplored regions of ethical life.

Brooks's 1875 lecture on courage was initially given at the twenty-first anniversary of the Salem Normal School. This was the two-year college that Fannie Fern Andrews attended and where Ella Lyman Cabot lectured at the turn of the century. As these women planned the production of *A Course on Citizenship*, it seems clear that they were intent on translating Brooks's description of moral behavior as the pursuit of "superior principles" into the stages of a moral curriculum. These stages were laid out in such a way that students were encouraged to imaginatively extend their preexisting loyalties and sympathies into wider spheres of action—what began as the child's intimate connection to her home was to be transformed into a genuine loyalty to her neighborhood, her nation, and her international community. This was the practical, pedagogical method that Royce repeatedly employed in his lectures on loyalty in the early years of the 1900s. In his courses, he would begin with an example of ethical action that occurred "close to home," in a place and time that his students could understand. In so doing, he exposed the principle that guided this given action. He would then ask his students to consider whether this principle could be pursued in other settings, or more accurately, whether this principle could achieve greater fulfillment if it served as the guiding force of other activities in other realms.[37] Cabot describes this process in detail in the introduction to *A Course in Citizenship*. In a passage that could have been extracted from the *Philosophy of Loyalty*, she writes, "Throw a pebble into stream. From a small center the ever-widening circles radiate till they reach the other shore. So loyalty to the simplest ties may enlarge circle by circle in the stream of a child's growing life till they reach the shore of good will among all men."[38]

AN ODD COUPLE: INTERNATIONALISM AND AMERICAN THOUGHT

But how wide can one's loyalties be? How inclusive can American loyalties be, while still remaining distinctly American? These are the questions of an "exceptional" nation, one that has always cherished the idea that its destiny was distinct from the rest of the world. In the last three hundred years, loyalty to the international community has often run counter to the nationalistic commitments that many Americans have held. Cabot's mature thought rejects the narrow nationalism that has often taken hold of the American mind, and she attempts to loosen this stranglehold that continues to jeopardize international cooperation. The selection of her peace heroes, who reflected a wide range of ethnic and gender identities, sets the stage for the argument that the nation needs to reframe the complex relationship of its citizenry and its relationship to the broader global community. A very similar move is made by Jane Addams, who crafts her political theory on the domestic front, gains insight from her experience in the Chicago settlement movement, and applies this insight in addressing international crises.

Starting on the home front, Cabot claims that the vitality and longevity of the United States depends on the cultural and political pluralism that has come to define its history. This stands in contrast to the nagging fear, one that remains hard to shake for many Americans, that diversity threatens national cohesion. Cabot tries to address this fear in *Our Part in the World*, writing that, "American life is made rich and fruitful by the gifts and services of many nationalities. . . . Thus the contact of different races can cease to be a source of contention and scorn and become a source of strength and blessing."[39] This comment would remain rather abstract if she did not conclude the statement by insisting that her students "recognize the rights and feelings of the Chinese laundryman, the Italian fruit dealer and the Jewish tailor."[40] Cabot pointedly mentions the "unmentionables" of American society, those individuals who were marginalized at the turn of the century on the basis of their ethnicity and cultural identity. Cabot acknowledged this marginalization and realized that the nation has often failed to recognize the strength of diversity. Indeed, she gave a clear-eyed and critical assessment of times when American policies have stifled or subordinated cultural differences. In her writings, she recounts the reactions of Harriet Beecher Stowe and Abraham Lincoln to the institution of slavery in the early nineteenth century. Her account is occasionally romantic, but it conveys the disgust she has for practices that reduce human beings to mere means on the basis of cultural differences. Cabot claims that "the powerful of the nation were against them," but both of these individuals fought against the dominant mindset and its associated institutions.[41]

Cabot generalizes the lesson learned from the actions of Stowe and Lincoln, applying it to a wider international sphere:

> If any of you have a chance to strike at slavery in whatever form it may take,—the rule of the boss, the crushing of Armenians, the overworking of children, the subjugation of little nations, the degradation of women,—hit it a hard blow and God will be with you.[42]

This is an interesting intellectual slight of hand. While Cabot begins by addressing intolerance and oppression as it manifested itself within the United States, she is very quick to turn her attention to problematic cases that emerge on the global stage, suggesting that "foreign" instances of injustice warrant our immediate and intimate concern. Additionally, in this passage, she indicates that slavery is not only a crime against a particular group of people, but a crime against humanity and *our* humanity. This stance would be extended in the human rights discourse that gathered momentum in the wake of World War I and continues to this day. A second point emerges from Cabot's text: she maintains that the eradication of one type of oppression may entail more complex efforts to combat its other forms. She encourages us to take on, simultaneously, instances of labor abuse, genocide, aggressive invasion, and sexism and gender discrimination. In so doing, she points to the overlapping interests of a variety of civil rights and human rights organizations, an overlap that would be cemented in the middle decades of the twentieth century.

Cabot's re-visioning of *A Course on Citizenship* and *Our Part in the World* is significant in light of criticisms that recent political theorists have leveled against classical American thought. Cornell West comments that the Dewey's social and political thought falls short to the extent that it aims at a cultural transformation that "has the flavor of small-scale homogeneous communities."[43] A similar criticism could be made of James and Royce, who both occasionally suggest that the international system might work better if its communities could be set up like their Irving Street neighborhood. West goes on to criticize Dewey for relying too heavily on pedagogical and dialogical modes of political-cultural reform, suggesting that there is a definite sense in Dewey that we can simply talk through the cultural crises and economic disparities that beset our time.[44] West suggests that sometimes talking just won't do. Dewey's notion of culture does not include robust political organizations that could dramatically alter policy or public mindset. Dewey's latent conservatism is apparent when he first caricatures, and then fiercely criticizes, the revolutionary mindset that gained a footing in Marxism. Without assessing the accuracy of West's claims, we might ask whether Cabot is susceptible to the same criticisms. Growing up in the homogenous community of the Boston elite, we might expect Cabot to err more grievously than Dewey in failing to acknowledge difference in its many forms. This author, however, is often able to transcend her social and economic position, insisting that her students respect cultural diversity and the unique contributions that various communities make to the patchwork of American culture. This comes to the fore in the chapter in *A Course on Citizenship* titled, "The Contribution of Each Race to the Nation." She also states quite clearly that her students are to "hit a hard blow" against slavery in its many forms, including intolerance for diversity.[45] Hitting back and "talking back" against authority are modes of communication that Dewey, in the early years of the century, wanted to avoid at almost any cost; it is significant that Cabot, a woman of the American aristocracy, suggests that there might be a time for each.

The efforts to combat slavery may begin at home for Cabot, but they are quickly taken abroad. This is clear in the care that she expresses in regard to the Armenian genocide of 1916. Her interest may be attributed to the hopeful idealism of the Wilsonian era or to the Christian idealism that occasionally marks her writing. On this second point, we might expect Cabot to echo Royce; he also cites the mistreatment of the Armenians by the Turks in his "Problem of Job" (1898), appealing to Christian scripture as he argues that his readers have a responsibility to respond to the human suffering experienced in Armenia. Cabot's rationale, however, departs from Royce's early idealism in a significant respect. Both Royce and President Wilson were at times criticized for their wishful thinking and big ideas. Royce was discounted by his pragmatic neighbors for ignoring the flesh and blood facts of the real world that never fully conformed to his wishful thoughts. Similarly, Wilson was criticized by his "realist" opponents for his support of the League of Nations in 1918, on the grounds that while internationalism was admirable in theory, it would be disastrous in practice.

Cabot responds to these sorts of criticisms in providing the practical justification for American engagement in international affairs. Instead of appealing to diffuse ideals, she underscores the concrete forms of interconnectivity that increasingly defined the global community at the turn of the century. While she cites and agrees with Wilson's words on April 2, 1917, that, "The world must be made safe for democracy," she grounds these words in pragmatic foreign policy.[46] She writes that, "The entire world is linked together. Touch any part of the chain and the whole vibrates. The very day that Romania declared war against Austria, American wheat prices went down in price, for Romania began to supply the Allies."[47] The economic prosperity of the United States was, and is, integrally bound to the fate of other nation-states. In this passage, Cabot also attempted to demonstrate the ways in which her students' daily lives were tied to the products and goods of foreign countries—she gives the examples of beet sugar from Germany, wool from Australia, and linen from Ireland—all the while emphasizing that this dependency coincided with a moral obligation to tend to the welfare of other states.

Cabot's description of dependence and interdependence is interesting in two significant respects. First, she is willing to invert the typical story of international affairs, in which smaller, less powerful nations are dependent upon the United States for their safety and economic security. Instead, she states quite clearly that it is the United States that relies heavily on the goods of other nations. In effect, she suggests that seemingly subordinate nation-states, such as Germany and Ireland, make vital contributions to well-being of dominant superpowers. Second, her analysis attempts to overcome the divide between public and private interests. Here she attempts to demonstrate that international conflicts entail costs that are shouldered by individuals in their private lives. The flow of goods between nations does not merely affect the international stock markets, but the lives of those who both consume and produce these goods.

During their courtship Richard Cabot had recommended that Ella Lyman study Political Economy instead of philosophy. She does not take his suggestion. Here, Ella Lyman Cabot draws her intimate knowledge of international stock and trade into the field philosophy. Cabot believed that financial interdependence served as an organic form of international insurance that is similar to the kind that Royce developed beginning in 1909, and highlighted in "War and Insurance," delivered in 1914. According to Cabot, greater economic integration would guard against aggressive actions between international parties because this integration would lead to wider range of common interests. Along these lines, Royce suggested that nations contribute to a common monetary fund, a financial embodiment of common interests, which would insure against antagonism between vested parties. Such contributions would lead to the synthesis of public and private interests, discourage reckless actions that might jeopardize the collective, and encourage a sense of stability. Through this type of insurance policy, according to Royce, each nation and its citizens would realize the religious ideal, "Bear ye one another's burdens."[48]

The failure of the League of Nations, and the questionable success of the United Nations and the International Monetary Fund, casts doubt on Royce's proposal and on the hope that countries would be willing and able serve each other in times of need. "Exceptional" nations are rarely willing to shoulder the burdens of a foreign nation, for they regard national interest as being *sui generis*, that is to say, truly exceptional. This being said, it seems safer to assert that global economic integration helps to maintain some geopolitical stability among its participants and may provide a system to balance national self-interest and concern for foreign nations. Cabot is on the lookout for ways in which American self-interest can coincide with the purposes of other states and political entities. As early as 1889, prior to her formal philosophical studies, Cabot notes that the Biblical imperative used by Royce, "Bear ye one another's burdens," should be juxtaposed with the insistence that "Every man bears his own burden."[49] Indeed, these statements seem to emerge as counterpoints in the sixth chapter of Galatians. In this early reflection, however, she states that, "I believe them both and that the contradiction is not real."[50] This passing remark, made in a letter to Richard Cabot, opens out into a robust internationalism in which the American public is challenged to realize the burdens of other nations as their own. Realization is the process of seeing a once foreign topic, idea, person, or nation as intimately tied to our life goals and most cherished purposes; Ella Lyman Cabot points to the ties of international commerce as one possible way of encouraging this realization.

Addams expressed similar hopes in her 1902 Chautauqua Lectures, which would be revised in her *Newer Ideals of Peace* (1906). Here she encourages citizens to acknowledge and respond to the call of internationalism, envisioning a "patriotism which the intermingling of nations has forced upon us, instead of the patriotism which prevailed when each nation had to regard the others as enemies."[51] Like Cabot, Addams regarded "commercial interdependence" as a means of securing collective interests and thereby a collective future. Cabot and Addams both acknowledge that global capitalism in its current form invites serious questions about oppression, domination, and exclusion. Indeed, Addams moves away from her idea of economic interdependence in her *Newer Ideals of Peace* in 1906 on these grounds, suggesting that an obsession with economic success may merely fuel imperialism and militarism. Cabot, however, maintains that a sense of reciprocity fostered in international trade provides a natural form of Roycean insurance against bellicosity and carries with it the responsibility to tend to the interests of other nations and their citizenry. She voices this suggestion with an important caveat that speaks to Addams's concern: she argues that tending to the welfare of other states does not necessarily, or even often, entail military intervention in the affairs of foreign powers. To identify the dependence of America on other nations is not an invitation to invade these nations on the grounds of national security. Cabot is quite clear on this point. Military means are to be used only as a last resort when a nation faces a clear and present danger to its sovereignty and its ideals; indeed Cabot is even more cautious, stating that only in this case "*may* war be right."[52] She continues, revealing her faith in diplomacy and the power of patience: "But we must always say as a last resort, that is after all honorable means have failed, for the prevention of war, like the prevention of disease, is mainly due to a right state of living before the crisis comes."[53] Cabot's approach to foreign affairs appeals to particular ideals—sovereignty, democracy, and the rule of law—but it does not set freedom on the march. Instead, Cabot carefully weighs the consequences of military interventionism against the risks of not taking action. She recognizes that prevention and peaceful reconciliation is always preferable to the forced and unstable peace that conclude many military conflicts, and she realizes that thinking is a practical activity that can effect political chance, at home and abroad. To this effect, Cabot notices that war is often the easiest possible course of action. It is thoughtful reflection and motivating dialogue that is hard to come by: "Deep thinking is tough work; and often harder than deep ploughing of a field and much harder than shouldering a gun."[54] In a nation that remains obsessed with the ideals of activity and progress, Cabot's emphasis on deep thinking and reflection remains as necessary as it is unusual.

CONCLUSION: LOYALTY FROM THE GROUND UP

Ella Lyman Cabot was an idealist in the most literal sense of the word. She believed that ideas mattered in the course of human activity and that ethical education depends as much on moral vision (*eido*) as it does on forceful action. Deep thinking, according to Cabot, involves seeing the "why" that underpins the "how" of activism. When we think deeply, Cabot suspects that we will notice that certain actions are not necessary, or natural, or even advisable. Reflection must temper the pragmatic desire to effect change in the world of human affairs. This is something that Cabot claims is often lost on Dewey and James in their enthusiastic plans for social and political reform. While James proposes that the "gilded youth" be drafted into civil service in order to simulate the hardships of war, Cabot has her doubts about the wisdom of idealizing militarism in any form. James often seems to suggest that warfare, as the odd mixture of boyhood lark and vision quest, is a way of enlivening the body and spirit. Cabot, on the other hand, does not advocate hardihood for the sake of hardihood (a position that James repeatedly expresses), but rather suggests that our strenuous efforts must be made in the spirit of loyalty to a moral cause. Identifying this moral cause does not involve more activity, but rather more reflection. In this regard, Cabot echoes Socrates' comment to Crito that forceful movements are good only to the degree that they are pointed in the right direction. What human beings need is not just a "good workout" but to work out the thoughtful pursuits and causes of a meaningful life. Loyalty is not a matter of brawn, but of brains.

If we return to most of Cabot's "peace heroes" we can identify a variety of causes worthy of our loyal dedication: the emancipation of slaves, the rights of women, the defense of vulnerable nations, and the care of the sick. She chooses her heroes not on the basis of the *intensity* of their actions, but on the ideals that guide their lives. At the heart of each ideal is a "superior principle" that Royce terms a "loyalty to loyalty." This loyalty to loyalty involves pursuing causes that enable others to be loyal to their own interests and purposes. For example, the emancipation of slaves was a cause worthy of loyalty to the extent that it allowed African Americans to freely form a new and personal set of loyalties and commitments—in other words, to advance the cause of loyalty in an increasing number of forms. It is worth noting that this general moral principle is neither exclusionary nor totalizing.

Imagine for a moment that Cabot had introduced her course on citizenship with the ethical command: "Be loyal to loyalty." Imagine that she tried to analyze the technical meaning and logical justification of this imperative for her young students. One hardly has to imagine the vacant stares, confused looks, and restless legs. In a certain sense, it is easy to understand how Royce's instruction to be "loyal to loyalty" may be construed as an abstract tautology, as a general direction to obey an even more general principle. If a teacher began by outlining the lofty goal of universal and ever-growing loyalty, many students would remain "out of touch," unable to grasp the meaning of a difficult concept. Cabot's course in ethics and citizenship is effective and interesting to the extent that she teaches Royce's philosophy of loyalty not as a concept, but as a unique way of life. She teaches the lesson of loyalty from the ground up, focusing on the concrete ways in which her students can embody and emulate ethical behaviors. The moral exemplars that she develops seize the imagination *even before* the case for particular ethical principles is made. Before they know it, students who act out these stories have begun to develop a moral sense and reflect commitments that can be made explicit in the later stages of ethical training. When they are made explicit, these concepts have already taken root in the lives and activities of Cabot's readers. In effect we discover that *Our Part in the World* is not some abstract destination, but rather an actual place where we can get down to the thoughtful business of living.

NOTES

1. William James, *Talks to Teachers on Psychology* (Boston: Holt, 1900), 241.
2. A 139/369.
3. Josiah Royce, *The Philosophy of Loyalty* (New York: Macmillan Press, 1908), 260. There is an interesting correspondence between this passage and Thomas Carlyle's *On Heroes, Hero-Worship and the Heroic in History*. In this book, one that influences both Royce and Cabot, Carlyle writes: "Hero-worship is the deepest root of all; the tap-root, from which in a great degree all the rest were nourished and grow. . . . Worship of a Hero is transcendent admiration of a Great Man. I say great men are still admirable; I say there is, at bottom, nothing else admirable! No nobler feeling than this of admiration for one higher than himself dwells in

the breast of men." In Thomas Carlyle, *On Heroes, Hero-Worship and the Heroic in History* (London: Chapman Publishing, 1894), 10. What is especially interesting is that Cabot widens the conception of hero beyond the "Great Man" to include women.

4. Josiah Royce, *The Philosophy of Loyalty* (New York: Macmillan, 1920), 262.
5. Ella Lyman Cabot, *Ethics for Children* (New York: Houghton Mifflin, 1910), 2.
6. Ella Lyman Cabot, *Seven Ages of Childhood* (New York: Houghton Mifflin, 1921), 45.
7. Cabot, *Seven Ages of Childhood*, 45.
8. Cabot, *Seven Ages of Childhood*, 40.
9. Cabot, *Ethics for Children*, 61.
10. Here we come across the aspect of the moral imagination that Steven Fesmire has highlighted in the work of John Dewey. Steven Fesmire, *John Dewey and the Moral Imagination: Pragmatism in Ethics* (Bloomington: University of Indiana Press, 2003).
11. Cited in Oliver Wendell Holmes, *Emerson* (New York: Houghton Mifflin, 1885), 297.
12. Holmes, *Emerson*, 297.
13. HUG 1755. Box 64. Lecture V. p. 2.
14. Ella Lyman Cabot, ed., *A Course in Citizenship* (New York: Houghton Mifflin, 1914), 129.
15. Cabot, *A Course in Citizenship*, xiv.
16. Ella Lyman Cabot, *Everyday Ethics* (New York: Henry Holt and Co., 1906), 207.
17. Sarah Gertrude Millin, *Rhodes* (London: Chatto and Windus, 1933), 138.
18. Royce's appreciation for cultural diversity is reflected in *Race Questions and Provincialism* (1908) and in the articles, written prior to 1908, that found their way into this book. For example, in 1902, Royce encourages a respect for local loyalties in "Provincialism: A Plea for Stronger Local Sentiment to Restrain National Heedlessness," an address that he gives at the Iowa meeting of the Phi Beta Kappa Society in June 1902. See HUG 1755. Box 47.
19. HUG 1755. Folder 92. p. 4a.
20. HUG 1755. Folder 92. p. 4.
21. HUG 1755. Folder 92. p. 24.
22. HUG 1755. Folder 92. p. 64.
23. HUG 1755. Folder 92. p. 90.
24. Friedrich Holderlin, cited in Martin Heidegger, "The Question Concerning Technology," in *The Basic Writings of Martin Heidegger*, ed. David Krell (New York: HarperCollins, 1993), 333.
25. Cabot, *Everyday Ethics*, 173.
26. Cabot, *Everyday Ethics*, 147.
27. Cabot, *Everyday Ethics*, 117.
28. Cabot, *Everyday Ethics*, 117.
29. Henry David Thoreau, *Walden and Civil Disobedience* (New York: Sparks Publishing, 2005), 268.
30. Cornell West, *The American Evasion of Philosophy: A Genealogy of Pragmatism* (Milwaukee: University of Wisconsin, 1989).
31. Cabot, *Everyday Ethics*, ix.
32. Cabot, *Everyday Ethics*, 236.
33. Cabot, *Everyday Ethics*, 236.
34. Cabot, *Everyday Ethics*, 236.
35. Cabot, *Everyday Ethics*, 237.
36. William James, *Talks to Teachers on Psychology* (Boston: Holt, 1900), 291.
37. Royce makes this process explicit in *The Problem of Christianity* (1913) when he states that his lectures have expanded the sphere of loyalty by beginning with "the more natural or the more primitive types of loyalty,—types such as grow out of family life, and tribal solidarity and war" and moving progressively to more inclusive forms. See Josiah Royce, *The Problem of Christianity* (New York: Macmillan and Co., 1913), 170.
38. Cabot, *Everyday Ethics*, xviii.
39. Ella Lyman Cabot, *Our Part in the World* (Boston: Beacon Press, 1918), 194.
40. Cabot, *Our Part in the World*, 194.
41. Cabot, *Our Part in the World*, 46.

42. Cabot, *Our Part in the World*, 47.
43. West, *The American Evasion of Philosophy*.
44. West, *The American Evasion of Philosophy*.
45. Cabot, *Our Part in the World*, 45.
46. Cabot, *Our Part in the World*, 89.
47. Cabot, *Our Part in the World*, 84.
48. Josiah Royce, *War and Insurance* (New York: Macmillan, 1914), xlviii.
49. A 139/319.
50. A 139/319.
51. Cited in Jane Addams, *Newer Ideals of Peace* (University of Illinois Press, 1907), xvi.
52. Addams, *Newer Ideals of Peace*, 106.
53. Addams, *Newer Ideals of Peace*, 106.
54. Addams, *Newer Ideals of Peace*, 106.

Chapter Seven

"Thought Is Never at Rest": Ella Lyman Cabot and the Struggle of Idealism

Even the most famous authors have their hidden passages. One of Emerson's is scrawled on a loose sheet and tucked into a notebook from 1870 titled "The Law of Mind." Here, an aging man looks back on the power of recollection: "I do not think violent changes of opinion often occur in strong men. As far as I know, they do not often see new lights, and turn sharp corners: but commonly, after 20 or 50 years, you shall find the individual turn to his earlier tendencies."[1] After forty years, the Cabots returned to their point of departure, to a book that they had shared as newlyweds on the hills of northern Italy, to the many scenes that they had memorized through years of an extraordinary union. They returned, in the twilight of Ella Lyman Cabot's life, to the passages from the *Divine Comedy*.

Rereading any book is a journey of both expectancy and immediacy. We have some idea as to the destination, and remain on the lookout for the path marks that guided us in the past. Indeed, there is some comfortable pleasure in the familiar approach. A specific terminus, however, is not what calls us forward in our rereading. In part, it is a vague but definite sense of direction that keeps us on the move. In part, it is that the well loved book has changed in our time apart. The mutability of the text is a reflection of the reader's angle of vision that has been widened by the passage of time. Certain bits of text stand out on a second pass, others recede, and still others are not read at all. We are drawn into unexpected openings in the text and the immediacy seizes us anew. These textual clearings look like places that we have never seen before.

When the Cabots reread the *Divine Comedy* in the summer of 1934, Ella Lyman Cabot remembered something of the youthful exuberance and hopeful idealism of 1894. The world had changed, however, and it seems very likely that Dante's masterpiece had also been transformed for this American Beatrice. The Victorian idealism that she had known as a young woman had finally faded in the face of imperialism, a Great War, and a greater Depression—factors that had destroyed the high hopes of Western civilization. American Transcendentalism and utopianism had been destroyed, or at least transmogrified, when these social and political factors had jeopardized the uniquely American project of creating a heaven on earth. The celestial city, in Josiah Royce's words, was very much "out of sight."[2] The world had been inherited, temporarily, by pragmatists with more "realistic" visions, but they too had been blamed for the crises of the early twentieth century and were forced to relinquish control. Their rhetoric of practical consequences, progressive education, and political reconciliation seemed out of kilter with a world governed by physical necessity, marred by radical injustice, and defined by social and political strife. The department of social ethics at Harvard that the Cabots had spearheaded at the turn of the century had run aground by 1927. In 1928, the couple attempted to revive the philosophical conferences that Royce had proposed at the turn of the century as a way of bringing philosophy down to earth, but Royce was gone and the Cabots' friends in academia were too busy publishing to tarry with such "applied" projects. The age of professional philosophy had begun in New England and classical American philosophy receded into that supposedly barren field of intellectual history. This was the setting for the Cabots' rereading of the *Divine Comedy*, a book that had launched their study of philosophy and religion and that maintained the intimate connection between ideas and action.

Dante's *Divine Comedy* begs to be reread. Its hundred cantos expand and contract, held together in its flexible *terza rima*, creating a living text that lives and moves and has its being as an organic whole. Its metrical complexity, one that reflects order and novelty, is rivaled only by its depictions of the workings of nature and the human mind. Indeed, the draw of the *Divine Comedy* lies in its uncanny ability to return its readers to nature, and more specifically, to the inner life of *human* nature.

As Virgil leads Dante through the Inferno, we are presented with an ascending typology of human dispositions: self-love, violence, and malice. This is the stuff of life, presented in all of its immediacy and jarring detail. Let us take the rare opportunity to be honest—this is the stuff of *our* lives. If the pragmatic mandate is to attend to human experience, this book is a good place to start. Dante's brilliance was not in his ability to render, with excruciating accuracy, the shortcomings and triumphs of our moral struggle, but rather to enshrine these renderings of everyday life in the eternity of the hereafter. This is, after all, a story of the afterlife. The fixity and familiarity of the Inferno is particularly frightening; no one cares to twaddle in this not so imaginary place. The spheres of the Inferno and Paradiso neither change with the passing years nor give way to one another in a type of moving progression. Achilles and Cleopatra, two individuals who were overcome by sensual desire, will always be found in the second sphere of the Inferno. Similarly, Thomas Aquinas and Saint Bonaventure will always be found in the fourth circle of Paradiso. Some things do not change in our rereading. We are able to return to these static snapshots of heaven and hell in order to catch sight of ourselves, to get an unmoving glimpse of human nature in the uncanny mirror that Dante provides.

While some characters of the *Comedy* remain permanently stuck in their respective spheres, Dante suggests that others might move freely through an array of spiritual realms. Sandwiched between the eternity of heaven and hell, purgatory exists in time, and its inhabitants spend this time in the tasks of repentance and atonement. This mountain isle provides the allegorical stage for the passion play of a moral existence. This is not a story of a distant hereafter, but a spiritual instruction manual for this life. On each cornice of purgatory, Dante discovers the struggles of virtue and the pitfalls of vice. This point was not lost on the Cabots, who repeatedly found themselves in similar ethical trials. Ella Lyman Cabot was intimately familiar with the interpretation of the *Divine Comedy* presented by her granduncle James Russell Lowell, who had single handedly made a place for Dante in nineteenth-century New England. She listens carefully to Lowell when he describes the ethical import of the *Divine Comedy*:

> Let us consider briefly what was the plan of the Divina Commedia and Dante's aim in writing it, which, if not to justify, was at least to illustrate, for warning and example, the ways of God to man. The higher intention of the poem was to set forth the result of sin, or unwisdom, and of virtue, or wisdom, in this life and consequently in the life to come which is but the continuation and fulfillment of this.[3]

The cantos of purgatory reflect Lowell's claim, depicting the actual work that is entailed in pursuing an ethical ideal; it is on these formidable slopes that the business of life is done, where dreams and hopes are lost and found. And they *are* lost and found. There is no easy way through purgatory. Even the Cabots found out that the best laid plans often turn out badly and that good intentions can easily go astray. We slip and struggle with our ethical burdens, rocks that tumble down steep hills that seem to have no bottom. Unfortunately, it does not take real genius or imaginative insight to empathize with the shades found on purgatory's first tier; we are all too familiar with the fallibility that is discovered on this mountain. What separates purgatory from hell, however, is the subtle sense that progress can be made despite, and perhaps in virtue of, these unavoidable struggles. This is a new form of idealism, the type that maintains that ideals are real and life-giving, but that their realization is partial and provisional. As Lowell states, "the poem is a diary of the human soul in its journey upwards from error through repentance to atonement with God."[4] No single sentence better describes the strain of American idealism with which Ella Lyman Cabot identified. Indeed, Royce's philosophical corpus could be outlined in precisely these terms. This form of idealism was initiated in *The Religious Aspect of Philosophy* (1885) with an argument for the possibility of error, took a darker existential turn in the Graham Lectures (1896) and "The Problem of Job" (1897), proceeded through *The World and the Individual* (1902) in its pursuit of an interpretative insight that might overcome error, and finally arrived at a lasting commitment to *The Hope of the Great Community* (1916). This final work continues to idealize forms of insight that can never be achieved in the span of one lifetime. This journey of atonement, away from error in the pursuit of an ideal, is the essence of Roycean idealism. *Its essence is in the struggle*; and as Royce states quite clearly in the "Problem of Job," the true idealist must be at home in wandering. More often than not, this is a lonely and uncomfortable domicile, but it is one that is made marginally more bearable by the belief that one pursues an ideal or cause that transcend one's "individual" life.

The transcendent character of such causes, however, are somewhat problematic for they appear, by definition, to be causes that will never be reached. They are, in fact, lost causes. In negotiating this tension, it is no coincidence that Royce turns to Dante in his *Lectures on Modern Idealism* as the archetype of an idealistic thinker. In these lectures, first delivered in 1906 at the peak of his exposure to the Cabots, Royce suggests that Dante's *Vita Nouva* presents the manner in which an individual can find meaning in the midst of struggle, in the pursuit of an ethical ideal that remains seemingly out of reach. In the *Vita Nouva*, Dante extends his pursuit of Beatrice, the elusive ideal of beatific love. Beatrice was a lost cause that made purgatory a bit more bearable.

LOST CAUSES, IDEALISM, AND PRAGMATISM

Richard Cabot was only partially correct when he called Ella Lyman Cabot his Beatrice. Like the idealization of Beatrice, she remained, both for her husband and for the broader Cambridge community, a largely hidden figure, an unknown ideal of chastity and devout ethical service. This American Beatrice had led Richard Cabot through many of his trials as an ethicist, as a doctor, and as a person. Looking back through the lens of contemporary feminism, Cabot appears as a tragic figure, tied to the imagination of her male companion. Unlike Dante's character, however, Ella Lyman Cabot was a full fledged participant in the working of the couple's moral projects and sensed with bone jarring clarity the obstacles that face ethical idealism. While Dante and Virgil tramp through the underworld, Beatrice remains a remote figment of their imagination. Ella Lyman Cabot, however, was not a character but rather a person who worked through the questions of human experience in order to pursue ideals of growth in her own life and in those of her familiars. Ada McCormick reflected on this fact after Cabot's death, stating that, "were ELC not here to influence RCC, he might lapse into boyish intolerance and become a prophet where he sits aloft and reaches down to pat heads."[5] Even before their marriage, Ella Lyman cut Richard Cabot down to size and forced both of them to face their ethical struggles without pretense. And struggle they did. While many of the trials of idealism that the Cabots faced led to new and innovative ideas and writings, others remain problematically unresolved. This concluding chapter does not seek to resolve these conflicts of life and philosophy, but only to expose the tensions that accompanied the Cabots' idealism. The causes that the couple pursued were, and in some cases remain, lost. A moment should be taken to reflect on the meaning and structure of at least one of these lost causes.

When Richard's older brother Ted, who had suffered from diabetes, fell ill with his final bout of consumption in 1893, a young Ella Lyman was on the scene as his primary companion during his last days. According to McCormick many of Lyman's friends had speculated that she had in fact fallen in love with Ted when she accompanied the Cabots to Saranac, New York for their summer camping trips beginning in the early 1890s. This is not a stretch. There was much to love about Ted Cabot. Head of the glee club at Harvard, president of his fraternity, captain of the University football squad, and exquisitely intelligent, he was the chosen child in a chosen family. Letters between *this* Cabot and Lyman indicate that *they* were reading Dante together in the spring of 1891. Ella, who was several years older than Ted's younger brother, Richard, was happy to be a part of Ted Cabot's group of friends and cherished the time spent together. As Ted's health declined, his mother and sister implored Ella Lyman to spend more time at the Cabot house, seeing that she was one of the few people with whom Ted still wished to spend time. Lyman obliged, spending weeks at a time with his family. Today, diabetes is a manageable disease, but at the turn of the century it was a rather nasty way to die. While only a few comments on Ted's death have been preserved in Ella Lyman Cabot's papers, one diary entry from the summer of 1893 seems to point to her relationship with this dying man. She writes:

> Hope never dies suddenly unless it is murdered. I even think that its ghost will haunt us. It asserts itself defiantly against all fact and reasoning and fear. You may trample it again and again but it does not die out. It is an unquenchable

fire. And this means something. It means most that on which the hope is founded is an immortal thing. Hope is the immortality of love and though its body may perish, its soul cannot die.[6]

What was this hope that Ella Lyman asserted defiantly against all fact and fear? Was it the hope for a fatally ill patient, or the hope of a person who seeks an impossible relationship, or perhaps the hope of a young woman philosopher in search of a meaningful intellectual life in a relatively unaccommodating world? These hopes did not die easily for Ella Lyman. She held out hope for Ted until the very end. She held out as long as possible before marrying his younger brother. Even in its most difficult moments, she held up this marriage as a philosophical experiment of idealism and feminism, hoping that it would yield personal and intellectual opportunities.

Throughout the fall of 1893, Richard routinely wrote to his mother and Ella concerning the care that was given to Ted, advising them on how to manage infection, what dietary restrictions would be most appropriate, and how to treat associated skin diseases. As Christopher Crenner has described, James Elliot Cabot wrote to Richard in October of this year, requesting that Richard become Ted's primary physician.[7] In Ted's last weeks, Richard, who had recently completed his medical training, agreed to assume responsibility for the healthcare of his ailing brother.

Richard Cabot's papers and correspondence are meticulously organized and meticulously redacted. The correspondence from 1893 cuts off sharply in October and does not pick up again for several months; no mention of Ted's disease exists in letters dated after November 4, 1893. Crenner accurately notes that this archival ellipsis obscures a family secret. This secret was also a trial that Ella and Richard Cabot would have to face as they crafted their ethical philosophies in the subsequent forty years. In one of the final letters to be preserved from 1893, Richard writes to Ella that, "Ted goes down hill steadily. . . . I can only be thankful for it as he does not suffer—the quicker the better now."[8] Richard's desire to limit Ted's suffering drew him, and Ella, into a profoundly difficult ethical position, one that would remain unknown to the Cabot's closest friends and relatives. In August of 1936, Richard Cabot broke the silence surrounding Ted's death, revealing to Ada McCormick his story of how, in his words, to "kill the person that you love the best."[9] Richard did love his brother Ted the best, idolizing this young man who was seven years his senior, commenting repeatedly on his enviable abilities at philosophy, a discipline Richard would later attempt to make his own. Richard Cabot remembered that to witness Ted's mind at work was "like being present—it is being present—at the creation of the world."[10] This idol, Ted, died on the 10th of November, 1893. His mouth and nose were covered by a towel soaked in chloroform, a towel held in place by Richard Cabot.

As Crenner has outlined, Richard Cabot was tortured with the decision to euthanize his brother. This struggle, however, was not as much an internal matter of heart as the struggle to convince his mother and father that it was the best course of action in regard to the treatment of their dying son. Elizabeth Cabot acquiesced rather quickly, but James Elliot Cabot was slow to give his permission. In his interview with McCormick, Richard Cabot recounted the many nights that were spent shuttling between Ted's bed and his father's study to convince the elder Cabot of the pain that Ted was experiencing. Richard maintained that his father eventually agreed to the plan that was carried out. Ted himself, however, was not given the chance to agree. Richard did not obtain his brother's consent as he moved forward with his act of mercy killing. In light of this, Ted's final moments are especially haunting.

Having preformed the chloroform procedure, Richard Cabot stepped away from Ted's bed and turned toward the door. As he grasped the doorknob and left the empty room, a familiar voice rose from bed: "Richard gave up too soon—I wasn't dead."[11] It seems likely that Richard Cabot's career as a medical ethicist began right here: at his brother's bedside, finishing the difficult task that he had begun several minutes earlier. The questions concerning a patient's right to life, issues of informed consent, and honesty in diagnosis and in treatment must have come home to him with unprecedented clarity. This formative moment of personal and familial crisis reverberated through both of the Cabots' philosophical works, appearing most prominently in their later writings. In *Adventures on the Borderlands of Ethics* (1926), Richard reflects on the frustration and fallibility of the physician: "Humiliatingly often our remedies do no good; our failures stare at us in dumb reproach out the sick man's eyes."[12] This reproach must have been especially painful when it was expressed in the dead eyes of his beloved brother.

At this point, it seems appropriate to return to William James's assessment of Richard Cabot, which was mentioned at the outset of this book. James was right to say that Richard Cabot was in the process of putting a new moral tone into the whole medical professional life of Boston, but he was not wholly accurate to suggest that Cabot did this out of a self-conscious sense that he or his wife were "very good."[13] Neither Richard nor Ella Lyman Cabot viewed themselves as "very good." Instead of embracing the comfortable view, held by most us, that our moral lives are already well ordered, both of these individuals understood that our ethical projects are always somewhat deficient. In light of this, we can return to Cabot's observation that Royce's philosophy underscored the tragic character of life's projects in ways that were neglected by his pragmatic counterparts. It was the recognition of the tragic shortcomings of ethical life that keeps one's life on the move, striving forward toward greater fulfillment. For the Cabots, there was never a time to sit back and say "good enough." In Ella Lyman Cabot's 1892 quotation book, one finds a trace of this sentiment in a passage from the *Divine Comedy*: "It is clear to me that our thought is never at rest unless Absolute truth enlightens it."[14] It is interesting that Cabot is drawn to this particular passage. Dante's fictional journey comes to rest—the story ends—only when he reaches Paradise, bathed in the light of the Absolute. Until that point, he witnesses and takes part in the strivings of purgatory, strivings that are oddly similar to the strivings of our worldly affairs. I would hold that Cabot's interest in this passage had more to do with this unique struggle than with the final destination of rest. This woman philosopher is particularly interested in the self discovery and personal growth that occur in the darkness and confusion of error or shortcoming. Ella Lyman Cabot was possessed by this tragic fact; it was one that both she and Royce believed to be at the heart of every form of idealism since the early modern era. For Cabot and Royce, idealism did not require an individual, in Royce's words, to possess "any peculiar revelation as to what the content of absolute truth might be."[15] Indeed, if or when one *did* acquire such a revelation, the philosophical story would reach its end. Likewise, the practical and ethical story would also be over, since the bearer of this revelation could cease her search for deeper insight or greater fulfillment.

This is the dogmatic idealism that Cabot and Royce both eschewed. Quoting Royce, Mary Mahowald writes that for this type of idealist, "truth must always be related 'to action, to practice, to the will.'"[16] In Royce's *Lectures on Modern Idealism*, he writes that idealists are to continually pursue the truth as "a construction, an activity, a creation, an attainment."[17] Due to our finite capacities, this attainment will always be partial, but this is not necessarily a reason to jettison idealism. Indeed, for Royce, the experience of our finite wanderings gives us a hint of the Absolute. This is the core of his error argument developed in the 1880s. The meaningfulness of any particular error and truth depend on an Absolute Knower that realizes the totality of both. While Royce and Cabot seem to distance themselves from this position, both of these thinkers emphasize the indispensible role that the Absolute plays in the directedness of future experience. The pragmatists of the day, such as James and Dewey, were possessed with the idea of growth and activity, but Royce and Cabot realize that without an Absolute cause, the practical activities of individuals and their communities are often best described as degenerate change rather than genuine growth. In Mahowald's account of Royce, she highlights the way in which the metaphysical speculations of the idealist—all of this talk about the Absolute—should be in the business of "directing our will, in defining our attitude toward the Universe, and making articulate and practical our ideals and resolutions."[18] It should not be in the business of idle talk about the Absolute, or in defining in no uncertain terms what this absolute ideal is or could be. Instead the idealist should diligently pursue ideals and objectives, even, and perhaps especially, those ideals that remain unattainable. That is to say that Cabot and Royce were the types of idealists who pursued lost causes.

The care of Ted Cabot is but one of many lost causes that Ella Lyman Cabot pursued. Many other events and topics could be explored along these lines. Her attempt to enter the field of philosophy, her efforts to pursue a teaching career, her struggles with productivity and self doubt, her ambivalence concerning childrearing, and her attempt to integrate progressive ideals and traditional religious values—all of these topics reflect the ways that distant ideals served as motivating causes that inevitably remained beyond Cabot's reach. In a recent presentation on lost causes and Royce's writings, Mahowald writes that:

> Probably like most of you, like most people, I have pursued other lost causes. These are all describable as lost because they posit impossibly reachable ideals. So why do I pursue them? Because by aiming to reach them through my practical decisions and actions, I believe their achievement is facilitated at least a little. And therein lies the pragmatic element of my idealism: as Royce would put it, the practical purposiveness of my ideals. Or as James might put it in his pragmatic theory of truth: pursuing these ideals really works.[19]

And they worked for Ella Lyman Cabot as well. The "practical purposiveness" of Cabot's ideals—the belief that women could be every bit as talented as men, that privilege entailed social responsibility, that marriage was to set one free rather than to constrain one's behavior—led Cabot to seize numerous opportunities in both the private and public spheres. Only a small number of these opportunities have been outlined in the previous pages. In her 1902 paper on the relation of chance to purpose, Cabot writes that, "Chances leap to meet the man with a strong purpose. . . . [T]he man of no particular purpose talks ruefully of chance in general, the man of purpose follows the game, says 'Here's my chance!' and takes it."[20] The writer of this passage was not a *man* of purposes, but rather a woman who pursued the broadest of causes with varying success. The expression "varying success" seems appropriate since, despite Cabot's stellar education and publishing record, she taught only one lecture course at the university level (at Berkeley in 1911–1912). She taught steadily at Pine Manor College in Wellesley, but the small size of this women's college stood in marked contrast to the breadth and depth of her Harvard–Radcliffe experience. Cabot was ahead of her time, or at least ahead of the time when women would take up the premier positions in the academic centers of New England. There is a reason why the first women philosophers, working at the end of nineteenth century, flourished only in the forward looking frontiers of St. Louis, Chicago, and Syracuse: the traditionalism and conservatism of the Northeast kept women like Ella Lyman Cabot "in their place" until the 1930s. As a member of the board of Radcliffe College (1902–1934), Cabot oversaw the coming of this more progressive age, but it was not her age.

Despite this, Ella Lyman Cabot pursued feminist ideals as only a Roycean idealist could. Mahowald points us to the way that pursuing objectives with "varying success" fit quite nicely with Royce's notion of an idea as being a "state of mind, or complex of states, that, when present, is consciously viewed as the *relatively completed embodiment* and therefore already as the *partial fulfillment of a purpose*."[21] In seeking the meaning of gender equality in the field of philosophy, Cabot pursued the "partial" or provisional fulfillment of a purpose. As Mahowald suggests, "despite the widespread assumption that idealism is incompatible with pragmatism, [Royce's] definition of an idea includes the pragmatic concepts of embodiment and purpose [practical intent]."[22] As Royce explains, the type of purpose that Cabot held dear could be best described as a lost cause to the extent that it outlived its pursuer. At this point, it seems wise to turn our attention back to the detailed discussion of interests in chapter five; indeed, Cabot's description of interests mirrors Royce's characterization of causes. Interests, according to Cabot, are life giving precisely to the degree that they are freely held, personally felt, and transcendent in nature. Interests are transcendent in two important related ways. First, they are future oriented, directed toward objectives that can be achieved only in coming moments. Second, at their best, interests are pursued by communities of individuals who are bound together by loyalty to a common cause. Here, we hear echoes of Cabot's claim that the art of life is "becoming other people"—who we are as individuals turns on our ability to become something else, and to do so in communities that support our growth. Lost causes are really only lost to discrete individuals, who pass away, rather tragically, in the course of a finite number of years. In the midst of this tragedy, however, lost causes are "found" and achieve greater fulfillment by communities whose life and purpose stretch into the distant future. It is not only the lost cause that outlives the individual who pursues it; it is also the case that communities literally "carry on," shouldering the weight of a cause that is yet to be fulfilled.

"TRUMPING CYNICISM"[23]: THE FUTURE OF IDEALISM

The foregoing chapters have highlighted several strands of a forgotten philosophy. I believe it is a philosophy that has been forgotten or, perhaps more accurately, overlooked, for a number of interesting reasons. Exploring these reasons might grant us fresh perspectives on our present society and the current state of professional philosophy. I will quickly retrace the path that I have tried to cut and attempt to take account of the new perspectives this study might grant.

Ella Lyman Cabot was born into a life of privilege, into the cultural and intellectual crucible of American philosophy. The wealth and social status of the Lyman family would have allowed this young woman to live quite comfortably within the narrow gender roles of nineteenth century Boston Brahmin culture. It would have allowed her to do so under the guise of "the proper" or "the good" or "the just." Privilege, in every age, comes hand in hand with the story of ethical righteousness. Ella Lyman Cabot, however, like Peirce in "The Fixation of Belief," did not believe this story. She knew that social acceptability should not be confused for the good or the true, and she, like Peirce, was deeply suspicious of what Peirce called the "moral terrorism" by which society often enforces its norms.[24] Starting at an early age, Cabot faced this terrorism with resolve and went against the grain, forming social relationships and a professional reputation that did not quite fit the standards of elite, Northeast culture. The development of the "Paper on Marriage," her abiding interest in professional philosophy, and her philanthropy and social service stood opposed to the expectations of her family and neighbors.

There is a tendency, or habit of thought, to think that one's present state—what one is doing right now—is morally sufficient. This is also to say that traditionalism or habit often doubles as moral rectitude. Habit is, after all, so comfortable. How could something so comfortable be wrong? *Quite easily*, Cabot answers. We, as a culture, do not like this type of answer. It strikes us as moralizing, or old fashioned, or retrograde. In fact, such answers are not old fashioned but rather forward looking, exploring possibilities that are often neglected in the humdrum, and unethical routine, of daily affairs. This is a point that I attempted to highlight in chapters three and four in the discussion of contingency, chance, and the moral imagination. Cabot's ethical stance did not culminate in a pronouncement on our moral dysfunction or laziness; rather, it terminates in a series of practical suggestions about how to make our lives better, both in the sense of more ethical and in the sense of more meaningful. Paying careful attention to the way that chance occurrences can translate into meaningful personal opportunities is not an abstract suggestion but rather one that allowed Cabot to seize upon the unique chances she was given as a student at Radcliffe, interacting with the greatest minds of her day. Similarly, her focus on the moral imagination was a product of her, as a woman working in a male dominated field, negotiating the barriers that she confronted. By the time Cabot arrived at President Hoover's White House dinner in 1930, she had grasped the fact that while certain avenues of personal development might be closed to her on the basis of gender, others might allow her to apply her philosophical studies in practical and wide ranging pursuits. This was the case with her involvement with the American Peace League, beginning in the second decade of the twentieth century, and in her extensive writing on moral psychology.

Cabot attempts to shift idealism away from its traditional rendering as being monistic and dogmatic toward a way of thinking that emphasizes possibility without foregoing purpose. This is no small task, especially in an age that seems determined to ignore its potential and to dismiss purpose as the outdated dream of a bygone age. The cynicism of our current age is, at least in part, understandable. It stems from a collective disappointment that the ideals that we once pursued remain unfulfilled. Yes, the pursuit of lost causes can generate cynicism and apathy instead of ongoing motivation. Ella Lyman Cabot's thinking, however, was both defined by a loyalty to lost causes and avoided, on the whole, the cynical sense that these causes were worthless. In this respect, her philosophy provides a helpful suggestion for our weary age, and perhaps, for the weary discipline of philosophy.

There is reason to be weary. The causes reflected in Cabot's writing and life are still only partially fulfilled. As Linda Alcoff recently observed, only twenty percent of professional philosophers are women.[25] Cabot's Paper on Marriage is brought into a new light when Alcoff explains the tension between the study of academic philosophy and the expectations and burdens of raising a family. Alcoff relates her hesitancy in continuing a pregnancy while working toward her masters in philosophy in a male dominated department, in classes led by professors who held the heteronormative belief that women ought to remain at home rather than venture out into academia.[26] Cabot also experienced this tension, and set the stage for women such as Alcoff and others who would manage to further the cause of gender equality in philosophy in more definite ways. This cause, however, remains problematically out of reach for many women. The entrenchment of this problem cannot be traced to a single cause. In an academic discipline that claims to have a corner on the understanding of ethical conduct, it may come as a surprise that women continue to be marginalized, discriminated against, and harassed. Perhaps this is because philosophers, as a general rule, believe that they are above reproach. Oddly enough, their "expertise" in ethics may make them unwilling or unable to recognize the moral blind spots in their own conduct or professional discipline. As Sally Haslanger's extensive scholarship has shown, women authors and articles on women's issues are systematically rejected at the premier philosophical journals.[27] Similarly, historical studies that might rework the canon of Western philosophy, so as to include women such as Ella Lyman Cabot, are often not even considered by reviewers at philosophical periodicals.

The irony in neglecting a thinker such as Ella Lyman Cabot is that it is her writing—focusing on the imagination, patience, insight, and loyalty to distant goals—might convince us to go in search of other lost figures and lost causes. It is her writing that could open us up to possibilities that might change our lives, that is, if we allow them to. In her assessment of the present state of women in philosophy, Alcoff writes that we must "fight the cynicism that such persistent problems can sometimes engender."[28] The recovery of the philosophy of Ella Lyman Cabot is but one small attempt to fight this cynicism, to pursue ideals that remain, *for the time being*, beyond our grasp.

NOTES

1. Collected Papers of Ralph Waldo Emerson. Houghton Library. Harvard University. bMS Am 1280.212 (15).
2. Josiah Royce, *The World and the Individual* (New York: Macmillan, 1920), 259.
3. James Russell Lowell, *Aids to the Study of Dante*, ed. Charles Allen Dinsmore et al. (New York: Houghton Mifflin, 1903), 416.
4. James Russell Lowell, "The Shadow of Dante," *The North American Review* 115 (1872), 148.
5. Richard Clarke Cabot Papers. Harvard University Archives. 4255.80. Box 1. "Research Material for Ada McCormick."
6. A 139/320.
7. Christopher Crenner, *Private Practice in the Early Twentieth Century Office of Dr. Richard Cabot* (Baltimore: Johns Hopkins University Press, 2005).
8. Cited in Crenner, *Private Practice*, 190.
9. HUG 4255.80. Box 4.
10. HUG 4255.80. Box 4, 190.
11. HUG 4255.80. Box 4, 194.
12. Richard Clarke Cabot, *Adventures on the Borderlands of Ethics* (New York: Houghton Mifflin, 1926), 27.
13. Cited in Linda Simon, *Genuine Reality: A Life of William James* (Chicago: University of Chicago Press, 1999), 358.
14. A 139/320.
15. Cited in Mary Mahowald, *An Idealistic Pragmatism* (The Hague: Martinus Nijhoff, 1972), 25.
16. Mahowald, *An Idealistic Pragmatism*, 25.
17. Mahowald, *An Idealistic Pragmatism*, 25.
18. Mahowald, *An Idealistic Pragmatism*, 6.
19. Mary Mahowald, "Lost Causes and Royce's Pragmatic Idealism." Presented at the 2009 meeting of the Society for the Advancement of American Philosophy. Permission to reprint was granted to the author.
20. A 139/320v.
21. Cited in A 139/320v.1.
22. Cited in A 139/320v.
23. This phrase, "trumping cynicism," appears often in the work of John McDermott. See John J. McDermott, *The Drama of Possibility* (New York: Fordham University Press, 2007), 476.
24. CP 358.
25. Linda Martin Alcoff, ed., *Singing in the Fire: Stories of Women in Philosophy* (Lanham, MD: Rowman & Littlefield Publishers, 2003).
26. Alcoff, *Singing in the Fire*, 2.

27. Haslanger has compiled a number of groundbreaking articles on these subjects in Sally Haslanger, "Changing the Culture of Philosophy: Not by Reason (Alone)" *Hypatia* 23, no. 2 (2008): 210–23.

28. Alcoff, *Singing in the Fire*, 9.

Appendix: Selected Writings of Ella Lyman Cabot

ASSORTED POETRY (1884–1915)

Reserve (Feb. 24, 1884)

    We live alone, thoughts that are deepest drawn
    And purest in our inner consciousness
    Abide undreamed by the common throng
    But to ourselves from God they wake to bless

    And yet though bitterness arises oft,
    Though in derision others dozed and laughed
    While we from highest fountain's draught
    The sweetest nectar for our spirits quaffed

    Still in the insight that comes but from prayer
    And through the visions that come but from love,
    Gaze we on angel's faces unaware
    And trust in man descends from God above.

    If that the moments are but short and faint
    That we to other souls do stand
    God's fellow-children may themselves acquaint
    Fixing in minutes space, eternity's great band

    Or yet unspoken there is a thing more deep
    Than words that may deceive or smiles that lie
    The being's self, sonnet for poet meet

The soul that cannot change and cannot die.

Oft we live on all silent with our friend
Trusting and loving, knowing not at all
Till that some flashes from the lightening rend
We see her moan and tremble but not fall.

Then we see the strength is from all high
A link to heaven sure though slender clean
Then can we love intenser, touch more nigh
And so to believe to trust and love again.

And so our trust in friends and men unfolds
And so our trust, great God of Love, in thee
Unveiled, eternal, to immortal souls
Infinite, unconcieved, who art and e'er shall be.

G. E. L. (George E. Lowell) (May 26, 1884)

Oh apple-blossoms, drop your snow-white leaves
    Alas! we weep;
The golden grain is gathered into sheaves
    The green we keep.
Our life is sadness, there is no soul but grieves
    Save those who sleep

The spring should be the time of laughing glee
    And man's best bliss
The axe stands waiting by the budding tree
    With poisoned kiss
And youth's bright promise, crushed by death we see,
    And life is this?

The birds are singing, the earth is bright,
    But he is dead,
The jeweled dewdrops sparkle in the light,
    But life has fled.
The flowers shed their fragrance, gladsome sight.
    Our hearts have bled.

Farewell to earthly pleasure, yet farewell;
    In God we trust.
The conquering anthem's changed to a funeral knell;
    The Lord is just.
Dark falls the pall of sorrow's silent spell;
    Dust turns to dust.

Philosophy and Nature (December 13, 1884)

What is our life? A sleep and a forgetting.
A happy rising and a painful setting
Bright with the aspirations of our youth
Dread with the fruitless searching after Truth

The sunlight's sparkling on the stream
The lilies node their heads and dream
The butterfly and bumble bee
Are seeking gold-dust airily

And is not purely truth our highest measure,
The greatest gift to man, and not merely pleasure
The highest gift, most absolute and new
Till when the precious words of wrong undo.

Look at the dewy glowing rose,
The fresh grass cooling all her glows
The deep blue fragrant summer sky
The insects buzzing as they fly.

Yet in the greatest life, not merely power,
Or wild ambitions that in bold hearts lower
Can be the deepest portion of the man
Without a love unfolding to mankind.

Untitled (Nov. 18, 1886)

What use in ponder, what use in solving
These old, old problems of the human soul!
Why not simplicity and sympathy,
An earnest and heartfelt striving towards life's goal
And a full fellowship of friendliness, that indeed
I would not bar from man, he should be free
Spite of vexed questions and unsure repose
To outstretched wide his arms in charity

For life shall ever be pleasure and pain
And noble yearnings up to duty, God.
Each as we seek the self-same end should help
With tenderness to widen and sustain
Our brothers yet be simple, truthful, aye.

God with His radiance maketh glad the sky.
Let us be glad, and we who feel within
The spark of endless life, let us help those whose eye

Vain seeking finds but bitterness, a cry.

I have been silent long, perchance I know not why.
Life's beauty deep has flooded in my way
Life's questions too, rapture and mystery.
Silent perhaps but to myself—
I trust I am more ready to take peace
With quicker understanding, wider though
In this wide world of God's, if less devout,
More consecrate, I hope, more ready for life's race.

M. W. H. (March 30, 1888)

The strength of other souls can be our strength,
The faith of deep—souled men become our own,
And as we lift our weary hands at length
We are not hopeless, utterly alone,
Because the blessing of the strong is ours.
If words could thank thee I would send them forth
To thank you for the hunger and the thirst
Thou gavest me for righteousness, a star
Deep set in holy skies, and thou at first
Known not but felt, thy courage makes me go
With earnestness, with patience, makes me know
That love and truth can triumph in despair
As god's sun lights the raindrop-saddened air.

Untitled (May 17, 1888)

There are long noontides when its seems that our lives
Will never change, how happy and how blest,
And watchful fear but for a moment strives
To lull itself with hope and be at rest.
'Tis changeless, all this flow of happy streams,
These treasured buds of friendship and of mirth,
These priceless gifts of health, and hallowed dreams
That make blue heaven near, not foot trod earth,
And then it comes so subtly and so still
In beauty or in joy yet not the same,
Another poem with only the old name,
New lines, not those that all our memory thrill
Cling to the old, yet brave accept the new
Life is all rich to him who dares to be true.

Werden (Feb. 4, 1889)

A world all fraught with pain,
Danger, and sudden shock,

But the triumphant soul
Standing a moveless rock,
Says "Werden," to become

Through all the hard-fought day,
With unknown future dread,
The soul which may not pray
For rescue lifts its head
With "Werden" to become

Oh faith, Oh courage strong,
Unspoken and half concealed,
To thee of right belong
The highest thing revealed
By "Werden" to become.

By thy strong, perfect life,
Lonely and sad yet true,
Thou showest amid all strife
The star that led us through
The Werden to become.

Insight (Feb. 4, 1889)

Make keen my ear, that I may never miss
One murmur of the voices of the infinite
That surge from human rapture, need and pain.
Make clear my eyes that, looking through a rift
Of clouded sky, I may not lose the star
Of beauty in a life that seems all sin.
Make sensitive my touch, that I may know
E'en through the blackness of unfathomed wrong
The need and tenderness of human souls
And thrill responsive to their slightest move.
And oh! Make strong my heart, and pure and wide
That touching, seeing, hearing this vast world,
Insight may find its truest way through love,
And pity know its deepest help in truth.

Untitled (May 19, 1889)

Victor! To write that word
Means in the field of battle to be scarred
With bitter piercing wounds,
And more than that
It means a conflict utterly more hard
In loneliness of spirit without sound.

Yet to be victor, this
Is power of future woven in one's soul,
New strength from weakness wrung,
Insight from snatches to the perfect whole.
It means assurance that we cannot fail,
Thought breathed in battle songs that heroes sung.

In glimpses such as these
We have power that is far beyond
What weaker moments teach.
Mine be the subtler strength
Won e'en from depths of loneliness and pain
Since triumph comes at length
Suffering is insight, bitterness is gain.

Solitudes (April 15, 1890)

Our lives are full of solitiudes
And wild untrodden ways,
Of haunts where ardent fancy broods
And smiling memory plays.
And budding hopes dream in the shade,
Deep-hidden like wood-bound glade.

Our lives are troubled with pain and woe
That we can never share
And not one human soul can know
The restless wave of care
That sweep with desolate roll
Over the lonely hung'ring soul.

Untitled

I love thee, oh, so dearly, Solitude,
On great wide pastures with the stars alone,
Or meadow green with four-leafed clover strewed,
By gay brooks tinkling words that are unknown
In music with its voice of noble praise
In thoughts that come with light from our days

And yet I love society if this
Mean meeting on high planes and soul to soul,
I love the sharing of redoubled bliss,
I love the laughter from pure fun that stole,
I love thy noble, fearless giving, all
That human lives can offer or can call;

And Solitude, I do but love thee when
Thou leadest me purer, stronger, back to men.

Untitled (1914)

Man does not keep his word, the word keeps him.
It is his armor against evil chance,
A shield from which all traitorous weapons glance,
A guard of stern, implacable cherubim

Man cannot break his word: The word outraged
Is still the master, man the wretched prey,
Rent, tortured, bleeding, whom Truth scorns to stay
Till all her dreadful vengence is assuaged

Look now on Europe. Belgium safe in pain,
Bleeding, betrayed, immortal, glorious,
Crowned with high crowns, three times victorious
Throned near the alter of her blessed slain.

And look at Germany, who tore the scroll,
Laughed at the compact, sneered at Truth and Faith;
Behold she learns in pangs of long-drawn breath
That little scrap of paper was her soul.

Untitled (August 1915)

Out of the new, the old. Each added year
Closer the well-knit strands of memory draws,
And in the holding of God's keeping here
No single stitch is dropped, no sound hath pause.
Into the old, the new. In song-filled ways,
In wreaths of scarlet berries and in dew,
In light that touch beloved eyes, in days
Of sunrise and sunset, all is new.

SELECTED PHILOSOPHICAL REFLECTIONS (1892–1902)

1892 Notebook (A 139/320v)

Insight and order Royce said are the elements essential to morality. Moral conduct involves 1) the power of appreciation of interests outside of your own, the recognition of the interests of others as real and 2) the ordering of our world out of chaos into self-possession. These are the two factors that cause all problems and all advance. We grow by newly acquired insight into moral truth by so enlarging our private self through love such that it becomes more and more a social self, bound up with the life of others—and by ordering our insight so that it becomes our permanent possession.

Royce's ethical motto: "Act so as to make more ties and stronger ones . . . that is to be LOYAL and loyalty includes sympathy and order."

March 14, 1892

The danger in living in a family and state surrounded by customs that seem unalterable and part of nature is that that very influence which is such an essential factor in one's development retards our swift advance. Family habits, so strong in their protective influence.

April 6, 1892

Dewey perhaps understates what Royce dwells on too much—the storm-stress aspects of life. Dewey's attitude is tremendously healthy . . . and he is not without feeling and appreciation as the half-unintentional touches in his books show. But could he possibly have such a wide sympathy as Royce with mystics and romanticists? Could he be as fair to them as Royce is? And if not is his position the best one! A healthy scorn for all things abstract and spiritual is a bracing tonic, but passion and pathos and the tragedy and mystery of life are real and sometimes so life-giving as to be the only world we can see and they must be met with understanding criticism not mere condemnation.

June 14, 1892

We owe Royce a very deep debt of gratitude for the courage and simplicity with which he has told of his own spiritual experiences. It is doubly convincing and inspiring because it is far more real when a man tells you in what a close way his philosophy coincides with his life. It helps me when I feel the faith, confidence and courage which his thought of the Absolute self gives to me. It moves me with grateful trust when he says: 'I have often found it deeply comforting in the most bitter moments.

The art of living is becoming other people. We are unfit to deal with the tragic vital world until we can see through others lives that we may anticipate, grapple, and respond to their need—living lives with—absolute understanding so that we can see all their point of view and beyond to what they really stand for. Oh God! Ever this lesson sink in deep!

Hope never dies suddenly unless it is murdered. I even think that its ghost will haunt us. It asserts itself defiantly against all fact and reasoning and fear. You may trample it again and again but it does not die out. It is an unquenchable fire. And this means something. It means most that on which the hope is founded is an immortal thing. Hope is the immortality of love and though its body may perish, its soul cannot die.

We talk about experience! Real experience teaches us everything in the world at once. I went to the concert to have it tell me the truth but her music murmured away on the surface and told me nothing. I know infinity but could not speak of it.

January 1893

Impersonal interests differ from personal in so far as they are impersonal such interests can be moulded to our tastes and our capacities, pursued ardently or given up without consulting anyone but ourselves. But when we deal with people, we are on harder and more delicate ground but the people are not merely our interests but are ends in themselves living sensitive beings capable of being hurt or helped as we may deal with them. Therefore I think all interests directly involving others must be dealt differently from impersonal interests. We can't postpone speaking an encouraging word to our friend as might postpone adding our accounts because something makes us too busy without hurting our relation to him but also it may be his efficiency in the world.

Men need women's experience and women men's, and need it in the future which the constant life together alone can give. No life can quite gain for itself by sympathy the richness of knowledge which men and women who love each other absorb from their close intimacy with each other and their children.

March 25, 1893

Live in the past! Live in the present! Live in the future! How impartial and unsatisfactory all of these are. Rather live as one being, for rationality consists precisely in that: in not forgetting, in not ignoring the past, present or future, but bringing all into the unity of a single purpose which is leavened in the past, is created in the present, and is growing toward, looking toward its future.

April 24, 1893

Moral sleeplessness may, I think be a danger for me. To be awake is good. To be sleepless is bad. It does not mark Richard because he is made so that alertness is food and refreshment. But not to have mental rest and quietness may be a strain for me. I can't physically bear very high of very continual mental pressure. I am sure it is the danger I run, as shown in sharp headaches and in the craving of my whole nature for solitude and the wild woods at times.

On Truth: Oh! Why can it not be given out and held forever to enrich the world? Why does God give us glimpses of eternity and let them vanish? Why will it ooze away until only its shadowy name is left. It cannot be wholly gone. Somehow, somewhere, it must live as music sent up to God.

From the dark shadowed chambers of the past music draws out again all we have known, all the dear tenderness of hand and voice softly sustaining with its strong pure love, all the old memories of courageous souls.

Poor instincts how you ache as you lay crushed and creased and scarred and bruised as a drag you out of view. Surely it is a strong love of truth which is willing to endure so much tugging and straining after the meaning of the buried life.

The Moral Life is a carrying out of purposes and it is in this insight that knowing your purposes is the one thing for every mother to teach in a myriad of ways and educational influences and for every boy and girl to endeavor to learn. Having purposes, concrete of widely embracing gives poise and cheer and bearing and eagerness to life. In its deepest meaning, a purpose is a creed.

Jesus was rejected by men; they had no use for him. So constantly we reject the best gifts offered to us.

If we cannot drink the cup to its dregs we shall be incapable of the poignant insight of tragedy. We shall be unable to go with the beloved so we shall lose them.

To live fully is to face the new unique moment with the panoply of the glory and awe of all centuries and nations around us.

Notebooks on Growth (1889–1900) (A 139/322v)

Growth is always creation not accretion, assimilation, or conservation . . . creation cannot be from death to life, but from life to more life . . . We are not really alive, not ourselves unless we are creating, assimilating into ourselves and giving out afresh. Americans are inventive and active minded to an unusual degree, but a fearfully large proportion of the population act passively and mechanically. We are parasites, sucking the life out of the past instead of contributing the new word. We don't earn our salt. We have hardly to learn that nothing is to be accepted passively, but all is to be faced imaginatively, not from a sense of superiority, but of indebtedness, of loyalty.

It's a rule of the game that on penalty of death no one shall use uniform phrases or acts save for the task of a new construction. We tend forever to slip into the ease and luxury of our old accustomed ways. A stranger disturbs our peace. We do not see that in the ruffling caused by the interruption may be our opportunity. For the stranger has a message be he a seer or a fool . . . everyday is a reconstruction period. If I can only work in my particular armchair or niche I am in so far making a story shell—acquiring moral arterial sclerosis. Not that I can instantly and by myself assimilate the difficulty, but that the sources of strength are in the reach of many.

In the creation of the work of art we have perhaps clearer growth than anywhere else accept in the execution of a well-conceived purpose. In each case we recognize growth as growth and not degenerate change because we made and know the ideal toward which we are working. We correct our failure by an appeal to an ideal. True, the ideal is a great deal more than we know and it also grows clearer when we express our aim but it is essentially ourselves and hence we can judge its progress or loss . . . ethics as well as art appeals to a whole (ideal) without which growth may be degeneration or rather all is chaos. In the creation of the work of art as in the creation of any purpose there is struggle and a sense of ineptitude and contrast with the ideal. But when we dwell in the whole we turn from the struggle to the completion involved in that struggle if it is true in itself—to the finished work of art and to religion.

The process of growth in music corresponds closely to the development of any idea or purpose. You know that by choice I am a physician, you may be surprised to find me next week exploring the Grand Canyon of Colorado. Such a project would seem to be in too distant a key from that original theme. The Explanation may be either that I have abandoned my profession and am playing a new tune of that there are relatives not as once apparent . . . And just as any purpose, unless deliberately abandoned, reaches out to the whole, every key can be reached from any starting point. The purpose determines rather how soon you will reach a given key rather than its absolute exclusion starting from growth . . . One reason that we don't see connections in growth is that we all have a liking to be miracle workers and burn our bridges after us instead of treasuring the steps as guides for those who come after. Nature has done the same with many links of animals and so we have suspected her to be a miracle worker . . . In view of this what next? The perceptual inquiry that connects the new with the old. Thoroughly to answer that question means to gather in all the significant and relevant past to a focus so that the alchemy of the newly emerging fact shall crystallize it into a unique and unheard of deed. The dogmas of the stormy past are inadequate to the stormy present. If the occasion is new so we must think anew and act anew.

To use the past—inherited physique, or brain, culture, joy, agony—so that is disentangles and liberates instead of enthralling that is creative life. The same net which trips and tangles us may be used to drag the great waters and hoist the shining salmon. That is the relation between past and present that reconciles them. . . . We need the past, every bit of it, for the sake of all our future. We cannot afford to forget although there must be many things that we store away till we are capable of assimilating them. We need all we can digest. For some experiences we must wait till our digestion grows stronger.

Habit, environment, circumstance, inheritance cannot then properly be called hindrances for they only hinder us insofar as we do not know how to use them. A million dollars, a great sorrow, an automobile, a broken leg, a down couch—all may be equally hindrances and helps according as we know how to use them. Helen Keller uses her dark and soundless world to reveal like the night sky the showing of the power of touch. A ten foot oar is most awkward till you use it for rowing. Creative power then is the foreseeing of fitness to our end.

Excerpt from Essay on *The World and the Individual* (1902) (A 139/372)

I think that the important part of Royce's view here is this: As long as we take the hard facts of the world without any purpose or any theory (which in Greek is *vision*) they simply delight or appall us . . . we are taken off our feet or knocked down by them: in any case we lose our balance. But to have a purpose is to look and order and learn eagerly from these strange facts of beauty and terror . . . our whole life's work is to find out who we are and what we mean . . . the desire for truth, for wide experience for study of philosophy is our homing instinct in a world wherein we stray and need wherein to fulfill ourselves.

The Relation of Chance to Purpose in Invention (1900–1902)*

In my last paper I reached the conclusion that it is through purpose that novelty is brought about. I propose in this paper to attach that doctrine. It will be purged and strengthened by a hand-to-hand encounter with its principal adversaries. I have called this paper the Relation of Chance to Purpose in Invention. I will define the three important words, in the title. In defining invention I assume without discussion both that there is nothing absolutely the same twice and nothing absolutely disconnected from the past. What we mean by invention must be, therefore, a relatively *significant* variation. We also have to distinguish between what is an invention for the individual who creates it and what is really new to society. In this paper I shall use invention as anything new and relatively valuable to the individual who works it out. I shall develop later the conception of chance. Here I will give simply its definition. Chance is the encounter of factors outside of our plans with our special end.

Next it is important to define what I mean by Purpose. There is a subtle temptation to make purpose an all embracing term. It is thoroughly obliging and at a moments notice will stretch to include the activities of jellyfish and bacteria, or at a pinch, take under its protecting wing the vaguest emotions which may chance years later to evolve into a plan.

Now just because purpose is an idea of central importance, it is best to keep its meaning from stretching so thin that it becomes a mere veil, a haze blurring our view of reality.

I know, of course, that there is and can be no fixed moment in the growth of an individual at which purpose begins and that it is rooted in what is less definite, but to keep myself to a standard of clearness, I shall say that an individual has a purpose when he has a deliberate plan of action. Here at once I am plunged into the midst of my discussion. There were within the idea of purpose as thus defined two distinguishable but inseparable aspects, that of discriminating or reflective attention and that of motor activity wherein the ideas to which we attend are manifested. These aspects may be briefly called thought or will. If it can be shown that the new does not and cannot be formed by either of these aspect thought or will, we shall have overthrown the claim of purpose to be the sufficient source of novelty.

(a) The relation of thought and novelty is very ably stated in a book by Souriau on the theory of invention and as I agree with his statement, though not wholly with his conclusion, I shall use several of his illustrations. Souriau begins by asking whether invention can be the product of deliberation and answers, that though it is true that we bring to every new problem a certain fund of thought, yet the really new is precisely what is never explained by thought, for if we already knew what we were to do or to make, it would not be original. Examples of this may be found anywhere in art. The poet who knows beforehand precisely what he has to say will not write a truly original poem. To succeed in being original, he must be open to chance suggestions; for instance from the rhyme. The poet chooses a word for the ending of his first line; the choice of this first ending brings up a limited number of words which rhyme with it, and these accidents of language themselves suggest to the poet a new idea and mold his conception. So the original orator is not he who plans every word and inflection of his speech at home, but he who is moved by the audience, moved by every chance incident in the meeting, moved even by the unexpected associations which his own words called up. We often speak of our end as if it were like a distant mountain top visible through all our walk and definitely the same all along. But any end which involves invention is changed in to process of fulfillment, otherwise it simply repeats our past idea or that of someone else. Hence the new cannot be the product of thought.

But though the function of thought is not to create, its value is still two-fold. *First*, to hasten discovery by increasing the number of our ideas and so the chance of forming a good one, and *second*, to restrain our ideas from wandering out of the field and to persuade us to retreat resolutely from blind alleys. Even the sterile critic is of value in this respect. He creates nothing, but by his persistent condemnation he tends to clear away rubbish and to lead the artist to discriminate between what is valuable and what is worthless. He never shows where the road to discovery is, but by his reiterated cry "you are off the path," he gives us a general restraint that is of value. Thus the function of thought is mainly negative. It restrains us within a limited area, it rejects absurdities, but for this very reason it is too conservative to create. Novelty is found by one who roves the world, not by one who stays always at home.

(b) Relation of Will to Novelty. Souriau's position that invention cannot be a product of thought is strengthened by the development of the thesis that the new cannot be willed in Prof. Royce's article on originality and consciousness (Studies of Good and Evil, p. 249).

The wish and intention to be original defeats itself and results in waywardness or in self imitation. "Originality must in general belong to the unconscious side of our life."

It cannot be due to will for I cannot will to do anything until I know what I am to do and I can only know by having done the act before. The initial act of the series must have been involuntary. So in learning to swim I cannot will to swim, I can only put myself in deep water and gasp and struggle until unconsciously and after a while I find the right combination of movements. "We imagine the will to be originative merely because very often by repeating old deeds we can get ourselves into unheard of situations, but it is life in such cases that contains novelties, it is not we who are original."

Originality and Chance

Now if invention is not due to deliberation or to will, if it can not be a product of intention on our part, it must be the result of what is beyond our plan, that is, of what turns up as far as we are concerned by chance. The question at once arises what is chance? In the first place it does not involve lawlessness. All effects in nature however complicated, have causes and hence there is no chance in the outer world. Again all human actions are determined by ends and there is no chance in the world of men though here, as in any complicated natural event, the difficulty of tracing intricate relations may give the appearance of lack of motive or cause. A man may, for example, be undecided what course to take because his desire for success struggles for his desire for honesty, but this, while it confuses the issue, does not any more tend to show that he acts without motives than the wind which blows the falling leaves upward tend to disprove the law of gravitation. There is no accident either in world of nature or of thought, but what we call chance is always the *encounter of factors of which our plans are unaware without own end.* For example, a ship is sunk by a glacier, the glacier is moved by wind and currents, the ship is steered in relation to the captain's purpose, with a full knowledge of the movements of these two bodies. The collision would have been seen to have been inevitable. Nevertheless, it was wholly outside of the plans of the captain and so seems to him accidental. A card player by chance turns up an ace. It is chance to him, although made inevitable by the shuffling and cutting of the cards. So again the case of a brick badly cemented and loosened by rain, which hits a man on his way to the office. The idea of chance as something without cause is illusory. But our perpetual ignorance, both of external events and of the full meaning of our own plans, makes what appears as chance a necessary and permanent factor in experience.

Now that we have established the powerlessness of thought or will to originate and have defined chance as the unforeseen factor which surprises our purpose, the ground is cleared for the discussion of the way in which chance brings novelty. Hints and signs of something beyond purpose were everywhere emerging in my paper on novelty, though I tended to suppress them there as unwelcome intruders who would injure my plan. Now that my purpose is broadened through the persistent self-assertion of these chance factors, they shall have their innings. I shall take up further aspects of the power not ourselves which makes invention and try to show *first*, that chance actually does enter into our purposes and *second*, that when we rigidly exclude chance, originality dies.

1. There is always chance in the birth of purpose.

    a. Either through the allurement of sight and sound, or
    b. Through the pressure of need.

    In either case if we exclude chance, originality dies.
2. Purpose is always changed in the process of *fulfillment* by the chances which meet it.

    a. Every plan we form is vague and

b. Ought to be vague for without chance suggestions we repeat.

3. The earliest dawnings of creative work appear in children associated with a marked element of chance. A little boy finds a piece of chain and more or less unconsciously balances it over a level bar. As his hands play with it he notices that one end goes up as the other goes down. The pulley idea is recalled and he looks about vaguely for something to attach to his hook. His luncheon basket is in sight and he eagerly seizes it, but now he needs a weight for the other end and some means of attachment. He thinks of a stone and runs out in the street to find one, and unable to find twine remembers or devises the powers of a handkerchief. Then he proceeds to what is for him the relatively original invention of an elevator.

In the analysis of this case we see (1) It was chance plus a greater interest in chains than e.g., in Latin grammar that made him see the chain. It was accidental groping which led him to balance the chain on the bar. It was imitation which suggested the construction of a pulley and the purpose of making an elevator arose rather as a result than a cause of activity.

Even in far more mature natures the birth of a purpose is a dark spot in which chance plays a large part. Charles Darwin was nearly dissuaded from taking the voyage in the Beagle (the critical event of his life which he spoke of later as his second birth), because his father thought it would appear disreputable that one who was to be a clergyman should be associated with roving explorers and rowdy sailors. Chance brought in his path friends who overcame his father's opposition, but even after the important decision to take the voyage was made, the birth of the definite place to trace the origin of species was due to an influx of chaotic facts (e.g., the myriad specimens drawn up by chance from the deep sea), rather than solely to a fixed intention.

Is not this typical and characteristic? Is not the starting point of invention the imperfect, the chaotic, the disorderly rather than the exclusively deliberate and definite? "The little beggars are doing just what I don't want them to," Darwin would say of his seedlings, but it was just because they would not conform to theory that they led him to really original work.

In artistic work the dawning of a plan seems often due to chance elements. An Indian box with dancing figures inscribed on it suggested to Massenet the ballet of his King of Lahore. The duel scene in Adam Bede jumped into George Eliot's mind one night at the theatre.

In short, as Stevenson says, "The world is so full of a number of things I am sure that we all should be happy as kings," and not only happy, but inventive. Lift up your eyes anywhere and something suggestive seems

almost sure to hit you, unless you are protected by the armour of _____.
We take the credit but the impetus and suggestion is forever flowing in from an endless, dazzling flight of objects of beauty or curiosity.

On the other hand when we exclude all chance elements from the birth of our purpose, we are decidedly apt not to get novelty at all. The sense that the deliberate watching of the birth of novelty kills it has wrought itself into the proverb, "A watched pot never boils." An element of mystery and even of unconsciousness hangs over the moment of creation.

"A man will not be observed in doing what he can do best. There is a certain magic about his prosperest action, which stullifies your power of observation. Every man is an impossibility till he is born, everything is impossible till we see a success."

Emerson, Experience III, 70.

The fact that roots grow only in the dark and that seeds must be buried has wider applications than in the realm of horticulture. It is most often out of the dark of unconsciousness that the greatest thoughts grow and the poems written for occasions and the deliberately commemorative pictures are usually the least original.

There is something like the swift movement of a juggler's hand and while we watch it a marvel has taken place not where we looked, but elsewhere. This does not seem accidental, but necessary; when we clearly foresee and perceive we simply unroll the old instead of evolving the really new.

"Power (says Emerson, Experience, p. 69) keeps quite another road than the turnpikes of choice and will, namely, the subterranean and invisible tunnels and channels of life. . . . Nature hates calculators, our chief experiences have been casual."

Hence a certain loosening of purpose and "abandon" is essential to originality. This is what Stevenson pleads for in the Apology for Idlers. (Virginibus Puerisque, p. 124).

"Look at your industrious fellows. They have no curiosity, they cannot give themselves over to random provocation . . . When they do not require to go to the office . . . the whole breathing world is a blank to them.

Many who have plied their book diligently come out of the study with an ancient and owl-like demeanor and prove dry, stockfish and dyspeptic in all the brighter parts of life.

I have attended a good many lectures in my time. I still remember that Emphyteusis is not a disease nor Stillide a crime. But though I would not willingly part with such scraps of science, I do not set the same store by them as by certain other odds and ends that I came by when playing truant . . . He may pitch on some tuft of lilacs over a burn . . . and there he may fall into a vein of kindly thought and see things in a new perspective . . . While others are filling their memory with a lumber of words, your truant may learn some really useful art.

In many of the examples I studied in my last paper on creation the element of *need* was prominent as a factor in creation and need is the pressure of something beyond himself on a man.

I touched on this doctrine of need in the account of the reinvention by schoolchildren of a loom to weave a rug, in the doctrine of Political Economy that *demand* creates supply; in the hunger for expression which impels the artist, in the attitude of missionary who looks only for that place where he is most needed. It is proverbial that Necessity is the mother of invention, and it expresses a profound truth and brings out the fact that all our well-laid schemes are less effective in forcing us to originality than the pressure of stringent circumstances. The tramp who has had no breakfast is surprisingly ingenious and original in his plans for wheedling a dinner out of a good natured cook, the man whose shoes wear out in the Labrador wilderness becomes as inventive in mending or supplementing them as is Edison. The word *need* has various usages and yet it is interesting to find that in all of the various implications we may say with truth that it is need rather than a deliberate intention which creates. Need is *necessity* and necessity (a constraining difficulty) is the extreme pressure of circumstances rather than a chosen plan. But again, need is a *want*, a nothingness, an aching void and out of the ache and void rather than out of the fullness of content, the satisfaction of a clear purpose the new life seems most normally to break its way. It is what we have *not* formulated rather than what we have that compels the new act.

Human nature abhors a vacuum and the sense of void calls forth latent powers. On a higher plane we find that the greatest men of genius and power are not satisfied to state their success in terms of their own will or purpose and appeal to need as almost *necessity*.

Luther exclaims, "Here stand I; God help me, I cannot do otherwise." Lowell (Poems 57) makes Columbus say "For me I have no choice . . . Here am I for what end God knows, not I. Westward still points the inexorable Soul . . . A hand is stretched to him from out the dark, which grasping without question he is led, where there is work which he must do for God." (If the will of God constrains me).

It is this I suppose which is the underlying truth in Butschli's mechanisms and vitalisms statement that the artist who makes the Parthenon is least of all his own designer. "Himself from God he could not free," and thus it was that he built better than he knew and that Nature gladly gave his temple place. The passive master lent his hand to the vast soul that o'er him planned."

B. So far I have spoken of the chance factors which entered into the *birth* of a purpose, but it is even more striking to find how *after* its deliberate start in life a purpose is molded by what it meets on the road. This is due primarily to the fact that every idea or plan we form is vague, it is a frame ready to hold a thousand different pictures. When, e.g., we speak of the sky as blue, this word blue still leaves open as possibilities an indefinite number of shades; when I say "I am going to move my arm to the left," even such a relatively definite statement admits within its scope scores of different motions of varying rate. In our most concrete plans we never foresee all the possibilities. The prudent surgeon knows that he must do his thinking ahead of the operation; he must face beforehand all the emergencies which may come up and make his decision how to meet each one. But with the best intentions he never succeeds, the situation is always different, unexpected, new; to meet it he has got to be inventive in some respect. This looseness or indefiniteness of any plan which might be considered a lack, is the centre of radiating opportunity. Each step in the fulfillment of a purpose suggests a partially new plan to the open-eyed.

Prof. Baldwin gives a delightful illustration of the effect of chance suggestion which changes and brings originality to a somewhat cramped purpose (Social and Ethical Interpretations in Mental Development, p. 106.) His little girl started to build a church out of blocks arranging the blocks, as she had been taught to do, in the form of a Greek cross. Suddenly the cross lines suggested to her something far more original and interesting than a church and she proceeded to add a second set of cross lines. "A church does not have two cross sections," said her father. "No," exclaimed the delighted inventor, "it is not a church, it's an animal with four legs and a tail."

(Abbott Thayer's Stevenson Memorial). Legouve (quoted by Paulhan Psychologle de l'Invention) tells how Rachel asked him to write a play for her and how in its conception everything centered round an intensely dramatic poisoning scene in which all Rachel's powers were to be displayed. But when almost ready to rehearse, Rachel declared that the poisoning scene ruined the play and made the character an impossible one, and gradually with much agony Legove came to agree with her and destroyed the scene for which the whole had been undertaken.

So Musset said, "I often turn against my favorite hereo and have him worsted by the enemy," and from a subtler point of view a contemporary author tells me that thought the plot of his drama turned on the suicide of the hero, that as the play became clearer, the hero absolutely refused to commit suicide. In this case the author came to see that the hero knew better than he and that by his refusal he had saved the play from melodrama. Our plan is vague and ought to be.

In chance suggestion is our opportunity for originating, and when our purpose is inflexible we tend to kill it by our efforts to keep it the same.

Emerson's daughter took her father to Egypt for refreshment and stimulus. He was most unhappy and restless, incessantly longing for home and the quiet of his study, but Miss Emerson had definitely planned that he should go to the second cataract and with unconscious ruthlessness of purpose she carried through very preconceived detail. Was it not perhaps for that very reason that Emerson found in travelling so little of a stimulus to fresh perception?

When our purpose draws its exclusive iron bands about us, we kill the life-giving tissues in our efforts to kill the invading germs of the haphazard.

The law of association leads us to repeat, unless our purpose is illumined by what it meets. If we try to speak words without any meaning, we begin glibly enough with a fair variety, but in a few minutes we are repeating. So profess giving the same courses year by year almost inevitably use the same words.

Now this tendency to repetition would be overwhelming, if it were not for the influence of outside forces, but fortunately for our originality we are never except in deep sleep or in times of great mental concentration, wholly unaffected by the world outside of our plans. We drive along the park making plans about a friend in a distant city, but the trees and houses and people we see affect us far more vividly than our vague uncolored memory and from the sight of them springs suddenly it may be, a new idea that will help that distant friend.

Every plan is and ought to be vague I said, and as this is so it is all along open to suggestion. It is then not strictly accurate to say that we *have* an idea and then express it. This seems to imply that it was there all along, but no, it is created as it goes. The words we accidentally use change more or less our original idea which was so vague as to allow much shifting. Write a paper on Charity and the words you use will change your predetermined ideas. In art again we invent by carrying out; our vague sketch develops very differently from what we meant, the notes he strikes by chance as he sits down to the piano suggest an improvisation to the musician; an accidental blot gives a new conception to the designer.

III. The function of Purpose and its relation to Chance. If we fully admit the play of the unforeseen in bringing novelty what becomes of purpose? Does it still remain true that purpose aids creative activity or is it all due to chance, i.e., to activities other than ours which we cannot anticipate?

My answer is (a) Without purpose there is no chance and (b) Any purpose in proportion to its width and strength changes chance to *my* chance.

As I said before, in defining the relation of chance to lawlessness there is no chance in the world without purpose. It moves steadily on its unastonished way (Glacier). "The event in itself is pure water, (Maeterlinck says in Wisdom and Destiny) and has neither savour or purpose or color."

(b) If it is true that without purpose there is no chance, a closer study of the cases of invention will show us that purpose is somewhere concealed even in the cases which are used to exalt chance.

I think you must have felt that in the cases of children's inventions or of the birth of Darwin's purpose to sail in the Beagle, there was a certain selective interest, though possibly it was not clear enough to be called purpose.

The case of Legouve's drama for Rachel where the development of the poisoning scene resulted in its destruction shows purpose nourishing itself on chance and triumphing because the destruction of the minor scene was caused by the fulfillment of the more fundamental purpose of success in the drama. So a man may start to defend a dogma which he thinks essential and finding it to be false, abandon it because to get at the truth is his deepest purpose.

Many of the examples which Souriau gives illustrate the necessity of a purpose to grasp the opportunities of the unexpected. It is perfectly true that the poet or artist who so fixedly plans his poem or picture that he leaves nothing open to chance will not be original, but equally true that the poet drifting in the arms of chance will find little but seaweed.

"God giveth to his beloved in sleep." "Yes," says Hegel, grimly, "but what they get is mostly dreams." It is wide awake vividness of interest that makes chance of value.

A couple of more or less apocryphal anecdotes about Newton will illustrate this. Newton said, according to one account, that he discovered the law of gravitation because he was always thinking of it. Another tradition says that he thought of it when he saw the apple fall, but of course without the (inchoate) plan of discovering the laws of nature he would never have worked out the significance of the apple's fall. We all see apples fall and think nothing more significant than I am glad it did not hit me, or there's something to eat.

It was the clearness and width of Newton's purpose that brought him the chance of seeing the significance of the apple's fall and this brings me to a distinction of importance which I call.

The relation of chance in general to *my* chance.

Any interest, affection or purpose is like a magnet to circumstance. In proportion to its strength and width it attracts to itself from greater and greater distances all that is akin. A striking case of the relation of "chance" to a magnetizing interest is given by Paulhan. (Psychologie de l'Invention).

Daguerre was experimenting with photography by exposing plates to light and one day he left a plate which had been exposed too short a time to have any image on it in a wardrobe. When he took it out later he found the picture on it and to discover the causes he tried the experiment again and again removing each time one of the articles in the wardrobe. Finally he found that the only thing which affected the photograph was a little box of mercury and after making more accurate tests with this he brought it into available use. Now, of course, there was "chance" in this, but I would only reveal its message to the seeker who had a definite intent.

Chances leap to meet the man with a strong purpose. I go along a country road and see nothing but dust and blurred foliage. My companion is excited at every step by a new discovery, a glacial scratch on the rock, a gentian in the marsh, or a footprint he cannot recognize. It is all because he has a vivid interest or purpose. To put the distinction briefly the man of no particular purpose talks ruefully of chance in general, the man of purpose follows the game, says "Here's my chance!" and takes it.

It is this truth which is expressed in Maeterlinck's Wisdom and Destiny (42). "Misfortune like water, expresses the form of the vase that contains it . . . Even as the soul may be wherein it seeks shelter, so will the event become tender or hateful, deadly or quick with life. To those around us there happen incessant and countless adventures whereof each it would seem contains a germ of heroism, but the adventure passes away and heroism there is none. But when Jesus met a Samaritan, met a few children, met an adulterous woman, then did humanity rise three times to the level of God."

One home-thrusting illustration may give point to my doctrine of the relation of chance and purpose, the illustration drawn from the relation of my paper tonight to the Seminary. It is in part a matter of chance what I say. During the weeks I have thought about it I have encountered many things not directly concerned with it which yet have affected it, but he reason I noticed and held these ideas or illustrations has been on account of the magnetism of my interest in chance and my purpose of writing a paper. So to each of you— there will be, I hope, something unexpected in my paper and yet each will seize what is akin to his central purpose or interest.

Mr. Yerkes will consider the relation to variation of species, Mr. Hocking the primacy of chance or purpose, Mr. Bacon whether my substitution of *my* chance for chance is valid.

If, however, nay of you is without an interest which is within the magnetic field of my suggestion, he will get just nothing at all, and the paper will in so far be a waste product. Or if his purpose is defined rigidly throughout, there will again be no chance of effect.

The situation may be exemplified by the purpose of catching trout in a mountain stream. If you sit by the stream without any rod you will probably see plenty of chances to catch trout, but they won't be chances for you. On the other hand if you resolutely and stubbornly thrust a clearly-hooked line into he water and push it deliberately toward each trout you see, you won't catch any either. New ideas are shyer than trout and even if they glide for a second into the hand of a man without a rod, he can't hold them unless he has the hook of purpose. Nevertheless, and he is the crux of the situation, we must conceal the hook and make random gyrating, illusive movements, almost forgetting that we are not the fly instead of the fisherman.

I shall now try to gather up the result of my analysis.

In the first place the idea of purpose has not lost its hold as an element in creative activity.

In the wide darkness that surrounds us it is our purpose and the purpose of those we love and so understand that a lone light and order our world and in so doing reveal our chance. As in a snowstorm, the numberless crystal flakes drift by us alluring and bewildering by their incessant movement and their strangely beautiful forms, so the myriad opportunities, joys, tragedies, mysteries glide silently by touching us for a moment and forever blending with the past at our feet while from the sky still whirl the endless flaked of the future.

What we get from all these opportunities depends wholly on our width and clearness of purpose; without a glimmer of purpose they are like snowflakes falling into the sea. Purpose is essential to the opportunity of original work, although as we saw purpose is also formed and molded by opportunity, suggestion, need and demand.

Nevertheless, I agree to the central meaning of all this criticism of the inadequacy of purpose to explain creation. The soul of the objection seems to me of vital significances and its meaning essentially this; "No man, and so no purpose, liveth to himself and no man dieth to himself."

The inadequacy, and in so far the falsity, of the idea of my purpose starting on its predetermined career to its chosen end is that it ignores 99/100 of the life of the world, which life, inclusive both unconsidered elements in himself and of the myriad streams of other purposes, inevitably asserts itself to mold, to frustrate, to fortify and enlighten his purpose.

Through criticism the concept of Purpose in relation to Invention has been purified and enlarged and in three aspects.

1. We have found that invention is the product of the *whole* man rather than of thought or will alone, and hence if anyone conceives his plan narrowly as attainable by deliberation alone, other elements in his nature, feelings, traditions, instincts, will come forward to mold it. Musset will turn against his favorite hero.

2. Invention is the product of the activity of the universe kept in focus for me by my plan, but not due to my plan alone, and hence, in so far as I think of my plan as independent, it is surprised and perhaps overthrown by the plans, activities and needs of others. Rachel forces Legouve to see that his poisoning scene is not in place.

3. The doctrine of my last paper that a purpose can only keep the same through change is re-enforced here and if we follow the direction in which an inventive purpose goes in order to keep the same we shall find it pushing out toward and within the whole.

This is the corollary of the idea that the wider and clearer the purpose, the greater are its chances. Ultimately all is grist that comes to its mill.

Our central discovery in this analysis may be put in Emerson's phrase in the Essay on Fate. It is "the cropping out in our planted gardens of the core of the world.

WHOLENESS IN RELATION TO GROWTH (1900–1902)

Summary

1. Trial definitions of Wholeness.

    a. To know any whole is to know that there is nothing beyond.
    b. To know any whole is to know all there is.
    c. To know any whole is to know that which is finished or forever the same.
    d. To know any whole is to know the universal aspect.

2. Failure of these definitions and reconstruction of the Whole as involving Growth. The whole is a system of ordered parts.

    a. To know Wholeness is to be interested or immanent.
    b. To know Wholeness is to be transcendent.
    c. To know Wholeness is to reject or exclude the irrelevant.
    d. To know or possess Wholeness is to attain sameness through constant difference.

3. Final definition of Wholeness.

The whole is the _____ of creation through an ordering and rejecting purpose.

In digging the soil about the roots of my concept Growth I have struck several times hard against a rock too heavy for me to move. When one does that repeatedly there are two alternative courses of action, one can move to another country and abandon the rocky soil or one can ask the help of all one's neighbors in hoisting the rock. As I am attached to the concept of growth and don't want to move, I have adopted the latter course and shall tonight make my small effort to lift the rock with the hope of being aided by everyone present.

This rock whose face I am first of all to dig out from the surrounding soil is called Wholeness.

I shall try then first to define what is meant by Wholeness, and second to bring out its somewhat paradoxical and intricate relations to growth.

It is clear that the term Whole is used frequently, and on following it even in uncritical usage, we shall find a number of suggestive variations of meaning.

1. A whole is that which is absolute, self-contained and needs nothing outside; e.g., "Fear God and keep his commandments for this is the whole duty of man."
2. Closely related to this usage is that of completion. The Whole is that which is total, undiminished, from which nothing has been subtracted; e.g., a whole pack of cards consists of 52 or 53, if we include the Joker.
3. The whole as that which is perfect, finished, forever the same. Christ is described as the Author and Finisher of our faith because he is supposed to have enunciated the whole truth.
4. In a somewhat more technical sense the whole is the object of any universal judgment. "All animals need food."
5. Finally the whole is defined as a system of ordered parts (whole = sound and healthy).

These different definitions are not mutually exclusive, but each accents a somewhat different point:
The first defines Wholeness by its external limits or lack of limits.

1. To be whole is to have nothing beyond.

It would seem that the only way in which you could be sure you knew the whole of anything was by seeing that nothing was left. You know you've eaten the whole of your piece of cake when not a crumb remains. The child looks hopefully about for a mislaid fragment, but "No!" the mother assures him, "You've had it all."

This is all very well for the time being, but just as the child more than suspects that any piece of cake came off a loaf and so that there may be more in the closet or at worst in the fertile resources of the cook, so we older mortals cannot long rest satisfied in a conception of Wholeness as defined by nothing beyond.

Here, e.g., is the world of space, everywhere more space and nothing beyond.

But what after all is that nothing? We have not really got the whole if that nothing still haunts us.

Spencer's unknowable is by its very definition nothing to us; we can make nothing of it, but perhaps for that very reason it is peculiarly persistently haunting to thought and to desire. For curiously enough as soon as I realize that there is nothing beyond, that shadowy nothingness becomes a potent power of discontent embittering all that is.

What is the use of living if there is nothing beyond? Exclaims the agnostic. (If in this life only we have hope we are of all men most miserable).

A still deeper objection is bound up with the nature of knowledge. To have nothing beyond is not merely to be bounded as a fact by those limitations, for in that case there would still be beyond you the knowledge of that outer nothingness, i.e., there would still be something beyond.

To have nothing beyond must be to know there is nothing beyond, but to know there is nothing beyond is to have thoroughly explored the outlying regions or in other words, to know that there is something beyond, however unattractive or obscure.

Here we reach a curious result. We have not got the whole if there is nothing beyond.

(2) Let us try a second definition which corresponds to the first, but in a positive form. It may be that the definition of the whole as that which had nothing beyond it was unsatisfactory, mainly on account of its negative statement.

To know the whole is to know all there is. This is very comforting, nothing more could be asked. I remember an organist who at the end of each recital used to announce, "that is all." It was thoroughly reassuring. There was no danger of missing encores.

But after all, was it true that we knew the whole of that concert? We had come at the very beginning and stayed through the middle and to the very end. Yes, but might it not have been that just because we had heard every single note we did not know the whole. Who of us has ever really heard the whole of the Walkure? Is an aggregate, a sum total of the notes of an opera the whole of an opera? Assuredly not. (The whole of that opera = the universe).

There are people who want to keep everything in an aggregate. It's a pity to lose even a fragment, they want the whole. They preserve their pressed flowers, their olds shoes, every letter of business or pleasure, every scrap of twine. Nothing, indeed, is lost, except the wholeness they sought. That is crowded out by an aggregate of rubbish.

"Sentiment fills garrets," proclaimed a wise old lady as she sent her ancestral samples and warming pans to auction. It does worse than that, it not only clogs garrets, it destroys integrity.

Here I make another discovery. Wholeness involves rejections as well as acceptance. To get all there is, is not to attain wholeness for the whole is other than the aggregate.

(3) Let us try another definition. (Perhaps we have failed to find a definition of wholeness because we have dealt with a world of novelty and of degeneration.)

May it not be that to be whole is to be finished, same and permanent? That which keeps the same would seem to be whole because it neither develops any disturbing novelty nor obliterates wholeness by decay.

The Buddhists recognize this. It is the restless will and untamed desire which bars absorption in the whole. This belief is expressed in the dreams of Keats and Tennyson. (Parmenides on pure Being).

Keats in his ode on a Grecian urn has represented with exquisite sympathy the ideal of changelessness. All is forever the same and decay, change and loss are barred out. We have the wholeness of Perfection. Fair youth beneath the trees, thou can't not leave they song, ___ ever can those trees be bare . . . Ah! Happy happy that cannot shed. Your leaves ___ ever be the spring adien and hoppy melodist unviewed. Forever pepping songs forever new. . . . Where old age shall __ generation _____.

Tennyson's Lotus Eaters weary with "ever climbing up the climbing wave," rejoice in the land where "all things ever seem the same," where they can steep their brows in slumber's holy calm.

> "How sweet it were hearing the downward stream,
> With hall shut eyes ever to seem
> Falling asleep in a half dream,
> To dream and dream like yonder yellow light
> That will not have the myrrh-bush on the height."

The problem is, nevertheless, only complicated by this revised conception of wholeness as equivalent to sameness. The problem or sameness is an added difficulty as appeared at our Seminary several weeks ago.

How do we recognize sameness? How do we know the room is the same as it was last week? We answered at first because it has not changed. That was shown to be not true. The room has changed. I would go a step farther and say, we know the room is the same among other reasons *because it has changed*. If I came here ten years hence and saw everything just as it is I should say they must have got new furniture, for it is just as it used to be. So if Prof. Royce talks in just the same way two weeks running, I shall say;

"Prof. Royce is a changed man. He never used to repeat." In a world where growth and degeneration are normal sameness demands inevitably difference.

We sometimes see the type of advertisement which proclaims identity. "The old reliable shoe, the kind your grandmother wore, always made just the same for seventy years." But to be really the same, i.e., the best made, that which grandmother would want now, it must be markedly different. For what we ____ his not the indistinguishable, the duplicate, but that which hold the same relation to other shoes now. To be whole in the sense of complete or finished is in a moving world to be different and disintegrating, i.e., to lose wholeness. Still may _____.

(Wholeness is the subject of all universal affirmatives, (e.g., all experience is spatial.)

This usage of whole is expressed in any universal judgment. We know the whole because we know the universal element; we do not require the aggregate or the particular. When I say, all triangles have three sides, I am making a judgment about the *whole* of the triangle world, and I do not need to be troubled by the fact that there are a great many triangles I have never seen nor that the forthcoming triangles may be different. What I know is the nature of triangles as such and that nature holds throughout.

The universal judgment predicates a universal law of connection. No matter how many triangles there are they must conform.

We seem to have right to declare this because we are not dealing with a numerical totality, but with the fundamental nature of the subject which we are discussing.

The whole is here that which contains all its parts and is equally ready for an infinite number more.

Emerson's splendid lines "'Tis man's perdition to be safe, When for the truth he ought to die," are true of all men. They express the experiences of Judas or of Savoriarola, of Luther or John Brown with equal accuracy (for as Bosanquet says, "The affirmation of universal connection is not approached from the side of the individual units, but from the side of a common nature which binds them into a whole." Logic, I, 226.)

Still it may be said truly that without the construction of triangles we should never have known that all triangles had three sides, and without the history of mankind any statement about his moral nature would be meaningless.

In other words the universal element, free as it seems from dependence on particulars, is, nevertheless, not aloof from them. [Even necessary propositions (i.e., those which mean to be undeniable) have to be reworded and modified in relation to a growing world, e.g. The axiom parallel lines never meet has to change to parallel lines never meet except at infinity.]

1. Here we are driven to a conception of wholeness which shall welcome instead of repel growth. A whole is a system of ordered parts and as order involves purpose any whole is the expression of a purpose and any purpose implies growth.

Within this conception of purpose there are several interwoven strands of central importance which I shall proceed to develop.

1. The whole in any ordered system is immanent, i.e., the *process* is organic to the end.
2. The whole is transcendent or creative in that it rejects the irrelevant and develops the new.

In what ways does a purpose or ordered system bring wholeness? We know it best in a characteristically human experience. Any interest welds the life of a man to wholeness by linking its changes into a unity, by opening out new reaches of effort, by preventing disintegration, by excluding the irrelevant.

One of the most striking of the great figures that loom out of the background of American history is Ulysses Grant. We see him first as the drifter, dissipated and rapidly going to pieces. The swift disintegration of his career is about to wash away all traces of his name. We see him again as the man with a single controlling purpose. He has begun to be a man of integrity. Wholeness and purpose are one. It is true of any interest, however, small that it welds a man to wholeness. Instead of the dissipation of the club or the passive morning at home, in an armchair we see him doggedly setting forth to his office day by day. He has formed the purpose of earning enough money to be able to marry. It is not attained, but he has, as we say, *identified* himself with it. It controls him and molds him. A friend asks him to go hunting. He hesitates, but refuses. "On the whole, I think I had better not." To the whole he refers as his guide, it surrounds him as his most familiar presence.

This is what we mean when we call the high-minded man of our city men of integrity. They are men who throw their whole selves into what they do. They act in view of the whole impartially. They are supremely interested, but to be interested means to be in it, immanent, expressed in the *process* as well as in the end. And as we come to a second point. The contrast of process and end in which the former is drudgery and the latter reward is lost in any interesting work and interesting work is not work of any special type, but work in which one feels expressed. (e.g. catching perch, climbing Matterhorn).

II. But to be interested is work _____

In the process it is to be beyond and so judge the process, it is to be transcendent as well as immanent.

This is not a contradictory though it is a paradoxical statement.

We never know the whole of anything unless we are beyond it as well as in it. If we are wholly inside, surrounded by the walls and unaware of what is beyond we never are conscious of the whole in which we abide, so to be really "in it" we must be in a sense out of it, i.e., at once observer and player. This is exemplified by any great critic or any great actor. He feels intensely the movement of the drama, but he is not lost in it, but beyond and as it were over-seeing it. He grasps the whole and is not absorbed in it.

As Nettleship says, "The condition . . . of possession, of sympathy is that I should be in a sense outside the thing possessed or sympathized with. . . . The bigger the self the more things it stands outside and yet the more things it enters into." (Lectures and Phil. Remains I.)

From a somewhat different point of view we see that to know or possess a whole is to be transcendent because wholeness involves rejection.

We saw before that the aggregate not only was different from the whole but actually often obliterated the whole. The reason was that the wholeness we sought was a purpose, not an aggregate and any purpose demands rejection.

The carpenter making a box rejects the imperfect wood, the man earning his living rejects the invitation to go hunting, the plant rejects the innutritious oversupply of oxygen.

Huxley expresses well the contrast of living and inorganic or passive bodies by saying that the former move with reference to their own integrity and the latter do not.

Now to move with regard to your own integrity, that is with a view to keep whole, involves constant rejection as the obverse side of choice, acceptance. When the bicycle falls over it falls without regard to its own integrity and is as likely as not to be smashed; when the bicycle rider feels he is falling, he rejects the natural path of gravitation and leaps off on his feet. He wants to keep a whole skin and to do that he must definitely decline to enter on the path of least physical resistance.

This law that wholeness involves rejection applies equally to any moral decision. It is a youthful trait to desire to do everything and know everything, or at least to take part in all the activities of one's contemporaries. It is an effort to get the whole by acceptance only, but it defeats itself. The very first acceptance enforces the necessity of refusal, and we discover that to know anything we must refuse sternly to know other things.

If St. Paul learned to be all things to all men it was through such vigorous rejections as "If meat cause my brother to offend, I will eat not meat, No! not while the world standeth."

One more characteristic must be brought out. Any true whole or purpose keeps the same only by carrying further its inherent differences. This is the obverse side of what I spoke of before. Professor Royce is the same man because his purpose of writing philosophy is expressed not in identical, but in different essays. They are united of course by a system or by the purpose to express truth, but are thereby inevitably different. And as perpetually different we see that a true whole is infinite, not finished or finite.

Let us look at this in its two aspects.

1. The ended is never the whole.
2. The whole is the infinite or self-creative.

(a) The life of sharp, definite endings is always finite, never whole. The man whose work has definite endings is he who is doing automatic routine work; the man who breaks stones or lays bricks or makes button holes has his eight hour day or his specified hundreds and the job is done. The reason it is finished is that it is piece work and not whole work, but so glorious is human nature and so crammed with interest the living world that it is rare that even the button-hole maker or brick layer is cramped to the finitude of absolute endings. Spite of trade unions and physical weariness, the creative impulse, the impulse of wholeness and infinite, creep in and the brick layer looks to the structure rising above and through him and lays yet another brick out of hours or the button-hole maker puts a loving extra touch into a baby's night-gown. More and more does the creative spirit push its way through the darkness of drudgery in work that deals with any life or art.

(b) Any persistent purpose opens out to infinity.

Of course there is a sense in which purposes stop and interests are satisfied, but never so long as they continue to be interests. I can__ at any time shut my eyes and not see the undone work of planting _____ flower-bulbs which are withering. So I can refuse to see the new _____ opportunity opened out by the completion of my first scheme. But this is only through blindness. We focus our eyes always on some centre and must and ____ must to see at all, but round every such centre there is a penumbra_____ absolutely continuous with our focus. In proportion was we are awake _____ (and few of us are, except in rare moments) we see more than to our_____ darker moments lies in shadow and turn our eyes where we will there is _____ always more and it is never sharply sundered from our central aim, but is simply the wider, truer vision of the same fact. Suppose as I did that my aim is a philanthropic one, that my central interest is in people. I may think at first that if I give them enough to live on all round my end will be accomplished, but any carrying out of this aim will lead me farther.

"Not alms, but a friend," the Associated Charities takes as its motto, but to be a real friend demands both a wide and a thorough and concentrated knowledge of everything in the world; We are usually satisfied with less, but in so far as we are loyal to the ideal of friendship we cannot be. I cannot be the best friend without understanding at first hand all that my friend case for.

A stupendous task, but only the beginning of my mission. The true friend not only must share his friend's life, but must open to him all other interests that may enrich and broaden him. To be a perfect friend to a single man you must love and sympathize with all men and the whole world of interests. No one is insane enough to try to do this all at once; it would defeat its own end as effectually as the attempt would do to gain a year's growth by eating a year's food at a meal. But the single purpose of being a true and loyal friend to any soul involves this endless growth. One step more, you might suppose per impossible that after many _____ you could encompass the wisdom of the ages and the world _____ men and be at liberty to rest, but far from it; Your diligent st_____ the universe has enriched that universe and given you interests w_____ at the start you did not dream of. Your sympathy with men has mou_____ men who require more and more subtle forms of sympathy.

("Be ye perfect even as your Father in heaven is perfect." It ____ only tremulously or exaltedly that we dare to face such a conception and yet every tiny interest we admit and loyally cherish reaches out and demands this ideal.) The infinite is what we seek.

I offer then, as a possible definition of wholeness = "Wholeness is perpetual creation through an ordering or rejecting purpose," and in this tentative shape I offer it to the Seminary in order that through

TYPES OF UNITY (UNDATED)

The category of unity underlies, in a way, all others, for they are all efforts to unify. This makes the possible expression of unity indefinite but I have tried tonight to characterize briefly and solely from the point of view of their unity a few of the most typical categories, and on the basis of this analysis to consider the place of unity in thought and to indicate the relation of the one to the Many.

A. *The mathematical Unity*	*Conceptual Unity*
The thing.	Quantity.
The Individual (popular usage)	
B. *Matter.*	*Unity as Explanation*
Substance.	
Force and Law.	
Atomic Theory (Modern)	
C. *The Organism*	Unity as Independence

Evolution.

D. Cause (Martineau)　　　　　Organic Unity or Individuality
Purpose, Thought, Ideal.
Aesthetic Unity.
Schelling's Idealism
The unconscious (v. Hartmann)

E. Peace

Unity as Precluding Definition

When we look at this collection of type we see running through them a certain thread which groups them in something like the order here given. At the top of the list I have placed those conceptions of unity in which it is used chiefly as a separator, an excluder, an ultimate element, repellant of intrusion. Here the one by its exclusion of the many really asserts them most prominently. The one is just such as is fitted for repetition; it is that which can be easily and conveniently repeated and exists chiefly for this.

This is unity primarily as unit.

At the end of the list I have placed conceptions in which the essential feature is the lack of features, conceptions in which the many is deliberately exercised or gently ignored. At this end of the scale thought distinctions are at a minimum and we approach the immediate (pure sensation) while at the other end the conceptual is at a maximum.

Between these two extremes are those types in which the one and the many are combined in various ways; this arrangement I meant to be logical not historical. I have grouped these more familiar unities in three classes, and I have tried to arrange their members in such a way that the classes melt into each other at the edges.

There are, however, marked differences, as well as likenesses in each member within any group and so I shall characterize each one separately.

I.

The mathematical unity is the symbol of hypothesis itself. It is precisely that without which we cannot get started in our calculations. This very ultimateness makes it universally available. It serves to measure anything, cows, diamonds, or bricks, feathers or lead. Because it is hypothetical and so far arbitrary it can be exact. It is cut off clearly from everything else and there need be no indefiniteness or blurring of meaning. It is exact and separate and so can repeat itself indefinitely. It has then the character of regulator as well as separator, but the power of relating seems the outcome of the separation.

The nature of the mathematical unit becomes metaphysically important to notice when we study such conception of God as the Unitarian, Trinitarian or the Polytheistic ideas.

The Thing of Common sense is a much more shifting conception. It seems, as we said, to include continuity in Time, but also has a marked inclination to define itself by discontinuity in space, and to insist on this character of separateness as a sign of its unity. It is often used as a unit to express any kind of data as when we say "Give me *anything*; I care for *nothing* in this World" and here it has the universal character without the accuracy of the numerical unit and also can be used as relater. In such phrases "Mark all my things with a B." Count all the things in that room it seems equivalent to the mathematical unit and has the same hypothetical or arbitrary character infinitely convenient because not concerned with the specific nature of what it relates. If instead of being able to say "Put my things in the valise" we had to enumerate each article we should appreciate how hard it would be to do without the wide and slovenly unity expressed by the word Thing.

Stress may, of course, be laid on the internal Unity of the thing and then it would differ from the unit, but his ordinary use is far reaching rather than distinct in character. After a search for an exhaustive list of what could be called things one would be tempted to decide that there were more things in heaven and earth than could be dreamt of in philosophy.

#3. The individual in its full significance is too important to touch on here, but it is interesting to notice its points of contact in popular usage with the unit and the thing.

It also is primarily a separator. The man of marked individuality is the distinguished man, the man cut off clearly from the common crowd, though we should also have to add that the distinguished man was the man of wealthy relations within his own character. He is, however, unique and this uniqueness makes the individual indefinable and apparently arbitrary.

If we dwell on the use of the word Individualist in its contrast to Socialist we get even closer to the conception of the unit. The individualistic view is: "Every man for himself, each one to count as one" and this definition has all the separateness and arbitrariness the great convenience of the numerical unit. The crank, the eccentric express the extreme of individuality in the sense of that which separates. This is of course a loose and popular usage. In its almost thoughtful meaning the man of greatest individuality is he whose unique expression springs from his width of relations to his race. He is at once most universal and most individual.

II.

In the 2nd group attention is turned from the assertion of separateness to an attempt at explanation. But this explanation means after all the finding everywhere of a certain hypothetical identity, so that it does not differ so very much from the 1st class in which though the stress was laid on separation, there must always have been the identity necessary to enumeration. To reduce everything to the term of things, is not so very different from reducing everything to the term of matter, except for the attempt at explanation in the later. The single substance, Force or Law is behind and below the facts it identifies, it supports and explains, is indeed thought of as their reality, or at any rate all that is truly important about them, yet it is often thought of as indifferent to the specific or the accidental nature of what it explains. What the Substance or the Atomic laws don't explain is not taken account of, but yet it is not distinctly assigned elsewhere or denied existence. Attention is simply not turned that way.

Matter e.g., is that One which is common to many diverse things without becoming infected with their diversity. It can take many a shapes, but is not itself the shaper.

(b) The conception of substance has had so many different meanings that it is confusing to analyze, but it has a tendency to hold itself independent of its accidents and though it explains them not to be explained by them, Its lies below the surface differences but is not itself differentiated by them. It abides through Time and Change but is not itself affected by them.

Its range of meaning from that which is completely independent of its accidents to that which fulfills the *purpose* of anything is suggestive as uniting under one term two of our types of unity.

(c) Force again is that which can slumber in potentiality or flash up in explosive actuality preserving thereby a continuity amid apparent discreteness. Its chief difference from Substance is this dynamic character which we shall see markedly in the 4th group, but it is like substance in that the appearance of discretion is not more fully explained than are the accidents. Force in its slumber is easily one but when it passes into many objects and yet is identified with none, we question the unity. The potential is clearly not the actual but if not how does it become actual? The unity does not seem inherent. Hegel points out (in the Phanomenologis) how the analysis of the nature of Force leads us to the idea of *Law* as the real unity as that which shows that it is of the nature of Force to rest in movement.

(d) Law is an attempt to lay the burden of the unity more on consciousness. It accents the one Order in the apparently disorderly, but it does not explain or hold itself responsible for the illusion of disorder, and when it takes from in various laws it leads to diversity and even contradiction, unless indeed we insist that all laws are really one and that there is no essential difference in them.

Atomistically constituted matter is the modern attempt to unite the advantages of the conceptions of unity so far described. It has a mathematical unit as its basis, it is one and yet many, it is a permanent and unchanging substance common to all things and capable of taking any form. It is also more conscious than the previous conceptions of the diversities which it underlies. Its manifoldness is intended as an orderly reflection of the manifoldness of sense. The laws of atomic motion are continuously in force and account for the mysteries of action at a distance and for such apparent disorders and catastrophes as plagues and earthquakes. The ultimate catastrophes are taken charge of, responsibility is assumed and the 72 elements are made part of the original hypothesis and so covered by its wing and taken up into its unity.

The type of unity embodied in the idea of an organism is hard to express because the conception often vacillates in popular usage between the conception of a teleological unity on the one hand and of a mechanism on the other. On the one hand the organic is the very stronghold of unity. It seems to involve complete interdependence. Organic is used as equivalent to fundamental. No superficial unity, but an organic one. An organic disease is one bound up with the central parts of the physical being, inseparable from him. The inorganic in science is that which is less intertwined into unity, which can be severed without violation of its essential character.

Yet there is a point of view from which the unity is treated as rather due to human weakness or to a convenient method of statement than as expressing any reality. The phenomena in this view remain many and independent. No blame attaches to them, whatever unity we may be compelled to see in them. This aspect comes out especially in the popular conception of evolution.

IV.

It is only when we reach our next division, that of purposes and ideals, that we seem to have a right to unify the facts in such a way because they are inextricably intertwined. As unifiers of fact the conceptions of this group lie behind the facts as do the conceptions already described. They run through many details as a common element and are capable of taking any forms; like matter, they have permanence through change and continuity within the discrete; like substance they have the same habit of retiring in possibility or coming out into clear acts like that noted in the laws of force.

But purposes, ideals, thoughts are far more interwoven with the facts with which they are concerned than were the conceptions of substance of force. The diverse is their diversity, the qualities are their own life, illusions are a normal expression of their law; the contingent is at its minimum. Indeed they are in this respect much more like the type of the organism. We may take the conception of the organism in such a sense that it is the same as that of the purpose, but the latter is a less illusive term and brings out not only the fact that *diversity* is of the essence of its unity but also that *growth* and all it implies is involved. These two characteristics of 1. Immanence and of 2. Growth, in this type of unity, so changes its character that they are worth considering a little more in detail. 1. In the first place the complete immanence of the idea in the facts makes it seem sometimes as if there were no unity. A man's acts it is said give expression to his ideal, but as his ideal is meaningless without the acts, it sometimes seems as if the ideal was only a description of the acts. In the older theories of conscience, it stood somewhat apart from the turmoil, took account of the various motives and circumstances and judged what was right, but such theories as that of Prof. Dewey, in which there is no judge, but the clear vision of all the facts concerned is the right action where virtue is knowledge seems to many so to unify as to exclude the unifier. The relation is as difficult to state as life itself, for it is life rewarded. We are tempted as I said, at times to say there is no real unity in the immanence of a purpose; but on the other hand without the unity of a purpose we get not multiplicity but chaos. The football game or the playing of an orchestra is a pandemonium unless one has an idea of its unity of purpose. With it, and especially in proportion as we understand it thoroughly, the details become clear, and explanation is complete and we are led to accent the unity as all important.

2. When however we dwell on the idea of growth which is involved in purpose and especially accented in the ideal, the unity seems lost again.

Nothing is ever exact or finished in this kind of unity; it is always pointing off to something more and can never be exhaustively stated. The unity is one of tendency, of direction, it cannot be expressed in static terms. The thing is *going one way* and not another, but it is going on a symmetrical track that cannot be mathematically foretold.

The unity is so subtle a conception that it can never be accurately stated. The English common law is a good example of this type of unity. The Roman law was so definite and finished a unit that it could be written on table of brass, but the English law grows step by step, and its unity is flexible enough to include the unknown future. Here we see how far we have got away from the mathematical unit with its convenient exactness, and separateness.

I have been characterizing so far the central members of my group, and what I have said does not apply to the two extremes, that of the Cause as used by Martineau and that of the Unconscious as used by Van Hartmann. These are so close to the groups which precede and follow them that one hesitates whether perhaps it would not be better to include them under these heads. Martineau's one cause though intended to be a teleological unity, is throughout clearly stated as separate from its effects. He feels as Prof. Howison does that the complete immanence of the cause would destroy its conscious and distinct character though I should gather that Martineau's dread was the merging of the Creator in his creation and Prof. Howison's that of merging the separate individuality of the creature in the unity of the whole. Both tend to pluralism or dualism, to a separation of details from principle which we find characteristic of the non-teleological unities like force and substance.

Both specially insists on the necessity of keeping the separation clear lest we slip into Buddhism, and we see how the dread is justified when we pass to the criticisms of Schelling's idealism (especially as viewed by Hegel) and to Van Hartmann's Unconscious. The reproach of Pantheism indicated that the reproacher finds in the doctrine criticized too close an identity of the one and the many. The wiping out of all difference and the casting it in the gulf of the Absolute is to them but the night in which all cows are black, and but a step from our last group.

Unities of the type of the peace of the old-fashioned heaven where there was no sin or struggle or sorrow, or the Nirvana of the Orientals do not lend themselves easily to characterization on account of their lack of features. They seem to be chiefly the negation of the many in one or another form. So it is when we dwell on any continuity solely. The account of the line as made up of infinite points does not tend to recall to us the character of any continuous theory or process, for it seems to accent separateness rather than continuity. Unities whose essence is continuity seem to be closer to sensation, less intelligible, more mysterious than those hitherto referred to. We can be conveyed by so discrete an instrument as conscious thought.

They explicitly and confessedly accomplish that washing out of particularity and difference of which conceptions of the Substance type are so often accused.

So much for our different types of Unity.

Now it seems clear to think at all is to unify in some of these senses. Even Hume in denying the real relation of cause and effect, had to explain how there was such a popular belief in the category. If we never see more than sequence, we yet have an inveterate tendency to unify into some category, for even sequence as the following of one particular set of events rather than another presupposes a kind of unity. Even those who land in pluralism have to vigorously search for unity, and the result of finding an ultimate pluralism is closely connected with that of declaring the world unintelligible. (Logic, I Chapt. III.) Mill e.g., in saying that the unity of any thing or person was but a subjective inference from association drew from it the conclusion that any inference was likely to be wrong and hence that we can have no sure knowledge.

Kant's in the darkest period of his skepticism was drawn toward the light by admitting and even accenting the fact that though we cannot know things in themselves, we yet to be sane at all must unify, and this unity beginning as a confession of weakness ended in the assertion of the validity of the categories for all scientific thought.

Starting as subjective they came out of the conflict of later thought (though not for Kant) as in the truest sense objective, the meaning of objective having undergone a change from "real apart from thought" to "scientific" and subjective from the "human point of view" to the momentary or prejudiced or illusive which thoroughly shifted their positions.

To think, to judge at all, we must unify, it is a necessity for all human thought. Kant said even chaos is still a category, even zero has unity. It is from this point of view that Prof. Everett says in the Science of Thought (page 192) "From the beginning to the end of philosophy, taking in systems the most frivolous and the most opposed, they all have this in common that they affirm the absolute unity of the universe. They are all alike searching for the principle of Unity.

In similar fashion Mr. Ritchie (*Mind*, Oct. 1698) says "Ultimate contingency or incoherence does not have any meaning. Out and out pluralism makes any assertion impossible. . . . The only test of reality is the test of coherence in thought, so that any one who throws doubt on coherence throws doubt on our *knowing* any reality at all" (*Mind*, p. 453).

So much for the place of unity in the thinking process. I turn now to a brief consideration of the problem of the one and many. I have been dwelling upon the necessity of some unity in all thought.

But as Plato in the Parmenides and Hegel in the Phanomemologi have shown, the one without the many vanishes; it is inexpressible, without form or character. To get the one perfectly pure is inevitably to pour out the baby with the bath, and if this is so, can we not say that the many is just as important as the one?

The claim made by the Pluralists is commonly that those who unify leave out facts and so do not really unify the whole but rather shut their eyes to the data left outside their narrow pigeonholes; and surely they say it is just as important to account for facts as to have the order got by turning your back on the confusion in your room.

To call the articles in a room one because they are all furniture suppresses the very patent fact that they are many. To a man who did not know our terminology the word furniture would undoubtedly seem a singular note plural term, and thereby be misleading. Conceptual unity is no real unity however much it may be true that we have to speak of a pile of stones, or a handful of chestnuts. As Hegel said it is but to dip all our facts in one color and then exalt in their uniformity of tone. The difference of position seems hopeless to reconcile unless we agree upon some test. Now if we take the test of unity to be interdependence in our groups so that no part could be spared without seriously affecting the whole we may raise the question of unity in these types of cases which we have been considering.

1. The mathematical unit.
2. Substance (Atomic)
3. The organic unity.
4. The unity of a work of art. Purpose, union of thought, and feeling.
5. The mystic unity.

From this point of view a heap of stones, a pile of wood, a bundle of clothes would be many rather than one because the removal of a decided portion of their members would not affect the unity. There would still be a heap of stones if part were gone.

If, however, the mathematical measure is exact as in a ton of coal, a cord of wood, or a quart of peas, unity would according to this test predominate. Take away half the peas and there is no longer a quart but a pint. But the ton of coal can be expressed as 2,000 lbs. and the quart as four gills and the idea of the many seems about as prominent as that of the one. The mathematical unity though, as I said, is a starting point, a necessary hypothesis so accents its own separateness from the rest of the world, that it calls our attention to the many as a child's insistence that he is good suggests to us that he is probably naughty.

The case is very different when our unit is of the type of a jury or a four part chorus. There each member is not only a numerical factor necessary in computation, but an essential part. The _____ jurors (to use Dosaquet's example) are not fully jurors without the 12th. For they can make no oath and make no judgment. The chorus is not itself without the tenor. The Separateness of the units is subordinated to their cooperation. In such cases as those of our second group under the conceptions of substance law or force, we hesitate somewhat as to whether there is enough interdependence for unity. Are the facts really dependent on the laws or are the laws only either summaries of the facts or a convenient name to embody them? If the laws are only this we are dealing with the many after all; and if they are more than this we seem to get dualism instead of unity. For the laws in this case, to use illustration of Hegel's are like the judging self who stands in superior isolation from the world it estimates. Here the interdependence of parts and whole is not complete. A similar question comes up with substance and accident. Harper in following the Scholastics brings up this problem (p. 195). The rose is separate from its redness, though the redness of the rose is not separable from the rose. The superiority of the substance to its accidents seems to give us a duality rather than a unity.

3rd. We can compare this with the case of a more organic unity. The simile of the vine and the branches wherein the branches cannot bear fruit unless they abide in the vine and when separate wither, but also the vine without the branches is no true vine expresses this organic relation. The tree is many in its elements but it is throughout interdependent. Yet in any such organism there seem to be parts which do not essentially belong. The thorns of a vine can be cultivated out of existence without essentially changing the vine, the color or fur of the animal seems relatively unessential. We do not reach the thoroughly unified in the sense of interdependent until we consider the fourth group. I spoke before of how the unity of a purpose must include as a part of itself all the details that are concerned in its fulfillment, but this becomes more striking in the types of a work of art, in proportion to its adequacy to its ideal. In the greatest symphonies no note could be changed and leave the work essentially the same. A line of poetry is fine in proportion as every word is inevitably connected with the whole. The novel or the picture which contains what is irrelevant at once loses rank. Unity here must mean entire interdependence.

Now this is especially interesting because in a great work of art we are on the pinnacle of the mountain and feel close on either side of us the conscious unity of a purpose and the mysterious unity of feeling. It is suggestive to notice that the word harmony has both the meaning of the complete interdependence of the one and the many and in its other usage verges toward a featureless peace. The work of art it is often said cannot be explained, it is essentially to be experienced, felt. If we accent this side that the unity is one of feeling we are led down toward that last group of unities whose center is Nirvana.

Our test of interdependence here seems out of place, there is not enough separation for interdependence. We can hardly call such a conception unity for even to think of it interrupts the entire absorption in the one.

In studying these types of unity one notices:

1st. Their range from abstract thought to pure sensation.

2nd. The vacillating character, which most of them have when questioned.

3rd. Their effort to reconcile the one and the many by elimination of either element and by accenting one of the two as more essential and by insisting that they are really one.

4th. It is interesting to notice how some conceptions like conscience have been through the entire _____ and are still tinged from popular thought with something of the meaning of all.

Every man has his individual conscience, conscience is the one law which lies behind the many; conscience is but the expression in action of the many conditions, and finally conscience is the law of the heart whose assurance the manifold conflict of duties cannot touch.

5th. It is interesting to notice the linguistic forms which express the various grades of unity. Uniqueness, identity, individuality accent the side of exclusion rather than explanation. Union, wholeness are attempts to express with the one and the many, while fusion, simplicity, purity lease to the undifferentiated oneness.

6th. We may notice cases of the different types of unity more or less clearly in historic form. In the Roman, Hegel has pointed out many of these states where everyone was a legal person, in the revolt of the one against many in Stoicism; in the close unity of the traditional Greek state with its members; in the Mysticism and of course in the Bhuddistism we find such types.

The corollary that if unity is to have such a wide range of meaning for most people, the conflict of the one and the many is not likely to come to an end, is clear.

NOTE

* The manuscripts that were used for this transcription were often badly damaged and illegible. In cases where the writing could not be made out clearly, I have decided to leave the writing blank (These illegible words are designated with _____). These cases occur infrequently enough that it does not obscure the writing on the whole.

Index

Abbott, Francis, 11, 30n20
Addams, Jane, x, 20, 34, 59n6, 88, 106, 107–108, 110n55, 132, 137, 138, 153, 161n51; on education, 13, 88; and Hull House, 106; on peace, 10, 138, 143, 157
aesthetics, 6, 49, 90, 91; and harmony, 50
altruism, 127, 128–132, 134
Andrews, Fannie Fern, 143–144
Aristotle: on contingency, 64, 65–68; on ethics, 89, 125, 140; on habits, 140, 150
Augustine, 125
autonomy, 26, 56, 117–118, 123–124, 140, 146, 147; vs. self-sacrifice, 127–132, 133, 113

Barton, Clara, 147
"Beatrice Relation," 3, 4, 30n3, 165; as a feminist project, 25–26; as the idealization of women, 23–25, 166; as a spiritual enterprise, 21–26
beauty, 99, 100, 106, 180, 181, 188, 192
Brooks, Reverend James, 151, 152
Buddhism, 214

Cabot, James, 5
Cabot, Richard, vii, ix, x, xiii, xvii, 6, 7, 8, 9, 10, 11, 13, 14, 15, 19, 26–27, 30n13, 33, 36, 44, 51, 59n11, 98, 99, 105, 108n4, 109n42, 132, 156, 166–169, 175n7; on marriage, 1–5, 27, 14–15, 21, 22; on the "work cure", 113–116, 118–123, 130, 133–134, 135n15
Cabot, Susan, 7
Cabot, Ted: death of, 167–169; friendship with Ella Lyman Cabot, 9, 171
Calkins, Mary Whiton, 112
celibacy, 7, 20–22, 99, 114
chastity, 21, 24, 166. *See also* "Beatrice Relation"
Child, Lydia Maria, 92, 133
childlessness, 20–21, 31n44, 99, 171
civil disobedience, 148, 151–152, 160n29
community: the formation of, 39, 35, 54–57, 58, 62n73; international order, 138, 146, 153, 155–156; as limiting individual capabilities, xiv, 7, 18, 30n29, 31n30, 38–39, 126–129; as regulative ideal, 152, 153, 165, xiii, xv, 15, 38, 40, 47, 59n15, 60n23; service to, 122, 127–129
conflict resolution, 35, 54, 145–146, 156–157, 181–182
contingency, xiv, 63–82, 83n11, 173, 215. *See also* Aristotle; James, William; Peirce, Charles Sanders
courage, 38; the lack of, 151; moral courage, 38, 150–153; of women, 150–151
culture, 125

Dante, ix, 1–4, 63, 167, 175n4; and the Inferno, 63–64; on purgatory, 165–166; on women, 3–4
Darwin, Charles, 68–69, 76, 77, 147, 192
Davidson, Thomas, 6, 112
death: and the cult of the dead, 33; Ella Lyman Cabot's, viii, 105; as existential imperative, 73, 149
democracy, 54, 137–138, 146, 155
Dewey, John, viii, ix, 41, 87–108, 170; on democracy, 12, 13; on education, xv, 120, 130, 132; on the moral imagination, xv, 87–88; and tragedy, xi, 37
Dix, Dorothea, 147–148
double-consciousness. *See* Du Bois, W. E. B.
Du Bois, W. E. B., 133–134
duty: imperfect, 125–127; of self-expression, 123–128. *See also* Kant, Immanuel

Eliot, George, 23–25
Emerson, Ralph Waldo, vii, x, xiv, 5, 11, 25, 94, 100, 101, 149, 163, 193, 195; on chance, 74–76; on the creation of the individual, 80, 82, 141–142; on the imagination, 77–80, 93
empathy. *See* sympathy
evolution, 56, 68–69, 71
experience: the concept of, 46; the lessons of, 96–97

Fay, Melusina, 14
feminism, x, xiii, 4, 15, 20, 22, 24, 104; contemporary, 22; and double-bind, 17; as reflected in moral exemplars, 147, 150–152; as reflected in personal experience, 24–25
Follett, Mary Parker, x, xiv, 35, 54–58, 61n69–62n79, 62n81, 122, 132, 135n27, 145, 146, 149, 157, 141
freedom, 3, 4, 9, 10, 22, 24–25, 27, 56, 71, 121, 124, 131–133, 138, 141
Fuller, Margaret, 5, 6–7, 12, 92, 94, 133
fugitive slave law, 148

Gilman, Charlotte Perkins, 13, 20, 27, 34, 38, 114, 116–117, 134n11
Green, Thomas Hill, 8, 31n30, 31n37, 15, 18, 89, 115
growth, 98, 100

habits: on the breaking of, 26, 70, 77, 184; on the formation of, 140–141, 150; in moral life, 72, 82n4, 84n54, 106, 140–141, 150, 152, 173, 188
Hague Peace Conference, 143
Harris, William Torrey, xi, 150
Hegel, Georg, 11, 15, 55, 114, 125, 126, 129, 197, 211, 214, 215, 216, 217
Hocking, William Ernest, 98
honesty, 169, 190
Hume, David, 89–90, 91, 108n9, 214

idealism, ix, xii, xv, 1, 3, 5, 6, 12, 15, 21, 22–23, 25, 28, 37, 38, 54, 61n69, 71, 149, 151, 155, 163, 165–168, 169–170, 171, 175n19, 208, 214; relation to Pragmatism, xvi, 25, 41–45, 172, 174
imagination, vii, xii, xiii, xv, 52, 65, 72, 78–81, 84n66, 87–108, 109n21, 120, 127, 138, 139, 141, 143, 144, 159, 160n10, 173, 175. *See also* Dewey, John; Emerson, Ralph Waldo; Kant, Immanuel
imperialism, 103, 138, 145, 147, 149, 157, 163
insight, 99–100
international relations, xiii, 35, 137–159

James, Henry, 4, 26–27
James, William, vii, xiii, 2, 6, 7, 10, 11, 12, 13, 27, 28, 30n2, 31n61, 33, 35, 36, 41–42, 43, 53, 56, 60n24, 61n66, 62n80, 65, 100, 102, 107, 109n36, 110n54, 111–113, 119–121, 130, 131–132, 133, 134n2, 135n16, 138, 139, 143, 149, 151, 154, 158, 159n1, 160n35, 169–170, 171, 175n13
Jim Crow Laws, 148
Johnson, Samuel, 80
justice, xvi, 89, 101, 112, 124, 143, 149, 151, 154, 163

Kant, Immanuel, 5, 15, 42, 109n13, 114, 123, 135n39, 215; on duty, xv, 95; on the duty of self-respect, 124, 125–127, 127–130, 135n34; on the imagination, 80, 89–92, 94–96, 97–98, 101, 107
Kies, Marrietta, 127

Lincoln, Abraham, 153
Locke, Alain, 38
Lowell, Anna, 116
Lowell, James Russell, ix, 165, 175n4
lost causes, xvi, 166–172
loyalty, xiii, 18, 25, 39, 40, 42, 60n23, 72, 52, 139–140, 144, 146, 152, 158, 175; to loyalty, 109n48, 158. *See also* Royce, Josiah

Marsh, James, 92
Martineau, James, 213
McCormick, Ada, xi–xii, 4, 27, 99, 121, 132, 136n58, 175n5
Mead, Lucia, 127
memory, 96
Mill, John Stuart, 111–112, 117
Mitchell, Weir, 116
moral emotions, 99–103; danger of, 103–108

novelty, 189–193; and growth, 76–77; and purpose, 72–75

"The Paper on Marriage", 4, 7, 13–17, 173, 174
Parker, Theodore, 92
Peirce, Benjamin, 111
Peirce, Charles Sanders, xiv, 28, 42, 44–45; on chance, 65–72; on fate, 68–70; on freedom, 72; on the pragmatic maxim, 6; relation to Emerson, 75; on truth, 173
Plato, 78, 89, 114, 215
power: the concept of, 55–58. *See also* Follett, Mary Parker
pragmatism: definition of, 5–6, 27–28, 42, 43, 51; Ella Lyman Cabot's criticism of, xi; and feminism, xvi; and idealism, xii, 42, 151, 166
Progressive movement, 54
Proust, Marcel, 96

racism, 144–145
rest cure, 116
Rhodes, Cecil, 145–146
Romanticism, ix, 14
Royce, Josiah, 7–8, 36–42, 45–46, 47–48; on his disagreements with Dewey, 41; on imitation, 22, 105, 139–143; on lost causes, 166–172; on loyalty, 40, 54–56; Philosophical Conference of 1903, 41

Santayana, George, 11–12
Schiller, Friedrich, 80
self-sacrifice, 127–128, 129, 22. *See also* duty: self-expression
slavery, 148, 153, 154, 155
Smith, Adam, 89–90, 91, 108n10
Socrates, 158
Spencer, Herbert, 68, 202
Stevenson, Robert Louis, 16
Stowe, Harriet Beecher, 153
sympathy: and the moral imagination, xv, 10, 37, 40, 42, 43

Taft, William, 143
Thoreau, Henry David, 29, 43, 102, 148
Transcendentalism, ix, 5–7, 163
Tychism, 63–67, 70. *See also* Peirce, Charles Sanders

Whitehead, Alfred North, 105
Whitehead, Evelyn, 105
Wilson, Woodrow, 155
womanhood, 7–9; the oppression involved in, 43, 115, 116, 118, 123, 125, 131; the Victorian concept of, 6, 7, 10, 13, 14, 16, 21, 25, 31n47, 92, 100, 104, 111, 112, 115
work cure, 122

About the Author

John J. Kaag is assistant professor of philosophy at the University of Massachusetts Lowell. He received his B.A. and M.A. in philosophy from Penn State University, his M.Phil. in International Relations from the University of Cambridge (U.K.), and his Ph.D. from the University of Oregon. Before joining the faculty at UMass Lowell, he was a postdoctoral fellow at the American Academy of Arts and Sciences and the Harvard Humanities Center. He teaches American philosophy among other courses in the history of philosophy.

LINDENHURST MEMORIAL LIBRARY
LINDENHURST NEW YORK 11757